BUGIALLI'S ITALY

ALSO BY GIULIANO BUGIALLI

The Foods of Sicily and Sardinia and the Smaller Islands (1996)

The Best of Bugialli (1994)

Giuliano Bugialli's Foods of Tuscany (1992)

The Fine Art of Italian Cooking (1977 first edition, 1990 second edition)

Giuliano Bugialli's Classic Techniques of Italian Cooking (1989)

Bugialli on Pasta (1988)

Giuliano Bugialli's Foods of Italy (1984)

BUGIALLI'S ITALY

*Traditional Recipes from
the Regions of Italy*

❖

Giuliano Bugialli

Photography by John Dominis

William Morrow and Company, Inc. / New York

In memory of Fabrizio Vitaletti and Audrey Berman,
the greatest gourmets and the greatest friends
I have ever known

Library of Congress Cataloging-in-Publication Data

Bugialli, Giuliano.
    Bugialli's Italy : traditional recipes from the regions of Italy :
companion to the National Public Television series / Giuliano
Bugialli ; photography by John Dominis.—1st ed.
      p.   cm.
    Includes index.
    ISBN 0-688-15864-1
    1. Cookery, Italian.   2. Bugialli's Italy (Television program)
I. Bugialli's Italy (Television program)   II. Title.
TX723.B7575   1998
641.5945—dc21   98-5670
                                                                    CIP

Printed in the United States of America

First Edition

1   2   3   4   5   6   7   8   9   1 0

BOOK DESIGN BY NAI CHANG

www.williammorrow.com

CONTENTS

MAIN COURSES 193

DESSERTS 253

ACKNOWLEDGMENTS

For the dishes: Tognana—Treviso, Italy
For the glasses: Luigi Bormioli—Parma, Italy
For the linens: Tessilarte—Florence, Italy
For the cookware: All-Clad—USA
For the small electric appliances: Kitchen-Aid—USA

Palm Bay Imports USA

Rocca delle Macie Winery in Tuscany
Sella & Mosca Winery in Sardinia
Cavit Winery in Trentino
Fattoria dei Barbi Winery in Montalcino, Tuscany
Marchesi di Barolo Winery in Piedmont
Bertani Winery in Veneto
Fassati Winery in Tuscany
Fazi Battaglia in the Marches

All the crew of my TV series *Bugialli's Italy,* and Luigi del Mastro, executive producer, and Hal Gurnee, director.

Thanks to all the restaurants, specialty food stores, and friends throughout Italy for their help.

Special thanks to my sympathetic and helpful editor, Pam Hoenig.

My thanks to my agent, Carl DeSantis, and, as always, to Henry Weinberg for his help in so many ways.

INTRODUCTION

I suppose each person's conception of a subject or place is unique, though many may agree on most things about it. My Italy, that is, "Bugialli's Italy," is made up of its great regional traditions, its long history, its remarkable landscape and architecture, the color of its seas and skies, its mountains and hills, flora and fauna. And I admit that it is also the sum of my personal tastes and my love for my country and its food. For me, the center, of course, must be gastronomy. And all of the above enter into it—all the culture, the art and history, and the visual setting from which the ingredients arise contribute to the aesthetics of the dishes and their presentation.

The only way to show how one sees and experiences one's native country is to travel through its regions, great and small cities, and share with the people their gastronomic loves and experiences. Though I include recipes from many different regions to show a panorama, three very picturesque ones are highlighted: Lazio and Rome, Veneto, and Friuli in the far north. Other regions are not neglected—certainly not my native Tuscany, or Piedmont, Abruzzi, Puglia, and others. I really don't prefer any regions above the others—I do love all of Italy—but I had to choose several that present the most contrasting extremes of the country. "My" Italy is the traditional one, and the main criterion for the dishes is authenticity. I take pains to verify the recipes by finding multiple sources from the place itself and tasting the dish in its native habitat. There are some recipes included here that are hard to find, or even unpublished in Italy, because they are so local. Some people do not agree with my passion for authenticity. They ask, if the recipe tastes all right, what difference does tradition make? My prejudice is that recipes that have been tasted over a long period have stood "the test of time" and survived many changes of taste. And undoubtedly these traditional dishes tell you much about the values of a region. I have no interest in pedantic scholarship for its own sake, only in revealing as much as I can about a colorful, fun-loving people through the food they have long preserved.

Our generation is not the first to be concerned about "health food." Sixteenth-century Italian cookbooks are full of notations about what is healthy to eat and which is the best season in which to eat it. Italy produces excellent butter in Parma and other areas, but Italian cooks long ago reduced its use for health reasons.

The concern with finding new ingredients has been a constant in Italy. Some Asian ingredients once were common in Italy but through the years, for whatever reason, came to be used less. These include mustard greens, pea pods, and ginger. A country as creative as Italy is always looking to add new things, but novelty alone is not enough; the dishes must have a quality equal to its own traditional ones. In fact, Italians are the first to try something new, but they will quickly drop it if it doesn't work for them.

In order to obtain the classic textures, I suggest such things as using a copper bowl and wire whisk to beat egg whites, because this makes the ingredients airier. Once you know the traditional technique, you can get the feeling for the result and learn to obtain it with other, perhaps more convenient appliances.

A variety of utensils is useful for obtaining the best result in a wide range of recipes. Copper bowls are useful for an evenness in pastry creams and zabaione. Terra-cotta pots produce a rounded, smooth, full flavor for sauces and soups. Of course, modern steel pots are also a must for a variety of uses.

The recipes stress authentic ingredients because I want you to know what the original ingredients are. For those that are difficult to obtain, I do suggest alternatives.

Italians do not generally use dried herbs, so fresh ones are preferable for these recipes. In Italy, in seasons during which herbs are difficult to obtain, we use them preserved in coarse salt or, as with basil for pesto, in olive oil. Sage, rosemary, and oregano stored under salt may last with full flavor for many months.

For recipes that call for pancetta, that is, salt-cured unsmoked bacon, I sometimes substitute prosciutto, because in Italy much pancetta, the type sometimes called *rigatino*, is quite lean, with alternating layers of meat and fat, and prosciutto is closer to it than fattier pancetta.

A note about ricotta: Today most manufacturers sell ricotta in 15-ounce containers, and I have made adjustments to the recipes accordingly.

Here are some techniques you'll need to refer to throughout the book.

Making Pasta by Hand or with a Manual Pasta Machine

To prepare the pasta dough, place the flour in a mound on a pasta board. Use a fork to make a well in the center. Place the eggs and salt and any other ingredients specified in the recipe in the well, and mix them together with a fork. Then, still using the fork, begin to incorporate the flour from the inside of the well, always incorporating fresh flour from the lower part of the well and pushing it under the dough that is forming to keep it from sticking to the board. Remove any pieces of dough that stick to the fork and incorporate them. Then, gather the dough together and set to one side of the board. Scrape the board with a pastry scraper, gathering together all the unincorporated flour, and sprinkle this flour over the board.

Start kneading the dough on the board, using the palm of one hand and folding the dough over with the other hand. The dough will gradually absorb more of the flour; do not sprinkle flour over it. Continue kneading until the dough is no longer wet and all but 4 to 5 tablespoons of the flour have been incorporated. If you intend to stretch the dough by hand, knead for about 5 minutes; if you intend to use a pasta machine, knead for only 2 to 3 minutes. The dough should now be smooth and elastic.

To Stretch the Dough by Hand Using a Rolling Pin

First, knead the dough for an additional 10 minutes, incorporating some but not all of the flour remaining on the board. Then place the center of the rolling pin over the ball of dough and gently roll the pin forward, then backward. This is the basic rolling motion, which should be repeated until the dough is thin and elastic.

To stretch the dough to an even thickness, fold the edge of the dough closest to you up over the rolling pin and roll up the sheet of dough around the pin, moving your fingers from the center outward along the edge of the pasta sheet to even out the edges. Then, with a quick, jerky movement, roll the pin one or two turns away from you so that the edge of the pasta sheet slaps against the board (this stretches the edge of the sheet). Flip the pin over and unroll the sheet away from you so that the underside is now on top.

As you roll out the pasta, alternate the back-and-forth motion with a side-to-side stretching motion. Turn so that you are working at a right angle to your original position, and roll the pin backward, then forward across the dough from this angle until the sheet is stretched to a little less than 1/8 inch thick. Roll up the sheet over the pin, flip the pin over, and unroll the sheet so that the underside is on top. Continue rolling and stretching the pasta sheet until it is the thickness specified in the recipe.

To Stretch the Dough Using a Manual Pasta Machine

(If the pasta dough is made from more than 2 eggs, divide the dough into roughly 1-cup pieces and stretch each piece separately.) With the palm of your hand, flatten the ball of dough to a 1/2-inch thickness. Set the rollers at the widest setting and pass the dough through them. Lightly flour the dough on one side, fold it in thirds, and press down to seal the three layers. Starting with an open end of the dough, pass through the rollers again. Repeat this folding and rolling eight to ten times, until the dough is smooth and elastic.

Set the rollers to the next thinnest setting and roll the dough through the machine. Flour the pasta on both sides and pass through the next thinnest setting. Repeat flouring and rolling the dough until it is the thickness specified in the recipe.

Grating Oranges and Lemons

Place a piece of parchment paper or thick waxed paper over the holes of a hand grater. Hold the paper in place with one hand while moving the orange or lemon back and forth on the paper with the other. Work on different sections of the paper so the paper does not wear out. Use a rubber spatula to remove the grated lemon or orange rind from the paper. Do not use what is left inside the grater or any of the bitter white part of the peel.

Making Orange or Lemon Zests

Orange or lemon zests, thin strips of the colored part of the fruit, can be made most easily with a citrus zester or a vegetable peeler. Simply pull the zester from the top of the fruit to the base so that you end up with long, thin strips of zest. It is important not to catch any of the white pith, as it has a bitter flavor. Strips of zest can be cut from the fruit with a knife, although it is more difficult to make thin strips and to avoid the white pith.

Cleaning Artichokes

Cut off the end of the stems and trim off all of the darker outer skin of the stem. Remove as many rows of outer leaves as necessary until you arrive at those leaves in which you can see the separation between the green at the top and the light yellow at the bottom. Remove the top green part by pressing your thumb on the bottom yellow part of each leaf and, with your other hand, tearing off the top green part. When you reach the rows in which only the very top part of the leaves are green, cut off these tips completely with a knife.

To remove the hair and the choke, first cut all around the choke with a knife, then scoop out the choke and the attached hair, using a long-handled teaspoon. As each artichoke is cleaned, return it to a bowl with acidulated water until needed.

Preparing Balsamella

Melt the butter in a heavy saucepan, preferably copper or enamel, over low heat. When the butter reaches the frothing point, add the flour all at once. Mix very well with a wooden spoon.

Cook until the flour is completely incorporated (1 to 3 minutes, depending on the quantities). If any lumps form, dissolve them by crushing them against the side of the pan with a wooden spoon. Remove the pan from the heat and let it stand for 10 to 15 minutes.

While the butter-flour mixture is standing, heat the milk in another pan until it is very close to the boiling point. Put the saucepan with the butter-flour mixture over low heat and add all of the hot milk at once. Stir until the sauce is smooth.

When the sauce reaches the boiling point, add the salt and continue to stir gently while the sauce cooks slowly for about 10 minutes longer. Remove from the heat and transfer the sauce to a glass or crockery bowl. According to the recipe, use it immediately warm or press a sheet of buttered waxed paper over the sauce to prevent a skin from forming and let the sauce cool completely.

How to Tie Meat Like a Salami

To tie a piece of meat like a salami, cut a piece of string six times the length of the meat to be tied. Place the string under one of the short sides of the rolled-up meat (about 1½ inches from the end). Make a knot, leaving only enough string on one side to pull over and knot the first ring in the center. Bring the long end of the string down the meat, another 1½ inches, and hold the string in place with your finger. With the other hand, pull the string under and around again to the point where it is being held by your finger. Pass the end of the string over and then under (like a sailor's knot). Remove your finger, hold the short end of the string with one hand, and pull the other end tight with the other hand. Continue this process at 1½-inch intervals until you reach the opposite end of the meat. Stand the meat on one end and pull the remaining string over the top end to the underside of the meat. As it intersects with each ring of string, pull under and over, fastening in the same way as was done on the other side (it is no longer necessary to hold the string with your finger or to pull tight on this side). After the last intersection, tie a knot using the two ends of the string. When the meat is ready, you will need to cut the string in only one place in order to remove it.

Toasting Bread Crumbs

Bread crumbs bought in Italy are very finely ground and lightly toasted. Italian bread crumbs may be duplicated by toasting other bread crumbs for 15 minutes in an oven preheated to 375 degrees and finely grinding them in a food processor.

Toasting Nuts

To lightly toast almonds and other nuts, place them on a cookie sheet in an oven preheated to 375 degrees for 15 minutes.

ANTIPASTI
Appetizers

The antipasto course in Italy has a long and distinguished history. In the great Renaissance feasts, it consisted of numerous different dishes, as many as thirty hot ones and thirty at room temperature.

The antipasto table with a variety of room-temperature dishes has survived, certainly in many restaurants. But hot appetizers are still important, particularly in family and private settings in which the dishes may be freshly made. When the appetizer is served hot, it is more likely that only one dish will be served.

FRITTATA ALLE ERBE
Frittata with Aromatic Herbs
Makes 6 to 8 servings

This frittata in its original version contains a festival of many wild greens, the exact combination being found only in that area, mountainous Friuli. We can approximate it with a gathering of greens and herbs available to us here: spinach, chard, leeks, sage, parsley, basil, marjoram, mint, and rosemary, all fresh if possible. The blending of so many herbs creates a wonderful freshness and combines into a convincing and original flavor.

1½ pounds fresh spinach, large stems removed

1½ pounds fresh Swiss chard, large stems removed

Coarse-grained salt

1 medium-size leek, white part only, or 1 yellow onion, cleaned

3 tablespoons (1½ ounces) sweet butter

3 tablespoons extra virgin olive oil

3 ounces pancetta, cut into small pieces or coarsely ground

1 large fresh sage leaf

5 sprigs fresh Italian parsley, leaves only

5 fresh basil leaves

1 tablespoon fresh marjoram leaves or large pinch of dried marjoram

10 fresh mint leaves

1 heaping teaspoon fresh rosemary leaves

Salt and freshly ground black pepper

5 extra-large eggs

TO SERVE:

Fresh basil and Italian parsley leaves

Soak the spinach and Swiss chard in a large bowl of cold water for half an hour. Bring a large pot of cold water to a boil, add coarse salt to taste, then drain the vegetables, add them to the pot, and boil for 5 minutes.

Meanwhile, rinse the leek very well and finely chop it on a cutting board.

Place a large casserole with the butter and 2 tablespoons of the olive oil over medium heat; when the butter is melted, add the leek and pancetta and sauté until the leek is translucent, 3 to 4 minutes. Finely chop the sage, parsley, basil, marjoram, mint, and rosemary together on a cutting board. Add them to the casserole and sauté for 5 minutes more.

Drain the cooked spinach and chard and cool them under cold running water. Lightly squeeze them and coarsely chop them on a cutting board. Add them to the casserole, mix very well, and season with salt and pepper. Cook for 10 minutes more, mixing every so often. Transfer the contents of the casserole to a crockery or glass bowl and let rest until cool, about half an hour.

Using a fork, lightly beat the eggs with salt and pepper to taste and pour them onto the cooled vegetables. Mix very well. Heat a 10-inch omelet pan with the remaining tablespoon olive oil over medium heat. When the pan is evenly hot, add the egg mixture. Level the mixture with a fork and keep puncturing the bottom with the fork as the eggs set, to allow the liquid on top to move through to the bottom. This will help the eggs to cook uniformly. When the eggs are well set and the frittata is well detached from the bottom of the pan, put a plate, upside down, over the pan and reverse the pan, turning the frittata out onto the plate. Return the pan to the heat and carefully slide the frittata into the pan and cook the other side. After 30 seconds, when the eggs should be well set, reverse the frittata onto a serving platter. Cut into wedges and serve warm or at room temperature after a few hours with the basil and parsley leaves.

VENETO

TORTINO RIPIENO ALLA VENEZIANA
Stuffed Frittata Venetian Style

Makes 6 to 8 servings

In most *frittate,* the vegetables or meat are incorporated into the eggs in an integrated round "pancake." When the proportion of vegetables or meat to eggs is greater than usual, it is sometimes called a *tortino,* as it is when made with large pieces of artichoke. Veneto and Tuscany, among other regions, have stuffed *tortini* in which two thin *frittate* enclose a stuffing. This type of stuffed omelet appears as early as the sixteenth century in a Florentine cookbook and is called *ritortelli ripieni.* This rolled, thin, stuffed omelet is like the traditional Florentine *crespelle,* taken to France as "crêpes"; the *ritortelli,* however, substitute egg for the flour and milk.

Since Venice was subject to sieges, it has many dishes based on preserved foods such as confit and fried fish preserved with the *carpione* technique, that is, with vinegar and aromatic herbs. Canned tuna is another type of preserved food, here used for a stuffing. In Tuscany, *tortino ripieno* is stuffed with cooked fresh vegetables.

continued

15 sprigs fresh Italian parsley, leaves only

One 7-ounce can tuna packed in olive oil, preferably imported Italian, drained

3 whole anchovies preserved in salt (see Note) or 6 anchovy fillets packed in oil (optional), drained

2 large ripe but not overripe tomatoes (about 1 pound)

¼ cup extra virgin olive oil

Salt and freshly ground black pepper

1 small clove garlic, peeled and finely chopped

FOR THE *TORTINO*:

2 tablespoons extra virgin olive oil

7 extra-large eggs

Pinch of salt

TO SERVE:

Fresh Italian parsley leaves

Finely chop the parsley, tuna, and, if using, anchovies together on a cutting board. Cut each tomato into 6 slices. Place a large nonreactive skillet with 2 tablespoons of the olive oil in it over medium heat and when the oil is warm, add enough tomato slices to line the skillet. Season with salt, pepper, and a little of the chopped garlic. Sauté on both sides for less than a minute. The tomato slices should be soft but still retain their shape. Transfer the tomatoes to a large serving platter. Repeat with the remaining tomatoes, adding more of the oil as needed, and let them rest until needed.

Prepare the *tortino*. Place a nonstick 10-inch omelet pan with 1 tablespoon of the oil over medium heat. Meanwhile, use a fork to lightly beat the eggs in a crockery or glass bowl with a pinch of salt. When the oil and pan are evenly hot, add half of the beaten eggs. As the eggs set in the pan, keep puncturing the bottom. The top part should still be very soft. Gently slide the frittata onto a plate. Repeat with the remaining oil and beaten eggs and slide the second frittata onto a different plate. Transfer the first frittata back in the pan with the moist part on top. Arrange the tuna mixture over it, then top with the second frittata, the moist side down. Cook for less than a minute, shaking the pan several times. Gently transfer the *tortino* to a serving platter, arrange the tomato slices over it, sprinkle over the parsley leaves, and serve. Slice it like a pie.

NOTE: If using whole anchovies preserved in salt, clean them under cold running water to remove the bones and excess salt.

TORTA DI CARCIOFI
Sardinian Artichoke Torte

Makes 6 to 8 servings

This *torta,* round in shape—like most—features two very Sardinian ingredients, ricotta and arti-chokes. Their ricotta is made from the milk of the many sheep on the island, and they still use wild artichokes. But even with the domesticated form of the vegetable we can make this delicious *torta.* Ricotta in Sardinia is used primarily as a binder rather than for its special flavor, so cow's milk ricotta works just fine. The white wine used is just one more indication that Italians do not accept the idea that artichokes and wine do not go together.

It is worth noting that Genoa's famous *torta pasqualina*—like this one an Easter dish—uses most of the same ingredients, though it has the celebrated many layers of paper-thin pastry. Whether this reflects Genoa's long occupation of Sardinia, we don't know for sure.

Unique to this dish is the presence of celery leaves without the stalks. My own feeling is that these leaves are used not for flavor but for their symbolic meaning, and a further guess is that they promise good luck and riches.

1 lemon, cut in half

6 large artichokes

Coarse-grained salt

1 cup dry white wine

1 tablespoon unbleached all-purpose flour

½ cup cold water

3 ounces prosciutto or pancetta, in one piece

10 fresh sage leaves

FOR THE RICOTTA:

15 ounces whole-milk ricotta, drained

15 sprigs fresh Italian parsley, leaves only

1 small clove garlic, peeled

Leaves from 2 stalks celery

1 cup freshly grated Parmigiano cheese

4 extra-large eggs, separated

Salt and freshly ground black pepper

TO BAKE:

¼ cup (2 ounces) sweet butter to butter
     the form and the remaining butter
     cut into pats

About ¼ cup unbleached all-purpose flour

continued

Squeeze the lemon halves into a large bowl of cold water and add the artichokes to soak for half an hour. Clean the artichokes (page 4), removing the outer dark green leaves and the choke, and cut them into eighths. Return the cleaned artichokes to the acidulated water.

Bring a large pot of cold water to a boil, add coarse salt to taste and the wine, then dissolve the flour in the ½ cup water and add it to the pot. When the water returns to a boil, remove the artichokes from the acidulated water, put them in the boiling water, and cook for 6 to 7 minutes; they should be half cooked. Drain the artichokes, transfer them to a serving platter lined with paper towels to absorb excess water, and let cool, covered with wet paper towels or a wet kitchen towel, for half an hour. Finely grind the prosciutto or pancetta and sage together and put the mixture in a small bowl.

Mix the ricotta very well to smooth it out completely. Finely chop the parsley, garlic, and celery leaves together on a cutting board. Transfer to the bowl containing the ricotta, along with the Parmigiano and egg yolks. Season with salt and pepper. Mix together very well.

Preheat the oven to 375 degrees. Heavily butter the bottom and sides of a 10-inch round double cake pan and line the bottom with parchment paper. Lightly flour the sides of the pan. Arrange all the artichokes over the bottom of the pan, sprinkle the ground pancetta mixture over them, season with salt and pepper, and place the butter pats on top. Use a copper bowl and wire whisk to beat the egg whites to soft peaks, then gently fold them into the ricotta mixture. Pour the ricotta mixture over the artichokes and bake for 45 minutes. It is done when the top is golden and soft to the touch and has detached from the sides. Remove from the oven and let rest for at least 5 minutes before unmolding onto a large serving platter. The artichoke layer should be on top. Serve, slicing the *torta* like a pie. *Torta* may be eaten hot or at room temperature after a few hours.

UOVA AL TARTUFO
Truffled Eggs

Makes 4 servings

Most white truffles come from Italy, specifically Piedmont, from the areas of Asti and Alba. The Arno Valley in Tuscany has a small amount and they are used locally, since there are not enough to export. In order to obtain the optimum flavor and perfume, white truffles should be used uncooked, shaved over the finished cooked dish when it is served. They are rare, therefore expensive, but worth it because they are one of the great delicacies of the world. Italy is also the largest producer of black truffles, which, however, must be cooked to display their maximum flavor; they are found in Umbria.

One of the favorite ways of showcasing the truffle is in this simple egg dish, in which the raw egg is covered with a cheese-and-cream combination and baked. I first ate this in Piedmont, at the Marchesi di Barolo's winery. As usual, the uncooked truffle is shaved, as abundantly as you can afford, over the finished dish.

½ tablespoon (¼ ounce) unsalted butter,
    at room temperature
4 extra-large eggs
Salt and freshly ground black pepper
¾ cup heavy cream
¾ cup freshly grated Grana Padano cheese
    (see Note)
Pinch of freshly grated nutmeg

TO SERVE:
Slivers of fresh white truffle
4 small sprigs fresh Italian parsley
8 thin *crostini* (country-style bread cut into
    4-inch squares), lightly toasted

Preheat the oven to 375 degrees and lightly butter four 4-inch ceramic, china, or terra-cotta gratin dishes. Carefully break one egg into each of the dishes. Be sure the egg yolk is whole. Lightly season with salt and pepper. Mix the cream and cheese together in a small bowl and lightly season with salt, pepper, and nutmeg. Pour one-quarter of the mixture all around each egg yolk.

Place the dishes in the oven. The baking time varies from 9 minutes for soft cooked to 15 minutes fully cooked, as you wish. Shave the fresh truffles over the top, garnish with a sprig of the parsley, and serve immediately. Most people eat this dish using a fruit spoon together with the toasted *crostini*.

NOTE: Grana Padano and Parmigiano Reggiano are the two main types of Grana and were probably the first cheeses made in large wheels and aged and shipped far from their place of origin. They are to be eaten as is or grated to be used for different dishes.

While Parmigiano is made in the restricted area between Parma and Reggio Emilia, Grana Padano is produced over a larger area further north. They are made using similar methods and combining skim and whole milk. Each is preferred for the dishes of its own region, but both are used all over Italy and even throughout the world. They are among the world's most celebrated cheeses.

FRICO
Cheese Crêpe Appetizer
Makes 8 to 10 servings

Latteria is the generic cheese of Friuli. Still made in small *caseifici* (cheese factories), with only the milk from their own cows, the name *latteria* comes from the little shops that sell milk and local cheese. Latteria comes in many different versions, depending on location and aging. Because of the small artisan production of each farm, the cheese is not widely disseminated, even within Italy. Asiago cheese, from the Veneto province, is close enough to use as a substitute (adding a little Parmigiano makes it a little sweeter and brings it even closer to latteria), and it is more easily found abroad. (Friuli was until recently one of the "Tre Veneti," a collective name for what are now politically separate regions: Veneto, Friuli, and Alto Adige (South Tyrol). They are grouped together because having all belonged to Venice, they share many characteristics—certainly in their food and wine.)

Frico is a very popular appetizer in Friuli.

¾ pound aged latteria cheese or ½ pound   Extra virgin olive oil
     asiago cheese and ½ pound
     Parmigiano cheese

Coarsely grate the latteria cheese. If using the asiago and Parmigiano cheeses, coarsely grate the asiago and finely grate the Parmigiano, then mix them together.

Place a nonstick 8½-inch omelet pan over medium heat. Line a serving platter with paper towels and place a custard cup upside down on a plate. When the pan is hot, season it with a few drops of olive oil (the pan should be no more than 375 degrees, or else the cheese will burn) and sprinkle about 7 level tablespoons of grated cheese to evenly cover the surface of the pan. Let the cheese melt uniformly and lower the heat if the edges begin to turn darker than the center. After the cheese cooks for about 30 seconds, remove the pan from the heat and let cool for a few minutes; the cheese will set into a thin pancake or crêpe. Gradually loosen the *frico* from the pan, using a flat spatula, and turn it over. Be sure the pan is still well seasoned with oil, then place it back over the heat and cook for 30 seconds more. Slide the *frico* over the upside-down custard cup so it falls into the shape of a large embroidered cup. Let rest until cool, about 2 minutes. The cheese, as it cools, will get very crisp and crumbly. Transfer the cup-shaped *frico* to the prepared serving platter, open side up. Repeat the same procedure until all the cheese is used up. Serve the *frico* slightly warm or at room temperature.

ANITRA AL COCCIO
Duck Confit Venetian Style
Makes 8 servings

Because Venice was always subject to blockade, which would cut it off from its food sources, the Venetians developed a repertory of preserved foodstuffs that could be eaten during a siege. Eventually these preserved foods became part of the Venetian menu and remained favorites even under normal conditions. The English for preserved goose or duck, confit, as usual entered the English language through the French, *confit,* rather than the Italian, *conservata,* even though it was originally Italian. (The name *Venice* itself came into English not from the Italian *Venezia* but rather through the French *Venise.*)

Duck or goose preserved in its own fat is still a homemade staple in Venetian families and is used in a number of traditional dishes as a dressing. The meat may be served as an appetizer or a main dish, but is still usually served over something else, such as beans.

1 duck (about 5 pounds), Long Island type	6 large sage leaves, fresh or preserved in salt (page 2)
1½ tablespoons coarse-grained salt	2 juniper berries
1 large red onion, cleaned and thinly sliced	10 black peppercorns
4 large cloves garlic, peeled and coarsely chopped	Pinch of freshly grated nutmeg
	2 cups dry white wine
1 tablespoon fresh rosemary leaves, wrapped in a cheesecloth	Extra virgin olive oil as needed

Carefully wash the duck, dry it with paper towels, then cut it into 12 pieces. Place the duck pieces in a large crockery or glass bowl, sprinkle the salt all over, and mix very well. Cover the bowl with plastic wrap and refrigerate overnight. The next morning, transfer the duck to a casserole. Arrange the onion and garlic over the duck and add the rosemary bag as well as the sage, juniper berries, peppercorns, and nutmeg. Pour in the wine and set the casserole, covered, over medium heat. Simmer for 2 hours, being sure that the duck pieces cook evenly. Remove the casserole from the burner and let sit at room temperature, still covered, for 2 hours to cool.

continued

Place the duck pieces and all the juices and rendered fat, discarding the rosemary bag, in a glass jar, add enough olive oil to cover all the meat pieces, and refrigerate. After two days you may eat the duck, reheated with some of the oil, as it is or accompanied with boiled cannellini beans or a different legume. This preserved duck may last as long as a year stored in the refrigerator. It may be served as an appetizer or as a main course.

COLLI DI POLLO RIPIENI
Stuffed Chicken Necks
Makes 8 to 12 servings

In earlier times, a colorful casing was often used to enclose a forcemeat that would be served at a big celebration. A boned chicken or duck neck was one of a variety of such casings. I remember, as a child, at the big dinner following the wheat harvest, the meal started with oversize bowls of broth with the stuffed necks, still whole, floating in them. Chickens and ducks were raised especially to be ready for this dinner. To serve, the necks were sliced, but still eaten together with the broth. We still eat the stuffed necks in Italy, and no longer only for special occasions. Now most often they are served sliced, at room temperature without the broth, as an appetizer course.

4 large chicken necks, plucked but with the heads left on

FOR THE STUFFING:

5 blanched almonds

6 walnut halves

2 chicken livers, all fat and membranes removed

2 slices white bread, crusts removed

½ cup completely defatted chicken or meat broth, preferably homemade

5 large sprigs fresh Italian parsley, leaves only

1 medium-size clove garlic, peeled

2 tablespoons extra virgin olive oil

6 ounces veal or beef, in one piece

Salt and freshly ground black pepper

2 extra-large eggs

3 tablespoons freshly grated Parmigiano cheese

Large pinch of freshly grated nutmeg (optional)

TO COOK THE NECKS:

3 quarts cold water

1 medium-size red onion, cleaned

1 stalk celery

1 medium-size carrot, scraped

Coarse-grained salt

5 sprigs fresh Italian parsley, leaves only

2 medium-size cloves garlic, peeled

TO SERVE:

2 bunches arugula (*rucola* or *ruchetta*), cleaned and large stems removed

3 tablespoons extra virgin olive oil

A few drops red wine vinegar

Freshly ground black pepper

Fresh basil leaves

Bone the necks, being careful not to break the skin. Rinse very well and dry with paper towels. Let rest until needed.

Prepare the stuffing. Finely chop the almonds, walnuts, and chicken livers together on a board or in a blender or food processor. Soak the bread in the broth for 10 minutes. When ready, squeeze the broth out of the bread and put the bread into a bowl along with the chopped ingredients. Coarsely chop the parsley and garlic together on a cutting board.

Heat the olive oil in a small skillet over medium heat; when the oil is warm, add the chopped garlic mixture and sauté for 1 minute. Add the veal or beef and sauté until lightly golden all over. Season with salt and pepper. Remove the pan from the heat and let cool for half an hour. Grind everything together with a meat grinder fitted with the disk with the smallest holes, blender, or food processor into a bowl. Add the juices from the pan and mix very well. Add the eggs and Parmigiano cheese and mix again. Add the nut mixture to the bowl, season with salt and pepper and optional nutmeg, and mix everything with a wooden spoon.

Meanwhile, place the cold water in a casserole in which all the necks can be arranged in one layer over medium heat. Cut the onion, celery, and carrot into large pieces. When the water reaches a boil, add all the vegetables and coarse salt to taste and the parsley and garlic and simmer for 30 minutes. Fill the chicken necks with the prepared stuffing. Be careful not to add too much; otherwise the necks will split while cooking. The amount of stuffing resulting from the above quantities is *approximately* enough, as the size of chicken necks varies a lot. Sew up the cavities of the necks and tie the beaks with a string. Prick the necks with a needle in several places. Wrap the necks in separate pieces of cheesecloth and tie like a salami (see page 5). Set the necks in the broth, reduce the heat, and be sure the broth never reaches a full boil. The necks must be completely covered with broth. Simmer for 30 minutes, then transfer to a serving platter. Let cool completely, then refrigerate for at least 4 hours or, even better, overnight. Untie and unwrap the necks, then cut them into slices less than ½ inch thick. Line a serving platter with the arugula and arrange the slices of necks on it. Very lightly mix the olive oil and vinegar together and pour it over the meat. Season with a little black pepper and the basil leaves.

VARIATION: Served with a sauce, such as the one below, this dish would be used as a main course, not an appetizer.

FOR THE SAUCE:

¼ cup extra virgin olive oil

1 pound ripe tomatoes or drained canned
    tomatoes, preferably imported Italian

4 fresh basil leaves

Salt and freshly ground black pepper

Once the chicken necks are cooked and cooled, drain the broth, saving the liquid and vegetables. Coarsely chop the vegetables on a cutting board.

Heat the olive oil in a large nonreactive saucepan over medium heat; when the oil is warm, add the chopped vegetables and sauté for 5 minutes, stirring every so often with a wooden spoon. If fresh tomatoes are used, cut them into large pieces. Add the fresh or canned tomatoes to the pan along with the basil leaves, torn into pieces, and cook, stirring, for 5 minutes. Add all the reserved broth and bring to a simmer. Place the necks in the pan and simmer for 20 minutes, turning them twice. Transfer the necks to a platter and pass the sauce through a food mill fitted with the disk with the smallest holes into a clean casserole. Reduce the sauce for about 10 minutes over medium heat, seasoning with salt and pepper. By that time a quite thick sauce should have formed. When ready, slice the necks and serve with the sauce, reheated, and fresh basil leaves.

FARRO

❖

Farro (also known as spelt or emmer), a type of soft wheat, was the preferred wheat of the ancient Romans, and the repertory of dishes associated with it has been somewhat retained up to modern times. Those areas of Italy that favor the growth of this type of wheat have low hills surrounded by thick forests, with moist soil, and are cool but get lots of sun. When I recently went to visit a farro producer in Lunigiana in northern Tuscany, considered an especially good area for this crop, I was surprised after walking through a thick forest of chestnut trees to come upon a field of ripe farro, fenced in and protected as though it contained solid gold. Tuscany, Abruzzi, and Sicily produce the best farro, but the tradition of this wheat is so strong that one still finds farro dishes in most regions of Italy.

In Tuscany, this wheat is used for dishes in all courses, from appetizers to desserts. In Abruzzi, the main usage is in thick soups with cracked farro berries. The soft berries are most often used whole, but flour is also obtained from them, for making pasta, bread, and pastries. The soft wheat flour is a little more difficult to handle than durum flour, but the result is worth the extra trouble. Bread made with farro flour has somewhat the texture of a cake made with butter, and a slightly sour taste.

Farro must be soaked before cooking. The classic soaking time is 45 minutes in a bowl of cold water. After draining off the soaking water, the cooking time is most often 45 minutes, in a large amount of salted, already boiling water.

The farro is cooked and ready to be drained when it is completely opened, but still has a little bite. Farro may be boiled in advance and kept for several days, refrigerated and covered, in a large crockery or glass bowl.

Farro may be found in gourmet shops or health food stores.

FAGIOLATA DI FARRO
Farro and Roman Beans

Makes 12 servings

In this dish, the farro, borlotti beans, and string beans may be cooked individually in advance, but it is best when the sauce is prepared and combined with the other ingredients at the last moment.

FOR THE ROMAN BEANS:

8 ounces (1¼ cups) dried borlotti
    (Roman) beans, picked over

2 large fresh sage leaves

2 cloves garlic, peeled

2 tablespoons extra virgin olive oil

3 quarts cold water

Coarse-grained salt

FOR THE FARRO:

8 ounces (1⅓ cups) raw farro

Coarse-grained salt

FOR THE STRING BEANS:

1 pound very thin fresh string beans,
    ends removed

Coarse-grained salt

FOR THE SAUCE:

½ cup extra virgin olive oil

6 ounces pancetta, very finely ground

Salt and freshly ground black pepper

Hot red pepper flakes

TO SERVE:

20 sprigs fresh Italian parsley, leaves only,
    coarsely chopped

1 large ripe tomato (about 1 pound), diced

Soak the Roman beans in a bowl of cold water overnight. The next morning, drain the beans and put them in a medium-size casserole with the sage, garlic, oil, and 3 quarts water. Set the casserole over medium heat and simmer for about 45 minutes. By that time the beans should be almost cooked and soft. Season with coarse salt and cook for 5 minutes more.

Meanwhile, rinse the raw farro and soak it in a bowl of cold water for 45 minutes. Bring a large saucepan of cold water to a boil and add salt to taste. Drain the farro, add it to the saucepan, and cook for 45 minutes, stirring every so often with a wooden spoon. Drain the farro, transfer to a crockery or glass bowl, and let rest, covered with wet paper towels or kitchen towels, until cool, about 1 hour.

The string beans must also be cooked while the Roman beans and farro are cooking. Soak the string beans in a bowl of cold water for half an hour. Bring a large saucepan of cold water to a boil and add salt to taste, then the beans, and cook for 8 or 9 minutes; the beans should be cooked, still retaining their shape, but not be crunchy. Drain the string beans, transfer them to a crockery or glass bowl, and let cool, covered, with wet paper towels or a wet cotton kitchen towel for about 1 hour or until needed.

When ready, transfer the Roman beans, farro, and string beans to a larger bowl and place a medium-size saucepan with the olive oil for the sauce over medium heat. When the oil is warm, add the ground pancetta and sauté slowly for about 5 minutes. All the fat from the pancetta should be rendered and the meat very crisp. Season with salt, black pepper, and hot pepper. Sprinkle the parsley over the beans and farro, toss very well, and transfer everything to a large serving platter. Pour the pancetta and oil over the serving platter and serve with the diced tomato.

PANZANELLA DI FARRO
Farro Panzanella

Makes 6 to 8 servings

This Tuscan favorite is not successful when prepared with breads other than the classic unsalted crusty white or whole-wheat Tuscan bread. Toasting or frying other breads really does not solve the problem. A completely authentic alternative recipe is to make panzanella using boiled farro in place of the bread.

8 ounces (1⅓ cups) raw farro

Coarse-grained salt

1 pound ripe tomatoes, cut into 1-inch cubes

1 large red onion, cleaned and cut into 1-inch cubes or thinly sliced

½ cup extra virgin olive oil

2 to 4 tablespoons red wine vinegar, to your taste

Salt and freshly ground black pepper

15 large fresh basil leaves, torn into thirds

TO SERVE:

Fresh basil leaves

Soak the farro in a bowl of cold water for 45 minutes. Bring a large saucepan of cold water to a boil, add coarse salt to taste, then drain the farro and add it to the saucepan. Reduce the heat to medium and simmer for 45 minutes. Drain the farro, transfer it to a crockery or glass bowl and let rest, covered with wet paper towels or a wet kitchen towel until cool, about 1 hour. Mix the tomatoes and onion together and refrigerate, covered, until needed.

When ready, transfer the farro to a larger bowl, add the tomato mixture, season with the oil, vinegar, salt, and pepper and add the torn basil. Mix very well.

Transfer the contents to a large serving platter, scatter the whole basil leaves on top, and serve.

VARIATIONS: More ingredients may be added, one, two, or all of them:

* 2 hard-boiled eggs, shelled and quartered
* 4 anchovy fillets packed in oil, drained, and finely chopped
* 2 stalks celery, cut into small pieces

BRUSCHETTE AND FOCACCE

❖

Bruschette and *focacce*, though most often served as snacks, are sometimes used in place of an antipasto before the first course of a meal.

The word *bruschetta,* meaning "charcoal toasted," is really a Roman slang word, but it has come to be used more often for this type of snack than the more appropriate Tuscan word *fettunta,* meaning an "oiled slice." This dish originated during the olive harvest, when the fruit is pressed for its oil. Everyone wanted to taste the new oil, and they would pour it on a piece of toasted bread.

Bruschetta, or *fettunta*, is different from *crostini* in that the slice of bread is much more substantial and the emphasis is on the toasting and the oiling, rather than the topping, which is the case with *crostini. Crostini* are considered true *antipasti* rather than snacks.

Bruschette have become increasingly popular in recent years, evolving from the simple bread rubbed with garlic and oil to include different toppings. These types of *bruschette* are not true regional dishes, but are eaten all over Italy. For this reason, I do not identify them as regional dishes, but rather as "in the style of" a region, because the main ingredient(s) of the topping comes from that place.

BRUSCHETTA AI POMODORI
Bruschetta with Sautéed Tomato Slices

Makes 12

1½ pounds ripe tomatoes

¼ cup plus 6 tablespoons extra virgin
  olive oil

Salt and freshly ground black pepper

10 sprigs fresh Italian parsley, leaves only

2 medium-size cloves garlic, peeled

6 large fresh basil leaves

TO SERVE:

12 slices country-style bread, each about
  4 inches square

2 medium-size cloves garlic (optional),
  peeled

24 to 36 arugula (*rucola* or *ruchetta*) leaves
  (optional)

Cut the tomatoes into ½-inch-thick slices. Place a medium-size nonreactive skillet with 2 tablespoons of the oil over medium heat; when the oil is quite warm, add enough tomato slices to cover the bottom of the skillet. Lightly sauté the tomatoes for about 25 seconds on each side and season with salt and pepper. Transfer the tomatoes to a serving platter and sauté the remaining slices in the same way, adding a bit more oil each time.

Finely chop the parsley, garlic, and basil together on a cutting board and transfer to a small bowl. Add the remaining 6 tablespoons olive oil, season with salt and pepper, and mix very well.

Toast the bread over hot ash, in the oven, or in a toaster. While still very hot, if desired, rub the bread on one or both sides with the garlic. Place one or two slices of the tomatoes over each slice of bread, with or without two or three leaves of arugula, then pour some of the sauce over and serve warm.

BRUSCHETTA AI FAGIOLI
Bruschetta with Cannellini Beans

Makes 6

1 cup dried cannellini (white kidney) beans,
    picked over

3 fresh sage leaves

2 ounces pancetta or prosciutto, in one
    piece

1 large clove garlic, peeled

6 tablespoons extra virgin olive oil

Freshly ground black pepper

Coarse-grained salt

One 3½-ounce can tuna packed in olive oil,
    preferably imported Italian, drained

TO SERVE:

6 slices country-style bread, each about
    4 inches square

1 large clove garlic (optional), peeled

Fresh basil leaves

1 small red onion, cleaned and very thinly
    sliced

Soak the beans in a bowl of cold water overnight. Next morning, place a medium-size saucepan of cold water over medium heat, drain the beans, and add them to the saucepan along with the sage, pancetta or prosciutto, and garlic ground together, 2 tablespoons of the olive oil, and black pepper to taste. Simmer for 45 minutes. By that time the beans should be almost cooked, soft but still retaining their shape. Season with salt and cook for 2 or 3 minutes more. Drain the beans (you may save the bean broth to use as the starting broth for a soup) and put them in a bowl. Season with salt and pepper, add the remaining 4 tablespoons oil, and mix very well. Let the beans rest, covered, until they cool to room temperature, about half an hour.

When ready, toast the bread over coals, in the oven, or in the toaster. While still very hot, if desired, rub the bread on one or both sides with the garlic and arrange on a plate. Add the tuna to the beans and gently mix them together. Ladle the beans and some of their juices over the bread and serve with basil leaves and rings of the onion.

BRUSCHETTA DI PECORINO AL PEPE NERO
Bruschetta with Pecorino Cheese and Pepper

Makes 6

6 ounces not-very-aged Tuscan Pecorino
   cheese
3 tablespoons extra virgin olive oil
Freshly ground black pepper

TO SERVE:

6 slices country-style bread, each about
   4 inches square
1 large clove garlic (optional), peeled
3 tablespoons extra virgin olive oil
   (optional)
Fresh basil leaves (optional)

Remove the rind from the cheese and cut it into very small pieces. Place the cheese in a crockery or glass bowl, add the olive oil and a lot of black pepper, and toss very well. Toast the bread over coals, in the oven, or in the toaster. While still very hot, if desired, rub the bread on one or both sides with the garlic and top each slice with the marinated cheese and some of the olive oil. Serve, if desired, with ½ tablespoon of the olive oil drizzled over each slice and basil leaves.

BRUSCHETTA UMBRA
Bruschetta with Truffle

Makes 6

1 very small fresh or canned black truffle
   (available in specialty food stores)
3 tablespoons extra virgin olive oil
Salt and freshly ground black pepper

TO SERVE:

6 slices country-style bread, each about
   4 inches square, lightly toasted
1 large clove garlic (optional), peeled
2 large very ripe tomatoes

Finely chop the truffle, transfer to a small bowl, add the olive oil, and season with salt and pepper. Mix very well.

Toast the bread over coals, in the oven, or in the toaster. While still very hot, if desired, rub the bread on one or both sides with the garlic, then cut the tomatoes in half and rub the bread with the cut part of the tomatoes. Repeat many times so the bread absorbs the taste of the tomatoes. Arrange some of the truffle mixture over each slice and serve.

VARIATION: Rubbing the tomatoes against the bread is the classic way; a shortcut is to finely chop the tomatoes, place them on the bread, and cover with the chopped truffle.

IN THE STYLE OF VENETO

BRUSCHETTA AL CAVOLO
Bruschetta with Cabbage

Makes 6

2 ounces pancetta, in one piece

2 medium-size cloves garlic, peeled

1 pound Savoy cabbage leaves,
     large veins removed

3 tablespoons extra virgin olive oil

3 bay leaves

Salt and freshly ground black pepper

About 2 cups completely defatted chicken
     or meat broth or vegetable broth,
     preferably homemade

TO SERVE:

6 slices country-style bread, each about
     4 inches square

1 clove garlic (optional), peeled

Arugula (*rucola* or *ruchetta*) leaves

Finely grind the pancetta and garlic together. Cut the cabbage leaves into 1-inch-wide strips and soak them in a bowl of cold water for half an hour. Place a medium-size casserole with the olive oil over medium heat and when the oil is warm, add the ground ingredients. After a few seconds, drain the cabbage and add it to the casserole. Add the bay leaves and season with salt and pepper. Do not stir or mix. Pour in 1 cup of the broth, cover the casserole, and let simmer for 30 minutes, adding more broth if needed. Remove the bay leaves, stir the cabbage, and simmer until the cabbage falls apart, about another 30 minutes. Remove the casserole from the heat and, using a wooden spoon, try to mash the cabbage completely. Then transfer it to a crockery or glass bowl and let rest, covered, until completely cold, about 1 hour.

Toast the bread over coals, in the oven, or in the toaster. While still very hot, if desired, rub the bread on one or both sides with the garlic. Top the slices of bread with some of this cabbage "jam" and arugula leaves, if desired.

BRUSCHETTA DI CARCIOFI
Artichoke Bruschetta

Makes 6

1 lemon, cut in half

1 large artichoke (see page 4 for
  cleaning artichokes)

1 medium-size clove garlic, peeled

5 sprigs fresh Italian parsley, leaves only

3 tablespoons extra virgin olive oil

Salt and freshly ground black pepper

About 1 cup completely defatted chicken or
  meat broth, preferably homemade

TO SERVE:

6 slices country-style bread, each about
  4 inches square

1 clove garlic (optional), peeled

Extra virgin olive oil

6 large slivers Parmigiano cheese

Squeeze the lemon halves into a bowl of cold water. Add the artichoke and soak for half an hour. Remove the artichoke from the water and clean it, removing the tough, dark green outer leaves and choke, and cut it into eighths. Put the artichoke pieces back in the acidulated water to prevent discoloring. Finely chop the garlic and parsley together on a cutting board.

Heat the olive oil in a medium-size skillet over medium heat. When the oil is warm, add the chopped ingredients and lightly sauté for 2 minutes. Drain the artichoke pieces and add them to the skillet. Season with salt and pepper. Stir several times to be sure the artichoke does not stick to the bottom of the skillet.

Start adding the broth ¼ cup at a time; do not add any more broth until what has been added is completely absorbed. If the artichoke pieces are not very tender, cover the skillet; in 15 minutes they should be completely cooked and very soft. Taste for salt and pepper. Transfer the artichoke to a crockery or glass bowl and let cool for 15 minutes, then refrigerate, covered, until completely cold, about 1 hour.

Toast the bread over coals, in the oven, or in the toaster. Remove the artichoke from the refrigerator and use a fork to mash it a little. While the bread is still very hot, if desired, rub one or both sides with the garlic. Place a tablespoon of the artichoke paste over each slice of bread, then drizzle it with a few drops of olive oil and top with a large sliver of Parmigiano.

BRUSCHETTA AL POMODORO E CAPPERI

Bruschetta with Tomato and Capers

Makes 6

3 medium-size ripe tomatoes, blanched for
1 minute, peeled, seeded, and diced

2 tablespoons extra virgin olive oil

1 heaping tablespoon capers in wine
vinegar, drained

Salt and freshly ground black pepper

TO SERVE:

6 slices country-style bread, each about
4 inches square

1 clove garlic (optional), peeled

Fresh basil leaves

Place the tomatoes in a small crockery or glass bowl, add the olive oil and capers, and season with salt and pepper. Mix very well. Toast the bread over coals, in the oven, or in the toaster. While still very hot, if desired, rub one or both sides with the garlic, top the bread with some of the tomato mixture, and serve with the basil leaves.

CROSTINI

❖

Crostini are Italian canapés, consisting of a small piece of country bread or fried polenta with a topping. Most often they are spread with some type of liver pâté, but a variety of other toppings is used, including seafood and other meat pâtés, truffle paste, wild mushroom sauce, bean paste, cheese, and cured meats. *Crostini* are the most common type of simple appetizer, sometimes served on a plate with slices of salami and prosciutto. Cheese slices are almost never included on a cold appetizer plate with the meat slices.

Crostini most likely derive from the medieval practice of serving food on a bread slice rather than on a plate, the bread being used only as a receptacle to be discarded. The Italians have not adopted the trendy use of a sliced vegetable such as cucumber or zucchini in place of the bread or polenta.

TUSCANY

CROSTINI DI POLPETTONE
Canapés of Polpettone

Makes 24

1 whole *Polpettone Vestito* (page 219) or a piece of it, left in the refrigerator at least overnight	Country-style bread Sweet butter Capers in wine vinegar, drained

Cut the *polpettone* into slices not thicker than ½ inch. Trim each slice, removing the outside layer of prosciutto and the chicken skin, and cut into 2-inch squares. Cut the bread into slices, then into squares the same size as the meat. Lightly butter one side of the bread and fit a square of meat over it. Top with a few capers and serve.

CROSTINI DI MOZZARELLA E PROSCIUTTO
Canapés of Mozzarella and Prosciutto

Makes 4

5 teaspoons extra virgin olive oil

8 slices Italian bread, without sesame seeds, each about ¾ inch thick

2 ounces thinly sliced prosciutto

8 slices mozzarella cheese, each slice less than ½ inch thick, cut into the same shape as the bread (total weight about ½ pound)

Freshly ground black pepper

Fresh Italian parsley leaves

Preheat the oven to 375 degrees.

Use 1 teaspoon of the olive oil to lightly oil a jelly-roll pan. Arrange the slices of bread on the pan and pour ½ teaspoon of the oil over each slice. Top each canapé with 1 slice of prosciutto, then the mozzarella, and bake for about 12 minutes. By that time the cheese should be soft and warm, but not completely melted.

Transfer the *crostini* to a serving platter, season with black pepper, sprinkle with the parsley leaves, and serve hot.

PIZZE

❖

From Puglia we have two remarkable offshoots of the flatbread tradition: one a pizza, but with pockets (*puddica*), the other a stuffed focaccia shaped like a rolled-up sausage.

For most *pizze* and *schiacciate*, it is desirable to roll the dough out very thin, with very crispy and flaky results. But in Sicily or in the part of Italy south of Naples, we have also a number of classic *pizze* that are rather thick, with a softer consistency because inside the crust there is a real crumb. Also from that area are two types of stuffed pizza, one stuffed in advance between two layers of dough and a second in which the thick pizza is baked, then sliced open, stuffed, and sometimes put back in the oven to bake a little more. The two *pizze* presented here are directly connected to the famous Sicilian *guastedda*, a round flatbread, classically stuffed with cooked spleen and eaten as an Easter dish.

If we allow the *puddica* dough to rest sufficiently, once the pockets are made and stuffed, the dough will close over the pockets. In the *sfogliata* from Puglia, the dough is rolled out into a long ribbon. Both of these doughs contain some semolina flour mixed with the all-purpose. *Sfoglia* means "layer," and the word refers to the layer of dough for pasta. *Sfogliare* means "layering," and *pasta sfogliata* is puff pastry; *pâté feuilleté* is an exact French translation of those two words for this Florentine invention. *Larousse Gastronomique* gives an absurd etymology from a hypothetical pastry chef, of course French, supposedly named Feuillet. *Sfogliatella* is the famous Neapolitan layered dessert pastry, lightly stuffed with pastry cream between the layers.

PUDDICA

Pizza with Tomato Pockets

Makes 12 servings

FOR THE SPONGE:

1 cup plus 1 tablespoon unbleached
    all-purpose flour

¼ cup semolina flour

1 ounce fresh compressed yeast or
    2 packages active dry yeast

1 cup lukewarm or warm water, depending
    on the yeast

Pinch of salt

FOR THE TOMATOES:

1 pound very ripe tomatoes, blanched for
    1 minute, peeled, seeded, and cut into
    very small pieces, or cut into small
    pieces with skins and seeds

2 tablespoons extra virgin olive oil

Salt and freshly ground black pepper

Several pinches of dried oregano

FOR THE GARLIC:

6 large cloves garlic, peeled and cut into
    slivers or coarsely chopped

2 tablespoons extra virgin olive oil

Salt and freshly ground black pepper

Large pinch of dried oregano

FOR THE DOUGH:

About 3¼ cups unbleached all-purpose
    flour

¼ cup semolina flour

1 cup lukewarm water

2 tablespoons extra virgin olive oil

Salt

TO PREPARE THE PAN:

2 tablespoons extra virgin olive oil

FOR THE TOPPING:

¼ cup extra virgin olive oil

Salt and freshly ground black pepper

Several pinches of dried oregano

TO SERVE:

Coarse-grained salt (optional)

To make the sponge, mix together the cup of all-purpose flour with the semolina flour and place the mixture in a medium-size bowl. Make a well in the center. Dissolve the yeast in the lukewarm or warm water, then pour it into the well along with the salt. Use a wooden spoon to gradually incorporate the flour. Sprinkle the remaining tablespoon of flour over the top, cover the bowl with a cotton kitchen towel, and let rest in a warm place away from drafts until the sponge has doubled in size, about 1 hour. (Signs that the sponge has doubled in size are the disappearance of the tablespoon of flour or the formation of large cracks on top.)

continued

Meanwhile, prepare the stuffing. Place the tomatoes in a small crockery or glass bowl, add the olive oil, season with salt, pepper, and oregano and mix very well. Refrigerate, covered, until needed.

Place the garlic in a second small crockery or glass bowl, add the olive oil, and season with salt, pepper, and oregano. Refrigerate, covered, until needed.

Prepare the dough. When the sponge is ready, arrange the all-purpose flour mixed with the semolina flour in a mound on a large pastry board, then make a well in its center. Place the sponge in the well along with the water and olive oil and season with salt. Using a wooden spoon, mix together all the ingredients in the well. Start mixing with your hands, incorporating the flours from the inside rim of the well little by little until almost all the flour is incorporated. Start kneading in a folding motion, until all the flour is incorporated and the dough is elastic and smooth.

Grease a 15-inch round cake pan with the olive oil. Use a rolling pin to stretch the dough to the same size as the cake pan, then place the dough in the pan, spreading it out to reach the sides, if necessary. Place a piece of plastic wrap, then a cotton kitchen towel, over the pan and let the dough rest in a warm place away from drafts for 30 minutes. With your index finger make pockets all over the dough, filling them with the prepared tomatoes. Then make more pockets for the garlic. Drizzle the juices from the tomatoes and garlic all over the top of the *puddica* and season with the olive oil, salt, pepper, and oregano. Cover the pan with a piece of plastic wrap, then a cotton kitchen towel, and let rest in a warm place away from drafts until doubled in size, about 40 minutes.

Preheat the oven to 400 degrees. When the dough is ready, remove the towel and plastic wrap and bake until golden and crusty, about 40 minutes. Serve hot, with a little oil if necessary, and sprinkle with coarse salt if desired.

STUFFING VARIATION: In place of the tomatoes, the pockets may be stuffed with either coarsely chopped salami or with coarsely grated mozzarella cheese, seasoned with salt, pepper, and hot red pepper flakes. The pockets containing garlic remain unchanged.

PIZZA ALLA CAMPOFRANCO
Fancy Pizza

This pizza, made with a type of brioche pastry instead of bread dough, is a completely authentic pizza from Campania. It is associated with a village just outside of Naples called Campofranco. Brioche pastry is just as widespread in Italy as it is in France and since it is used for the very old and traditional fried sweet *bomboloni* (filled doughnuts), there is no reason to assume that it did not exist in Italy before the period of French influence. Also, what is possibly the most popular Italian breakfast pastry is also called brioche, though it contains less butter than the French version and is different in appearance.

The name is probably French, but quite frequently foods of Italian origin adopted French names in areas ruled by the French from the seventeenth to the nineteenth centuries, especially foods of the upper classes.

FOR THE SPONGE:
½ ounce compressed fresh yeast or
    1 package active dry yeast
5 tablespoons lukewarm or hot milk,
    depending on the yeast
½ cup unbleached all-purpose flour
Pinch of salt

FOR THE DOUGH:
¼ cup (2 ounces) sweet butter
4 extra-large eggs
1 teaspoon granulated sugar
Large pinch of fine salt
3 cups unbleached all-purpose flour
¼ cup lukewarm milk

FOR THE STUFFING:
1½ pounds ripe but not overripe tomatoes
3 large cloves garlic, peeled
¼ cup extra virgin olive oil
Salt and freshly ground black pepper
10 large fresh basil leaves

TO KNEAD THE DOUGH:
About ½ cup unbleached all-purpose flour

TO BAKE:
1½ tablespoons extra virgin olive oil
1 extra-large egg mixed together with
    1 tablespoon cold water

TO SERVE:
Fine salt
Fresh basil leaves

continued

Dissolve the yeast in the lukewarm or hot milk, then place the flour and salt in a small bowl and make a well in it. Pour the dissolved yeast into the well, then incorporate all the flour. Let the sponge rest, covered, in a warm place away from drafts, until doubled in size.

Meanwhile, melt the butter in a large metal bowl or in the bowl of a stand mixer placed over a pot of boiling water.

When the sponge is ready, mix by hand or in the mixer fitted with the paddle the melted butter with the eggs, adding them one at a time. Then add the sugar, salt, and risen sponge. Start adding the flour and milk a little at a time until all the ingredients are used up. Keep stirring until the dough is very shiny, about 1 minute. Cover the bowl and let the dough rest in a warm place away from drafts until doubled in size.

Prepare the stuffing. Cut the tomatoes into slices less than ½ inch thick and the garlic into thin slivers. Set a medium-size nonreactive skillet with the olive oil and garlic over medium heat; when the oil is warm, add the tomatoes and sauté for 1 minute on each side. Season with salt and pepper. Transfer the tomatoes and all their juices to a plate and let rest until cool, about 30 minutes.

Preheat the oven to 375 degrees and heavily oil a 14-inch round pizza pan with ¾-inch-high sides. Spread out the 2 ounces of flour on a pastry board. Transfer the dough to the board and knead for 1 minute, using the palms of your hands in a folding motion. Divide the dough into two pieces of one-third and two-thirds. Use a rolling pin to stretch the larger piece of dough out to a disk of about 15 inches in diameter. Transfer it to the prepared pan and line completely the bottom and sides. Arrange the tomatoes with all their juices over the dough and spread the basil leaves over the tomatoes. Stretch the second piece of dough into a disk the size of the bottom of the pan. Fit the layer of dough over the tomatoes and press the edges very well together. Lightly brush the top with the olive oil, then cover with plastic wrap and let rest until doubled in size, about half an hour. When ready, lightly brush the top with the egg mixture and bake for 30 minutes. Remove from the oven, sprinkle a little salt over, and serve with the basil leaves, slicing it into wedges.

STUFFING VARIATIONS

STUFFING 1: Layer over the bottom crust 1 pound ripe tomatoes, cut into pieces, cooked with 2 tablespoons olive oil and seasoned with salt and pepper; 3 ounces mozzarella cheese, coarsely grated; 5 thin slices prosciutto; and 5 tablespoons freshly grated Parmigiano cheese.

STUFFING 2: Boil 1½ pounds escarole in salted water, then sauté in 3 tablespoons olive oil, season with salt and pepper, and mix with 2 tablespoons capers in wine vinegar, drained, and about 15 Gaeta olives, pitted and cut into large pieces. Spread this over the bottom crust.

SFOGLIATA PUGLIESE

Pugliese Stuffed Focaccia

Makes 8 to 10 servings

FOR THE SPONGE:

1 cup plus 1 tablespoon unbleached
   all-purpose flour

¼ cup semolina flour

Pinch of salt

1 ounce fresh compressed yeast or
   2 packages active dry yeast

1 cup lukewarm or warm water, depending
   on the yeast

FOR THE STUFFING:

1½ pounds red onions, cleaned and thinly
   sliced

6 tablespoons extra virgin olive oil

1½ pounds ripe cherry tomatoes
   (like pugliesi "*pomodorini*"), halved

Salt and freshly ground black pepper

5 tablespoons capers in wine vinegar,
   drained

4 whole anchovies preserved in salt (see
   Note on page 10) or 8 anchovy fillets
   packed in oil, drained and coarsely
   chopped

20 sprigs fresh Italian parsley, leaves only,
   finely chopped

6 fresh basil leaves, torn into pieces

¾ cup freshly grated Pecorino Romano
   cheese

Hot red pepper flakes (optional)

FOR THE DOUGH:

4 cups unbleached all-purpose flour plus
   ½ cup for kneading after the second
   rising

¼ cup semolina flour

1¼ cups lukewarm water

3 tablespoons extra virgin olive oil

Salt

TO BAKE:

6 tablespoons extra virgin olive oil

TO SERVE:

Extra virgin olive oil and coarse salt

To make the sponge, mix the cup of all-purpose flour with the semolina flour and salt in a medium-size bowl. Make a well in the center. Dissolve the yeast in the water, then pour it into the well. Use a wooden spoon to gradually incorporate the flour. Sprinkle the remaining tablespoon of flour over the top, cover the bowl with a cotton kitchen towel, and let rest in a warm place away from drafts until the sponge has doubled in size, about 1 hour. (Signs that the sponge has doubled in size are the disappearance of the tablespoon of flour or the formation of large cracks on top.)

Meanwhile, prepare the stuffing. Place the onions and olive oil in a medium-size nonreactive skillet and set over low heat. Sauté the onions until translucent, about 5 minutes. Add the tomatoes and cook for 10 minutes, mixing every so often with a wooden spoon. Season with salt and pepper and cook for 2 minutes more. Transfer the contents of the skillet to a crockery or glass bowl and let cool for 1 hour. Add the remaining stuffing ingredients and mix well when the dough is ready to be stuffed.

Prepare the dough. When the sponge is ready, arrange the all-purpose flour mixed with the semolina flour in a mound on a large pastry board, then make a well in its center. Place the sponge in the well along with the water and olive oil and season with salt. Using a wooden spoon, mix together all the ingredients in the well. Start mixing with your hands, incorporating the flours from the inside rim of the well little by little until almost all the flour is incorporated. Start kneading in a folding motion, until all the flour is incorporated and the dough is elastic and smooth. Lightly oil a large bowl, place the dough in it, and cover the bowl first with plastic wrap, then with a kitchen towel. Let rest in a warm place away from drafts until doubled in size.

When ready, knead the risen dough with a little flour, then stretch it into a "ribbon" about 5 inches wide and about 2½ feet long. The thickness will be about ½ inch. Arrange the finished stuffing down the center of the dough along the entire length of the ribbon, leaving 2 inches empty at the two ends. Seal together the two sides of the ribbon for its entire length, enclosing the stuffing inside to resemble a very long sausage. Be sure there are no holes in the dough casing. Use 2 tablespoons of the olive oil to heavily oil a 15-inch round double cake pan (one with 3-inch-high sides). Carefully transfer the "sausage" to the pan, circling around the sides and continuing inward. One end of the ribbon will be in the center of the pan. Pour the remaining 4 tablespoons olive oil over the top, cover the pan first with plastic wrap and then with a kitchen towel, and let rise for 30 minutes.

Preheat the oven to 400 degrees. When ready, remove the towel and the plastic wrap and bake for 40 minutes. Remove from the oven, season with more oil and coarse salt, and serve, sliced, hot.

COLD APPETIZERS

❖

Among the cold dishes served as appetizers we sometimes find recipes that are called *insalate* or salads. These are never served as a salad course, usually because they involve a special sauce or marinade and contain ingredients beyond salad greens.

In Italy most cold dishes, even complicated galantines, are regarded primarily as appetizers and a formal meal still requires a hot main dish. In summer, eating an ambitious cold dish as the main course is an informal breaking of the general rule, most often allowed only at strictly family repasts.

ASPARAGI ALLA SALSA VERDE CON OLIVE

Asparagus with Green Sauce

Makes 4 to 6 servings

2 pounds asparagus, white bottom part
    removed
Coarse-grained salt
2 medium-size cloves garlic, peeled
1 tablespoon capers in wine vinegar, drained
2 whole anchovies preserved in salt
    (see Note on page 10) or 4 anchovy
    fillets packed in oil, drained

15 sprigs fresh Italian parsley, leaves only
⅓ cup extra virgin olive oil
Salt and freshly ground black pepper
6 large black Greek olives, pitted and
    coarsely chopped
Fresh basil leaves

Tie the asparagus together in a bunch. Set a medium-size stockpot of cold water over medium heat; when the water reaches a boil, place the asparagus standing up in the boiling water with coarse salt to taste. All the tips and some of the green part of the asparagus should be out of the water. Cover the pot and cook until the asparagus are cooked but not mushy. The cooking time depends on the size of the asparagus you use.

Meanwhile, cut the garlic into slivers, then chop together with the capers, anchovies, and parsley on a cutting board or in a blender or food processor. Transfer the chopped ingredients to a small bowl, add the olive oil, and season with salt and pepper.

Transfer the asparagus to a serving platter and cover them with a wet kitchen towel until cool, about half an hour. When ready, untie the asparagus and arrange them on the platter. Pour over the sauce, then sprinkle with the olives and basil leaves.

INSALATA DI SEDANO E FINOCCHI
Celery and Fennel Salad

Makes 6 servings

The celery and fennel, shaved as thin as the shavings from a truffle cutter and topped with slivers of Parmigiano, are transformed by the merest two teaspoons of authentic balsamic vinegar into something really special. The authentic D.O.C. balsamic vinegar Aceto Tradizionale Balsamico from Modena is very concentrated and expensive, like truffles, but is used in very small quantities as a rare delicacy. When using this D.O.C. vinegar, you realize the true quality of this ingredient.

4 white inner stalks celery, all strings removed

2 medium-size fennel bulbs, cleaned and cut into quarters

1 lemon

¼ cup extra virgin olive oil

Salt and freshly ground black pepper

2 teaspoons balsamic vinegar

1 large bunch arugula (*rucola* or *ruchetta*)

4 ounces Parmigiano cheese, cut into medium-size slivers

1 ounce walnuts, coarsely chopped

Fresh basil and Italian parsley leaves

Shelled walnuts in large pieces

Soak the celery and fennel in a bowl of cold water with the lemon, cut in half and squeezed, for half an hour. Drain the vegetables and use a truffle slicer or a mandoline to slice them very thin. Transfer the slices to a crockery or glass bowl and season with the oil, salt and pepper to taste, and the vinegar. Mix very well. Arrange the arugula leaves in a single layer on a serving platter, then arrange the vegetables in a layer over that. Over them lay the slivers of Parmigiano, then sprinkle with the chopped walnuts.

To serve, use a spatula so you can keep the layering as it is, without mixing the vegetables together with the cheese and nuts. Finally, sprinkle each portion with some basil and parsley leaves and a few walnut chunks.

CIPOLLE E TONNO IN INSALATA
Tuna-Flavored Onion Salad

Makes 6 to 8 servings

Canned tuna in Italy is packed in olive oil and is often paired with raw onions. One very popular dish is tuna and onions served with cooked beans and another is this dish, in which onions are flavored with an elaborately prepared marinade and bits of canned tuna. The marinade contains both white wine and its vinegar, garlic, and bay leaves, with a final touch of fresh parsley and basil.

The repertory of recipes involving canned tuna is quite distinct from the very large one involving fresh tuna, which is, of course, very plentiful in Italy and is a mainstay of Sicily and Southern Italy for substantial main dishes in place of meat.

1 pound yellow or white onions, cleaned

FOR THE POACHING BROTH:

1 cup cold water

1 cup white wine vinegar

1 cup dry white wine

3 large cloves garlic, peeled and cut into slivers

3 large bay leaves

Pinch of dried oregano

Coarse-grained salt

TO FINISH THE DISH:

4 ounces canned tuna packed in oil, preferably imported Italian, drained

6 tablespoons extra virgin olive oil

Salt and freshly ground black pepper

TO SERVE:

15 sprigs fresh Italian parsley, leaves only

10 large fresh basil leaves, torn into thirds

Thinly slice the onions and soak them in a large bowl of cold water for half an hour. Pour the cup of water, the vinegar, and wine into a medium-size saucepan, then add the garlic, bay leaves, oregano, and coarse salt. Set the pan over medium heat and simmer for half an hour.

In a small bowl, break up the tuna. Mix in the olive oil and season with salt and pepper. Drain the onions and place them in a large crockery or glass bowl. Strain the hot marinade and pour the hot liquid directly over the onions, then cover the bowl. Let rest for a few minutes, then refrigerate for 1 hour. Drain the marinade from the onions and transfer them to a serving platter. Add the tuna mixture and mix well. Sprinkle the parsley and basil over the top and serve.

PRIMI PIATTI
First Courses

Italian meals almost always have several courses. Antipasto is not always a must, but as their names indicate, the *primo piatto,* "first dish," and *secondo piatto,* second dish, are the bulwark of Italian dining. Antipasto is not counted as a numbered course; indeed, it means "before the meal" (not "before the pasta").

As is further explained under the subheading *"Minestre,"* before the mid-nineteenth century, this course was an elaborate soup, usually thick and spicy, with dumplings of vegetables, meat, or fish in it. This soup course remains in place in many other countries to this day, but in Italy it is only one possibility, indeed a minor one compared to the pasta repertory that came to dominate that course. Polenta dishes, made with coarsely ground grains, are survivals of the ancient world. In those times they could be made with wheat, barley, buckwheat, or millet and were often the only course in a working-class meal.

With the introduction of corn to Europe from the New World, that grain came to dominate polenta dishes. And rice, which was brought by the Spanish, was easily cultivated in Northern Italy and gave rise to many rice dishes, including the celebrated risotto. Strangely, though Italy is one of the main rice producers in Europe, it consumes relatively little of its own rice, which is mostly exported.

Despite these other first-dish categories, the *primo piatto* has become almost synonymous with pasta—fresh, dried, stuffed, and dressed with a great variety of sauces. And pasta, perhaps exaggeratedly, has come to symbolize Italian cooking for much of the world. All regions have their own pasta dishes. Dried pasta, because it has been used since ancient times in Southern Italy, long before Marco Polo did *not* bring it from China, has the largest repertory and now dominates in Central Italy as well. It is only in the North that rice occupies quite a large place and where *minestre* have held on the most firmly.

I include here a panorama of the first courses from many regions and hope that you make and enjoy these selected recipes.

FRESH PASTA

❖

Fresh pasta mixes some type of flour with a liquid to make a dough. The types of flour range from unbleached all-purpose wheat flour to semolina, soft wheat flour, rye, buckwheat, chick-pea or chestnut flour, cornmeal, and still others, as well as a combination of unbleached wheat flour and any or several of the above to increase their gluten content. The liquid may come from whole eggs, egg yolks, egg whites, oil, water, wine, milk, heavy cream, melted butter, or a combination of these. Most fresh pasta contains eggs, but there are some types that are eggless. These variations are largely dependent not only on what grows locally in the different regions but on the survival of certain traditional fresh pastas that date back several centuries to a period before wheat totally replaced some other types of flour, and when the use of eggs in dough was less widespread.

However, most fresh pastas are made primarily with unbleached all-purpose flour and eggs. I find no difference between the pasta that I make in Italy and the pasta that I make with unbleached all-purpose flour in the United States. The same is true of the wheat in other continental European countries. In Canada, the unbleached all-purpose flour is harder, so I use baker's flour, which is a bit softer. I do not use so-called "bread flour." In England I would use a harder flour than the "plain flour" normally used, which I find too soft to handle. And I see no advantage in using so-called "pasta flour" anywhere.

It is wise to add a pinch of salt to the pasta dough, not only for taste, but to prevent the pasta from crumbling as it dries a bit. It should be obvious that fresh home-made pasta will never turn into dried pasta, even if it dries completely. The only change as it dries is in the cooking time necessary, still only a matter of seconds, not minutes.

Fresh pasta is cooked, as is dried pasta, in a large quantity of boiling water, with coarse salt added after it boils and just before the pasta is added. It is cooked for a much shorter time. For fresh and dried pasta, it is a serious mistake to add oil to the cooking water or to rinse the pasta once it is cooked. It is a misconception to think that oil is necessary to keep the pasta from sticking together. What in fact happens is that the oil coats the pasta, making it impossible for the sauce to penetrate the pasta once sauced. In addition, rinsing pasta removes its "body" and makes it slippery. It is not done at all in Italy. It is done abroad in some restaurants to cool precooked pasta, which is then reheated instantly, not with the best results.

A very few pasta dishes require that the pasta be sautéed with the sauce just before serving; these are specifically *pasta strascicata* dishes, that is, "stir-sautéed." Do not do this with any other finished sauced pastas.

Fresh pasta should be soft when cooked and served. There is no such thing as *al dente* fresh pasta.

LAZIO

SPAGHETTI ALLA POMMAROLA CON MOZZARELLA
Spaghetti with Pommarola Sauce and Mozzarella

Makes 8 servings

Tomato sauce made with fresh vegetables is the most common sauce in Central and Northern Italy, and is a staple. In making it with fresh tomatoes, the vegetables are placed on top of the tomatoes in the pan, so they are really steamed—keeping the sauce lighter—and only the tomatoes are sautéed. Canned tomatoes may also be used with a good result.

Pommarola is usually made in large quantities and kept with a little olive oil poured over it in the refrigerator to be used over the period of about a week. Remember that Italians generally have some pasta every day as a first course. The *pommarola* may be frozen if it is made without salt; add it only after the sauce is defrosted and ready to be reheated and used.

In this Roman sauce the fresh mozzarella is added, uncooked, to the warm sauced pasta.

FOR THE *POMMAROLA* SAUCE:

1 medium-size red onion, cleaned

1 medium-size stalk celery

2 large cloves garlic, peeled

1 medium-size carrot, scraped

10 sprigs fresh Italian parsley, leaves only

8 large basil leaves, fresh or preserved in
    salt (page 2)

2 pounds very ripe tomatoes or drained
    canned tomatoes, preferably imported
    Italian

2 tablespoons extra virgin olive oil

Salt and freshly ground black pepper

2 tablespoons (1 ounce) sweet butter

1 pound dried spaghetti, preferably
    imported Italian, or fresh

TO MAKE FRESH SPAGHETTI:

3 cups unbleached all-purpose flour

3 teaspoons olive oil or vegetable oil

3 extra-large eggs

2 tablespoons stemmed, boiled, drained,
    squeezed dry, and finely chopped
    spinach

Pinch of salt

TO COOK THE PASTA:

Coarse-grained salt

TO SERVE:

8 ounces mozzarella cheese, preferably
    buffalo mozzarella, cut into small cubes

8 large fresh basil leaves

Prepare the *pommarola* sauce first. Very coarsely chop the onion, celery, garlic, carrot, parsley, and basil together on a cutting board. If fresh tomatoes are used, cut them into large pieces. Place the tomatoes in a medium-size nonreactive casserole, then add the onion mixture and olive oil. Do not mix. Set the casserole, covered, over low heat and cook for 1½ hours, shaking it every so often, but without mixing, to prevent the tomatoes from sticking to the bottom. Pass the contents of the casserole through a food mill fitted with the disk with the smallest holes into another casserole. Place over medium heat, season with salt and pepper to taste, and add the butter. Mix very well and let reduce for 15 minutes, stirring every so often with a wooden spoon. Let the sauce rest off the heat until needed. The sauce may be prepared up to one week in advance and kept, covered, in the refrigerator.

If using fresh spaghetti, prepare the pasta with the ingredients and quantities listed, placing the chopped spinach in the well of the flour with the other ingredients, according to the directions on page 3. Roll out the pasta to ⅛ inch thick (on a manual pasta machine that would be two settings before the last one) and cut into spaghetti. Let the pasta rest on paper or cotton kitchen towels until needed.

Bring a large pot of cold water to a boil and add coarse salt to taste. Add the pasta and cook for 1 to 3 minutes for fresh pasta, depending on the dryness, and 9 to 12 minutes for dried pasta, depending on the brand. Meanwhile, reheat the sauce, then drain the pasta and transfer it to a large, warmed bowl. Pour the sauce over, mix very well, and transfer to a large serving platter. Sprinkle the cubed mozzarella all over and serve immediately with the basil leaves.

Paparele and Stracci

Paparele and *stracci* are two regional fresh pastas, the first from Veneto, the second from Rome. *Paparele* is an egg pasta, its dough containing two unusual ingredients, semolina and milk. The pasta is cut much like tagliatelle, but a bit wider. *Paparele e Bisi*, in a Venetian manner, combines this pasta with peas.

Stracci have sweet paprika in the dough, unusual for Italy and especially for Rome, and are cut into squares. The dressing is almost the same sauce as in the meat dish *Coda alla Vaccinara*, with a few minor differences.

VENETO

PAPARELE E BISI
Paparele Pasta with Peas

Makes 6 to 8 servings

FOR THE PASTA:

2½ cups unbleached all-purpose flour

½ cup semolina flour

3 extra-large eggs

2 tablespoons milk

1 tablespoon (½ ounce) sweet butter, at
    room temperature

Pinch of salt

FOR THE SAUCE:

1 small red onion, cleaned

15 sprigs fresh Italian parsley, leaves only

6 tablespoons (3 ounces) sweet butter

3 ounces prosciutto or pancetta, ground

2 pounds shelled June peas or 2 pounds
    frozen tiny tender peas

Salt and freshly ground black pepper

About 2 cups completely defatted chicken
    or vegetable broth, preferably
    homemade

TO COOK THE PASTA:

Coarse-grained salt

TO SERVE:

¼ cup (2 ounces) sweet butter

Freshly grated Parmigiano cheese

Fresh Italian parsley leaves

Prepare the pasta with the ingredients and quantities listed above according to the directions on page 3, placing the butter in the well of the flour with the other ingredients. Roll out the pasta to a thickness of ¹⁄₁₆ inch (on a manual pasta machine that would be next to the last setting). Cut the pasta sheet into pieces about 10 inches long, then into *paparele*—a little bit wider than tagliatelle.

If you do not have the wider cutter attachment on your pasta machine, cut the pieces of pasta with a very sharp knife, not with a scalloped pastry wheel. Let the *paparele* rest on paper or kitchen towels until needed.

Prepare the sauce. Finely chop the onion and parsley together on a cutting board. Place a large skillet with the butter over medium heat; when the butter is melted, add the ground pancetta and onion mixture. Lightly sauté for almost 20 minutes over very low heat. When ready, raise the heat to medium, add the peas (if using frozen peas, do not defrost them), season with salt and pepper, and cook for 5 minutes, then start adding the broth ½ cup at a time, not adding more until the present addition has cooked down, until the peas are completely cooked but still retain their shape.

Place a medium-size pot of cold water over medium heat; when the water reaches a boil, add coarse salt to taste, then the pasta, and cook for 30 seconds to 1 minute, depending on its dryness. Meanwhile, place the butter in a large bowl and set the bowl over the boiling water to melt the butter. Drain the pasta, transfer it to the bowl containing the butter, mix very well, then pour in the contents of the skillet with all the peas and their juices. Mix very well, then transfer to a warmed serving dish and serve warm with the freshly grated Parmigiano and parsley leaves.

❖

STRACCI ALLA VACCINARA
Stracci Pasta with Vaccinara Sauce

Makes 8 servings

FOR THE SAUCE:

Coda alla Vaccinara (page 232)

FOR THE PASTA:

4 cups unbleached all-purpose flour

4 extra-large eggs

4 teaspoons olive oil or vegetable oil

4 teaspoons cold water

4 teaspoons sweet paprika

Pinch of salt

TO COOK THE PASTA:

Coarse-grained salt

TO SERVE:

Freshly grated Parmigiano cheese

Prepare the sauce with the ingredients and quantities listed on page 232, but the celery, which in that recipe is added at the end, should instead be chopped along with the other vegetables and added at the beginning. You will need 4 cups of the reduced and skimmed sauce for the amount of pasta you are going to prepare.

Prepare the pasta with the ingredients and quantities listed above according to the directions on page 3. Roll out the pasta to a thickness of about 1/16 inch (on a manual pasta machine that would be the next to last setting). Use a scalloped pastry wheel to cut the pasta sheets into *stracci*, pasta squares of about 3 inches.

Bring a large pot of cold water to a boil over medium heat, add coarse salt to taste, then the pasta, and cook for 1 to 2 minutes, depending on the dryness of the pasta. *Stracci* should not be completely soft. Drain the pasta, transfer to a large skillet containing 3 cups of the sauce over medium heat, and gently finish cooking the pasta, mixing constantly with a wooden spoon. Just before removing the pasta from the skillet, add the remaining cup of sauce and mix very well. Transfer to a large serving platter and serve hot with the freshly grated Parmigiano sprinkled all over.

Abruzzese Fresh Pasta Cut
with a "Guitar"

In Abruzzo, the region parallel to Rome and Lazio, on the Adriatic side of Italy, fresh pasta is still made on occasion by most families. And the unique aspect of their excellent pasta is the way it is cut. A wooden implement, about 19 inches long and 8 inches wide, is strung with metal strings on each side, which are used as cutters for the long sheet of pasta—one side for wider pasta, the other for finer strands. They call this implement or instrument the "guitar" and if you strum it, you will find that it is indeed tuned. Why? The reason is shrouded in the mystery of centuries. But there is no mystery to its use in our century. And the particular cut of the substantial strands of pasta is unique to Abruzzese pasta, which is used for a body of recipes, two of which follow. Both have semolina and saffron in the dough. Abruzzo, along with Calabria, has a strong taste for hot red pepper and uses it abundantly in many dishes, including these.

Maccheroni alla Chitarra uses the wider cut of the pasta and dresses it with a pancetta/onion sauce, serving it with basil, parsley, and grated pecorino cheese. *Chitarrina al Sugo di Peperoni* uses the thinner cut of pasta and is served with a sauce of peppers, onions, garlic, and pancetta or prosciutto, with a sprinkling of the usual grated pecorino cheese.

MACCHERONI ALLA CHITARRA
Pasta Cut with a "Guitar"

Makes 12 servings

FOR THE PASTA:

3 cups unbleached all-purpose flour

½ cup very fine semolina flour

4 extra-large eggs

2 tablespoons olive oil or vegetable oil

Pinch of salt

Large pinch of ground saffron

FOR THE SAUCE:

6 ounces pancetta, in one piece

1 large red onion, cleaned

10 fresh basil leaves

15 sprigs fresh Italian parsley, leaves only

½ cup extra virgin olive oil

Salt and freshly ground black pepper

Hot red pepper flakes

About 1 cup completely defatted chicken or meat broth, preferably homemade, or cold water

TO COOK THE PASTA:

Coarse-grained salt

TO SERVE:

Fresh basil leaves and Italian parsley leaves

Freshly grated aged Pecorino Romano cheese

Prepare the pasta with the ingredients and quantities listed above, placing the semolina flour and saffron in the well of the all-purpose flour with the other ingredients, according to the directions on page 3. Roll out the pasta to almost ⅛ inch thick (on a manual pasta machine that would be two settings before the last one) and cut into 8-inch-long pieces. Let the pasta rest until a very thin skin forms on it. When ready, place each piece of pasta over the "guitar" and, with a rolling pin, roll up and down several times so the strings of the guitar cut the pasta. Repeat with all the pieces of pasta, then let the pasta rest on paper or cotton kitchen towels until needed.

Prepare the sauce. Finely grind the pancetta in a meat grinder and finely chop the onion, basil, and parsley together on a cutting board. Heat the olive oil in a medium-size skillet over medium heat; when the oil is warm, add the pancetta and onion mixture. Sauté until the onion is translucent, about 15 minutes, stirring every so often. Season with salt, black pepper, and hot red pepper. Start adding the broth or water ¼ cup at a time and cook for 15 minutes more.

Bring a large pot of cold water to a boil, add coarse salt to taste, then the *maccheroni*, and cook for about 9 minutes. The *maccheroni* are quite thick and adding semolina flour to the dough makes the pasta very resistant, which is the classic texture for this regional pasta.

Drain the pasta, transfer to a large bowl, pour the sauce over, mix very well, and transfer to a large serving platter. Serve with the basil and parsley leaves and plenty of freshly grated Pecorino Romano cheese.

CHITARRINA AL SUGO DI PEPERONI
"Guitar" Pasta with Pepper Sauce
Makes 6 to 8 servings

FOR THE PASTA:

3 cups unbleached all-purpose flour

½ cup very fine semolina flour

4 extra-large eggs

2 tablespoons olive oil or vegetable oil

Large pinch of ground saffron

Pinch of salt

FOR THE SAUCE:

1½ pounds ripe tomatoes or drained canned
   tomatoes, preferably imported Italian

Coarse-grained salt

4 large yellow bell peppers

1 medium-size red onion, cleaned

2 small cloves garlic, peeled

Large pinch to ½ teaspoon hot red pepper
   flakes, to your taste

4 ounces pancetta or prosciutto, in one
   piece

½ cup extra virgin olive oil

1 to 1½ cups completely defatted chicken
   broth, preferably homemade

Salt and freshly ground black pepper

TO COOK THE PASTA:

Coarse-grained salt

TO SERVE:

Freshly grated Pecorino Romano cheese

Prepare the pasta with the ingredients and quantities listed above, placing the semolina flour, together with the eggs, olive oil, saffron, and salt, in the well of the all-purpose flour. Stretch the layer of pasta to ⅛ inch thick (on a manual pasta machine, that would be two settings before the last one).

Prepare the *chitarrina*. Let the pasta sheet rest on cotton kitchen towels until a very thin skin forms on it, then cut it into pieces 2 inches shorter than the length of the "guitar" strings. Use that side of the "guitar" with the strings closer together in order to cut the pasta into thin strands. Place each piece of pasta over the guitar and, with a rolling pin, roll up and down several times so the strings of the guitar cut the pasta. Repeat with all the pieces of pasta. Then let the cut pasta rest on cotton kitchen towels until needed.

Prepare the sauce. If using fresh tomatoes, blanch them in salted boiling water for a minute and remove their skins. Pass fresh or canned tomatoes through a food mill fitted with the disk with the smallest holes into a crockery or glass bowl. Skin the peppers by first singeing them or partially roasting them in the oven to loosen the skins (see page 176). Remove skins, stems, and seeds, then cut the peppers lengthwise into strips less than ½ inch wide. Finely chop the onion, garlic, and red pepper flakes together on a cutting board. Cut the pancetta or prosciutto into very small pieces.

Place a medium-size nonreactive casserole with the olive oil over medium heat; when the oil is warm, add the chopped onion mixture and sauté for 5 minutes, stirring every so often with a wooden spoon. Add the pancetta and cook for another 5 minutes. Add the peppers, lightly sauté for 3 more minutes, then pour in the strained tomatoes. Mix very well. Cover the casserole and continue to cook for 30 minutes, stirring every now and then with the wooden spoon and adding hot broth as more liquid is needed. After 15 minutes, season with salt and pepper.

Bring a large pot of cold water to a boil over medium heat, add coarse salt to taste, then the pasta, and cook for 1 to 3 minutes, depending on its dryness.

Meanwhile, warm a large serving platter. Ladle 2 cups of the hot sauce onto the platter, drain the pasta, arrange it over the sauce, and pour the remaining sauce over. Mix very well, sprinkle the Pecorino Romano on top, and serve.

CORZETTI STAMPATI CON TOCCO DI PESCE
"Stamped" Pasta with Fish Sauce

Makes 6 to 8 servings

Corzetti was the name of a Genoese coin, and the word was taken over to describe a coin-shaped pasta that is stamped on both sides. The pasta is made with all-purpose flour, whole-wheat flour, or chestnut flour, exclusively or in combination. The stamped pasta may be dressed with a number of different sauces. This recipe uses chestnut flour in combination with some all-purpose flour to make the coin-shaped pasta, and it is dressed with a fish sauce prepared with wine, bay leaves, and vegetables.

The wooden stamp used to make the pasta has a handle with a design on one end, while the cutter has another design on its reverse side. Traditionally, one design was usually the family crest and the other some symbol of the sea, of fertility, or of good luck. Many people in Genoa still have their old family stamps, and it is possible to find copies made at the present time.

FOR THE PASTA:

3½ cups unbleached all-purpose flour

1 cup fresh chestnut flour, imported from
    Italy or France (available in specialty
    food stores), or whole-wheat flour

1 cup cold water

1 extra-large egg

Pinch of salt

FOR THE SAUCE:

4 cups cold water

1 cup dry white wine

2 bay leaves

1 medium-size carrot, scraped and cut into
    large pieces

1 small red onion, cleaned and cut into
    pieces

Fine salt

5 black peppercorns

1 pound fish (a whole fish with head and tail
    removed or several different types of
    fish, but not oily ones)

Coarse-grained salt

1 lemon, cut in half

¼ cup extra virgin olive oil

1 medium-size red onion, cleaned and thinly
    sliced

15 sprigs fresh Italian parsley, leaves only

2 teaspoons rosemary leaves, fresh or
    preserved in salt (page 2), wrapped in
    cheesecloth

Salt and freshly ground black pepper

TO COOK THE PASTA:

Coarse-grained salt

1½ tablespoons sweet butter or extra virgin
    olive oil

TO SERVE:

Sprigs fresh marjoram or rosemary

Prepare the pasta with the ingredients and quantities listed above according to the directions on page 3. Roll out the pasta to ¹⁄₁₆ inch (on a manual pasta machine that would be the next to last setting). *Corzetti* stamps, made of wood, are in two pieces. The bottom piece serves two functions. Its bottom side is like a cookie cutter; the top side is carved to produce an image. The top piece has a handle and the bottom produces a second and different image. Cut the pasta sheet into disks using the cutter of the stamp and let them rest for several minutes on cotton kitchen or paper towels. Discard the pasta remnants. Place one of the prepared disks between the two carved images and press, producing a disk with a different image on each side. Continue until all the disks are stamped, lightly flouring the two carved sides each time. Let the *corzetti* rest at least 1 hour before using; otherwise the printed design will disappear in the boiling water.

Meanwhile, prepare the sauce. Place the water, wine, bay leaves, carrot, and onion cut in pieces in a medium-size casserole set over medium heat. When the water reaches a boil, add fine salt to taste and the peppercorns, reduce the heat to medium-low, and simmer for 20 minutes.

continued

Soak the fish in a bowl of cold water with a little coarse salt added and the lemon halves squeezed into it.

Strain and discard the vegetables from the broth, drain the fish, and add it to the broth. Simmer until the fish is barely cooked, about 10 minutes or less, depending on the thickness of the flesh and the quality of the fish. Transfer the fish to a cutting board and discard all the bones. Save the poaching broth.

When ready, bring a large pot of cold water to a boil over medium heat and place a skillet with the oil over low heat. When the oil is lukewarm, add the sliced onion and sauté for 2 minutes, then sprinkle the parsley over it and add the bag of rosemary. After a few seconds, add the fish and ½ cup of the reserved fish broth, seasoning with salt and pepper. When the broth is almost evaporated, pour in 1 cup more and simmer for another 15 minutes. Discard the bag of rosemary leaves. When the water in the stockpot reaches a boil, add coarse salt to taste, then the pasta, stir, and cook for 4 minutes or more, depending on the dryness of the pasta. Pasta should be completely cooked, but will be a bit resistant because there is water and only one egg in the dough. Drain the pasta, transfer to a large bowl with a little butter or oil, and mix very well. Each serving will be prepared with some of the pasta, some of the fish sauce on one side, and the sprigs of fresh marjoram or rosemary.

FREGOLA AL FORNO
Stewed Sardinian Pasta

Makes 8 to 10 servings

Fregola is a pasta made from unprocessed couscous, that is, coarsely ground wheat, and is the classic pasta of Sardinia; it is not well known in other parts of Italy. Fregola is technically a pasta, because it combines ground wheat with liquid. Sometimes it is prepared with saffron already mixed into the liquid, so there are two types available, plain fregola and saffron fregola. It also exists in different sizes, small fregola being utilized mostly in soups and the medium-sized and large fregola being served with sauces. Packaged fregola is increasingly available in gourmet shops and Italian markets, but it is easily made at home. Instructions for making it are at the end of this recipe.

12 cups completely defatted chicken broth, preferably homemade

Coarse-grained salt

1 pound dried large saffron fregola pasta (*fregola grossa*)

Large pinch of ground saffron, preferably Sardinian

3 ounces pancetta or prosciutto, in one piece

15 sprigs fresh Italian parsley, leaves only

5 tablespoons extra virgin olive oil

1 large red onion, cleaned and thinly sliced

2 large cloves garlic, peeled and finely chopped

Salt and freshly ground black pepper

2 tablespoons (1 ounce) sweet butter

1 cup freshly grated Pecorino Sardo or Pecorino Romano cheese

TO SERVE:

Freshly grated Pecorino Sardo or Pecorino Romano cheese

Fresh basil leaves

Taste the broth for salt and add coarse salt as needed. In a large pot bring the broth to a boil over medium heat, add the fregola and saffron, and cook until the pasta is *al dente*, about 20 minutes. Drain the pasta, leaving it in a little cooking broth and reserving 2 additional cups of the broth. Let the pasta rest in a crockery or glass bowl until the sauce is ready.

Coarsely grind the pancetta or prosciutto with a meat grinder and coarsely chop the parsley leaves on a cutting board. Place a medium-size skillet with the olive oil over medium heat; when the oil is warm, add the pancetta, parsley, onion, and garlic and sauté until the onion is translucent, about 5 minutes, adding some of the saved broth if needed. Season with salt and pepper.

Preheat the oven to 375 degrees. Heavily butter the bottom and sides of a medium-size oven-proof casserole, preferably made of terra-cotta. Arrange one-third of the fregola in the casserole and cover with one-third of the cheese, then one-third of the pancetta mixture. Repeat the layers two more times in the same order. The fregola should still be sitting in a little broth, so if it has absorbed all the liquid, add enough of the remaining saved cooking broth for the fregola to absorb while baking. Cover the casserole and bake for 20 minutes. Fregola should be completely cooked, but will still be resistant. Mix very well and serve from the casserole, with a little more cheese sprinkled over and the fresh basil leaves on top.

To make fregola: Spread out 1 pound couscous grains (not the precooked couscous) and, little by little, add drops of cold water to all the grains until ½ cup of water has been absorbed. Rub the grains between your hands to keep them separated as they swell. Mix together 2 large egg yolks, ½ teaspoon salt, and 2 large pinches of ground saffron and, using this liquid, repeat the above procedure of adding it to the grains. The swelling will increase considerably. Preheat the oven to 375 degrees. Spread the couscous over a cookie sheet, bake for 10 minutes, turn off the oven, and leave in the oven for 3 hours. Remove from the oven, let cool for 2 hours, and store in a closed jar until needed.

Stuffed Fresh Pastas

In the name *Tordelli di Fagioli*, the word *tordelli* might be thought to be some dialectal variation of *tortelli*, which, in Tuscany, refers to the stuffed pasta now often called ravioli—which, in earlier centuries, were indeed called tortelli. But *tordelli* refers instead to the shape of the pasta, thought to resemble the breast of the small birds *tordi*, which often eat so much that they look overstuffed. And of course the pasta itself is overstuffed, with a wonderful bean puree. The beans have been cooked with sage, the herb of choice in preparing *tordi*, or any kind of game bird.

Ravioli ai Filetti di Sogliole, from Le Marche, are stuffed quite simply with ricotta, parsley, and nutmeg, but the sauce is made from fillets of sole, which are left whole and served together with the ravioli. It is unusual to combine the meat that flavors the sauce with the pasta and even rarer to do it with a stuffed pasta.

Le Marche is on the Adriatic and has access to an abundant supply of Mediterranean (sometimes called "Dover") sole.

The producers of the marvelous San Daniele prosciutto insist that their choice product be served uncooked so that the unadorned prosciutto may be properly appreciated. During a festival in that beautiful hilltop town in Friuli, I wandered down a street and noticed on the menu of a trattoria a local homemade pasta called *fagottini*, which was described as served with slices of the local prosciutto. But when the dish came, there was prosciutto, chopped up in the stuffing itself, that was indeed cooked, along with uncooked slices. I was fascinated by the unusual shape of the "little package," which is what the name means, and particularly by the way it was cut and sealed in one motion, as you'll see below. It is a unique local pasta and deserves to be better known.

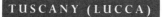
TORDELLI DI FAGIOLI

Tortelli Stuffed with Bean Puree

Makes 6 to 8 servings

FOR THE BEANS:

¾ cup dried cannellini (white kidney) beans, picked over

5 cups cold water

2 teaspoons extra virgin olive oil

5 medium-size sage leaves, fresh or preserved in salt (page 2)

Salt and freshly ground black pepper

Large pinch of hot red pepper flakes

5 medium-size cloves garlic, peeled

FOR THE TOMATOES:

5 tablespoons extra virgin olive oil

½ pound very ripe tomatoes or drained canned tomatoes, preferably imported Italian

5 large sage leaves, fresh or preserved in salt (page 2)

Salt and freshly ground black pepper

TO FINISH THE STUFFING:

½ cup freshly grated Parmigiano cheese

¼ cup very fine unseasoned bread crumbs, preferably homemade, lightly toasted

2 extra-large egg yolks

Salt and freshly ground black pepper

FOR THE PASTA:

3 cups unbleached all-purpose flour

4 extra-large eggs

Pinch of salt

FOR THE SAUCE:

5 tablespoons extra virgin olive oil

5 large sage leaves, fresh or preserved in salt (page 2)

5 large cloves garlic, unpeeled

3 pounds very ripe tomatoes or drained canned tomatoes, preferably imported Italian

Salt and freshly ground black pepper

TO COOK THE PASTA:

Coarse-grained salt

TO SERVE:

½ cup freshly grated Parmigiano cheese

Soak the beans overnight in a bowl of cold water. The next morning, drain and rinse the beans and place them in a small saucepan with the water, olive oil, sage, salt, black pepper, hot pepper, and garlic cloves and cook over medium heat until the beans are cooked and tender, about 45 minutes. Discard the garlic and sage.

continued

Meanwhile, prepare the tomatoes. Heat the olive oil in a medium-size nonreactive saucepan over low heat. If using fresh tomatoes, cut them into pieces, then add the tomatoes and sage to the saucepan and let cook for 15 minutes, stirring a few times. Season with salt and pepper. Drain the beans, add them to the tomatoes, and let cook for another 10 minutes, stirring a few times. Pass the contents of the saucepan through a food mill fitted with the disk with the smallest holes into a clean saucepan. Place the saucepan over medium heat. Reduce it for 5 minutes, constantly stirring so the beans won't stick to the bottom of the pan. Transfer to a crockery or glass bowl and let rest until cold, about a half hour.

When ready, add ½ cup of the cheese, the bread crumbs, and egg yolks to the tomato-bean mixture, mix well with a wooden spoon, add salt and pepper to taste, and refrigerate, covered, until needed.

Prepare the pasta with the ingredients and quantities listed above according to the directions on page 3. Roll out the pasta to a thickness less than 1/16 inch (on a manual pasta machine that would be next to the last setting). Prepare 2½-inch tortelli, following the directions for pasta on page 3 and using ½ tablespoon of stuffing for each. Let the tortelli rest on cotton towels until needed.

Prepare the sauce. Heat the olive oil in a medium-size nonreactive saucepan over medium heat. When the oil is warm, add the sage and unpeeled garlic cloves and sauté for 2 minutes. If using fresh tomatoes, cut them into pieces. Whether using fresh or canned tomatoes, pass them through a food mill fitted with the disk with the smallest holes into a small crockery or glass bowl. Discard the sage and garlic from the oil, add the tomatoes, reduce the heat to medium-low, and cook until you have a rather thick sauce, about 20 minutes, stirring every so often with a wooden spoon. Season with salt and pepper.

Bring a large pot of cold water to a boil, add coarse salt to taste, then the tortelli, and cook 1 to 3 minutes, depending on their dryness. Ladle ½ cup of the sauce into a large warmed serving platter, use a strainer-skimmer to transfer some of the cooked tortelli to the platter, then continue alternating layers of sauce and tortelli until everything is used up. The top layer should be sauce. Serve hot, with the Parmigiano sprinkled over each serving.

RAVIOLI AI FILETTI DI SOGLIOLE
Ravioli with Sole Sauce

Makes 6 servings

FOR THE STUFFING:

8 ounces ricotta, drained

2 extra-large egg yolks

1 cup freshly grated Parmigiano cheese

10 sprigs fresh Italian parsley, leaves only,
    finely chopped

Salt and freshly ground black pepper

Pinch of freshly grated nutmeg

FOR THE PASTA:

3 cups unbleached all-purpose flour

4 extra-large eggs

2 teaspoons olive oil or vegetable oil

Pinch of salt

FOR THE SAUCE:

4 sole fillets (2 whole sole, filleted), each
    fillet then cut in half down the middle

Coarse-grained salt

1 lemon, cut in half

1 small red onion, cleaned

1 medium-size clove garlic, peeled

1 stalk celery, very well scraped

10 sprigs fresh Italian parsley, leaves only

¾ cup extra virgin olive oil

1 pound ripe tomatoes or drained canned
    tomatoes, preferably imported Italian

Freshly ground black pepper

¼ cup dry white wine

TO COOK THE PASTA:

5 quarts cold water or completely defatted
    chicken or meat broth, preferably
    homemade

Coarse-grained salt

Prepare the stuffing. Place the ricotta in a small bowl, then add the egg yolks, Parmigiano, and parsley and mix very well. Season with salt and pepper and the nutmeg. Mix again and refrigerate, covered with plastic wrap, until needed.

Prepare the pasta with the ingredients and quantities listed above according to the directions on page 3. Roll out the pasta to less than ¹⁄₁₆ inch thick (on a manual pasta machine that would be the next to last setting). Place ½-tablespoon dots of the stuffing about 3 inches apart over the sheet of pasta. Cover with another sheet of pasta and press down between the dots of stuffing. Cut into rectangles with a pastry wheel. Be sure to seal the edges around the stuffing very well. Let the ravioli rest on cotton kitchen towels until needed.

Prepare the sauce. Place the sole fillets in a large bowl of cold water. Add a little coarse salt and squeeze in the juice from the lemon halves. Let sit for 30 minutes. Finely chop the onion, garlic, celery, and parsley together on a cutting board. Place a large nonreactive skillet with the olive oil over medium heat; when the oil is warm, add the chopped mixture and slowly sauté for 10 minutes, mixing with a wooden spoon. If fresh tomatoes are used, cut them into pieces. Whether using fresh or canned tomatoes, pass them through a food mill fitted with the disk with the smallest holes into a bowl and then add them to the skillet. Season with salt and pepper and reduce until the vegetables are soft, about 10 minutes. Place the drained sole fillets over the sauce in the skillet, cook for 1 minute, turn the fillets over, and add the wine. Cook for 2 to 3 minutes more.

Meanwhile, bring a large pot with the cold water or the broth to a boil over medium heat, add coarse salt to taste, then add the ravioli. Cook for 1 to 3 minutes, depending on their dryness. Use a skimmer to transfer the ravioli to a large serving platter, alternating layers of pasta and sauce. The top layer should be of sauce and all the fish fillets. Serve hot.

❖

FAGOTTINI DI SAN DANIELE
Little Pasta Packages with Prosciutto

Makes 6 servings

FOR THE STUFFING:

2 tablespoons (1 ounce) sweet butter

2 tablespoons extra virgin olive oil

1 whole chicken breast from a 3½-
   to 4-pound chicken with the skin on

1 bay leaf

2 sage leaves, fresh or preserved in salt
   (page 2)

Salt and freshly ground black pepper

4 ounces prosciutto, in one piece

2 extra-large egg yolks

¼ cup freshly grated Parmigiano cheese

Freshly grated nutmeg

FOR THE PASTA:

4 cups unbleached all-purpose flour

4 extra-large eggs

2 tablespoons milk

2 tablespoons olive oil or vegetable oil

Pinch of salt

FOR THE SAUCE:

1 medium-size red onion, cleaned

2 medium-size carrots, scraped

3 stalks celery

15 sprigs fresh Italian parsley, leaves only

5 fresh basil leaves

2 small cloves garlic, peeled

¼ cup (2 ounces) sweet butter

¼ cup extra virgin olive oil

1 cup dry white wine

2 cups completely defatted chicken or meat
   broth, preferably homemade

Salt and freshly ground black pepper

TO COOK THE PASTA:

Coarse-grained salt

TO SERVE:

¼ cup (2 ounces) sweet butter

6 thin slices prosciutto

Freshly ground black pepper

Freshly grated Grana Padano cheese

Prepare the stuffing. Heat the butter and olive oil together in a small skillet over medium heat. When the butter is melted, add the chicken breast, bay leaf, and sage and sauté over low heat for 20 minutes, turning the chicken breast several times. Season with salt and pepper. Remove the skillet from the heat. Transfer the chicken breast to a cutting board, saving all its juices in the skillet. Discard the bay leaf and sage, then bone the chicken breast, discarding the skin and bones. Finely chop or grind the chicken breast and prosciutto together, then transfer the mixture back to the skillet with all the juices. Mix very well, then place everything in a crockery or glass bowl. Add the egg yolks and grated Parmigiano and season with salt, pepper, and nutmeg. Mix very well. Cover the bowl with plastic wrap and refrigerate until needed.

Prepare the pasta with the ingredients and quantities listed above according to the directions on page 3. Roll out the pasta to a thickness of less than $\frac{1}{16}$ inch (on a manual pasta machine that would be the last setting). Cut the pasta sheet into 6-inch squares and immediately stuff the pasta. Once the pasta dries out even a little bit it will become impossible to seal the packages. Place a tablespoon of the stuffing in the center of the each square. Fold the pasta square in half to become a triangle, then, as you wrap a package, place a string just above the stuffing and make a knot; in this way the pasta will be cut evenly and closed at the same time. Do not press the edges, or the dough will become very tough. Let the packages rest on kitchen or paper towels until needed.

Prepare the sauce. Coarsely chop the onion, carrots, and celery together on a cutting board, then finely chop the parsley, basil, and garlic together. Combine it all together. Place a medium-size casserole with the butter and olive oil over medium heat; when the butter is melted, add the chopped mixture and lightly sauté until the onion is translucent, about 10 minutes. Add the wine, reduce the heat to low, and simmer for 15 minutes. Add the broth $\frac{1}{4}$ cup at a time, letting the broth cook down each time before adding more. Stir every so often with a wooden spoon. Add salt and pepper to taste. When all the broth is used up, a rather smooth vegetable sauce will have formed.

Bring a large pot of cold water to a boil, add coarse salt to taste, then the pasta, and cook for 1 to 3 minutes, depending on the dryness of the pasta. Melt the butter on a large serving platter set over boiling water. Place a slice of prosciutto on each serving plate. When the pasta is ready, transfer it to the platter to coat with the melted butter, then to the individual plates over the prosciutto slices. Ladle some of the sauce over, season with a little black pepper, and sprinkle over the grated Grana Padano. Serve hot.

❖

Large Stuffed Pastas

Large stuffed pastas, like the three following, though they require much work, are convenient because the elements may be prepared the day before. The pasta can be assembled and placed in the refrigerator in glass baking pans and baked just before eating on the next day.

Pasta Incartata ai Carciofi from Sicily is an unusual type of layered pasta, that is, lasagne, in which the bottom layer of pasta does not cover the sides of the pan and is not folded over the top layer at the end. The pasta layers are simply fitted on top of each other, with stuffing, in this case made from artichokes, placed in between.

The pasta itself contains chick-pea flour as well as wheat flour. Chick-pea flour is used in batters in Tuscany and Liguria as well as in Sicily, but making pasta with it is a strictly Sicilian thing to do. Though a smaller proportion of the chick-pea flour is used, it changes both the taste and texture of the all-purpose flour.

Pasta Ripiena di Melanzane is made with squares of fresh pasta, but only two layers of it, on the bottom and on top. In between are sandwiched fried eggplant slices or cubes in a tomato sauce with Parmigiano. In Sicily the combination of eggplant and pasta prevails, and generally the eggplant is fried before it is combined with the other ingredients. On the island *pasta alla norma* means "pasta in the normal manner," and refers to the Sicilian pastas with eggplant. The name has nothing to do with Bellini's opera, though he was a good Sicilian himself.

Ruote di Pasta Ripiene uses large rectangles of fresh pasta that are covered with a layer of stuffing. The composite is closed by rolling it up. The roll is then cut into ½-inch-thick slices, which produces the shape of a wheel, hence the name, "stuffed wheels of pasta." Note the variation in which there are two layers of pasta with two thinner layers of stuffing and a layer of boiled ham placed over the second layer of stuffing before everything is rolled up. When the roll is cut, the pinkish ham can be seen in the center of each "wheel." Both versions of stuffed wheels come from the Emilia-Romagna region.

PASTA INCARTATA AI CARCIOFI
Layered Pasta with Artichokes

Makes 8 to 10 servings

6 large artichokes

1 medium-size lemon, cut in half

15 sprigs fresh Italian parsley,
    leaves only

5 cloves garlic, peeled

3 tablespoons (1½ ounces) sweet butter

2 tablespoons extra virgin olive oil

3 cups completely defatted chicken broth,
    preferably homemade

Salt and freshly ground black pepper

FOR THE *BALSAMELLA* (BECHAMEL):

¼ cup (2 ounces) sweet butter

2 medium-size cloves garlic, peeled

¼ cup unbleached all-purpose flour

2¾ cups milk

Salt and freshly ground black pepper

Large pinch of freshly grated nutmeg

FOR THE PASTA:

1¾ cups unbleached all-purpose flour

1 cup chick-pea flour (see Note)

3 extra-large eggs

2 tablespoons olive oil or vegetable oil

1 tablespoon cold water

Large pinch of fine salt

A few twists of black pepper

TO COOK THE PASTA:

Coarse-grained salt

2 tablespoons olive oil or vegetable oil

TO BAKE:

¼ cup (2 ounces) sweet butter

4 ounces Pecorino Romano cheese, freshly
    grated

TO SERVE:

Freshly grated Pecorino Romano cheese

Clean the artichokes (see technique on page 4), removing all the green leaves and chokes, and cut them into 2-inch pieces. This should yield about 22 ounces of cleaned artichokes. Place them in a bowl of cold water with the juice of the squeezed lemon halves.

Finely chop the parsley and garlic together on a cutting board. Place a large nonreactive casserole with the butter and olive oil over medium heat; when the butter is almost melted, add the garlic mixture and sauté for 1 minute. Drain the artichokes and add them to the casserole. Cook for 2 minutes, then start to add the broth ½ cup a time. Do not add the next ½ cup until the first addition has almost entirely reduced. After 1 cup of broth has been used, season with salt and pepper, then continue adding the remaining ½ cups of broth. The artichokes must be completely cooked and soft but not mushy. Transfer them to a crockery or glass bowl and let rest, covered, until cool, about 1 hour.

Meanwhile, prepare the *balsamella* (see page 4) with the ingredients and quantities listed above, adding the whole cloves of garlic to the pan together with the butter. Transfer the sauce to a crockery or glass bowl, discard the garlic, and fit a piece of buttered waxed paper on top to prevent a skin from forming. Let rest until needed.

Prepare the pasta with the ingredients and quantities listed above according to the directions on page 3, placing the chick-pea flour in the well of the unbleached flour together with the other ingredients. Prepare the dough and roll it out to a thickness of less than 1/16 inch (on a manual pasta machine that would be the last setting). Cut the sheets of pasta into squares. Precook them in a large pot of salted boiling water, then transfer them to a bowl of cold water with the olive or vegetable oil added, and then onto dampened cotton kitchen towels. Let rest until needed. Be careful; pasta prepared with chick-pea flour is very delicate and breakable.

Assemble the dish. Preheat the oven to 375 degrees and butter a 13½ × 8¾ × 2-inch glass baking pan. Cut the remaining butter into pats. Make a layer of pasta on the bottom of the pan; over it arrange half of the artichokes. Then continue with a second layer of pasta, then half of the grated cheese together with one-third of the butter pats. Make a third layer of pasta, then half of the *balsamella*, and a fourth pasta layer topped with the remaining artichokes. Add a fifth layer of pasta and top with the remaining grated cheese mixed with half of the remaining butter. Cover with a final layer of pasta, then the remaining *balsamella* and the remaining butter. Bake until completely heated through, about 20 minutes. Serve with the grated Pecorino Romano.

NOTE: Chick-pea flour is available at Italian, Middle Eastern, and Indian groceries, as well as at gourmet shops.

PASTA RIPIENA DI MELANZANE
Pasta Stuffed with Eggplant
Makes 6 to 8 servings

FOR THE EGGPLANT STUFFING:

2½ pounds eggplant, the thinnest you can
   find, but not baby eggplant

1 tablespoon coarse-grained salt

2 cups vegetable oil (½ sunflower oil and
   ½ corn oil)

1½ cups unbleached all-purpose flour

Fine salt

FOR THE TOMATO SAUCE:

1 stalk celery

1 carrot, scraped

1 small red onion, cleaned

1 clove garlic, peeled

5 fresh basil leaves

5 sprigs fresh Italian parsley, leaves only

3½ pounds very ripe tomatoes or 3 pounds
   drained canned tomatoes, preferably
   imported Italian

6 tablespoons extra virgin olive oil

Salt and freshly ground black pepper

FOR THE *BALSAMELLA* (BECHAMEL):

½ cup (4 ounces) sweet butter

1 large clove garlic, peeled

¼ cup unbleached all-purpose flour

3¼ cups milk

Salt and freshly ground black pepper

Pinch of freshly grated nutmeg

FOR THE PASTA:

2¼ cups unbleached all-purpose flour

4 extra-large egg yolks

1 tablespoon olive oil or vegetable oil

2 tablespoons cold water

Pinch of salt

TO COOK THE PASTA:

Coarse-grained salt

2 tablespoons olive oil or vegetable oil

TO FINISH THE DISH:

3 extra-large eggs

1 cup freshly grated Parmigiano cheese

TO SERVE:

Fresh basil leaves

Peel the eggplant, cut them into ¾-inch cubes or ¼-inch-thick slices, and spread them out in a serving dish. Sprinkle the coarse salt over them and let stand for 1 hour.

Meanwhile, prepare the tomato sauce. Very coarsely chop together the celery, carrot, onion, garlic, basil, and parsley on a cutting board. If using fresh tomatoes, cut them into pieces. Place the tomatoes in a large nonreactive casserole and arrange over them the chopped mixture. Drizzle 3 tablespoons of the olive oil over the top and season with salt and pepper. Cover the casserole and let cook over low heat for at least 45 minutes, without mixing, but shaking the casserole occasionally to keep the tomatoes from sticking to the bottom. When ready, pass the contents of the casserole through a food mill fitted with the disk with the smallest holes into a smaller nonreactive casserole. Season with salt and pepper and add the remaining 3 tablespoons oil. Reduce the sauce over medium heat to a rather thick consistency, about 15 minutes. Remove from the heat, transfer the sauce to a crockery or glass bowl to cool for about 10 minutes, then refrigerate, covered with plastic wrap, until cold.

Prepare the *balsamella* with the ingredients and quantities listed above as instructed on page 4, adding the whole clove of garlic with the flour. Transfer the *balsamella* to a crockery or glass bowl. Then, let the *balsamella* cool with a sheet of buttered waxed paper pressed over it for at least half an hour. Discard the garlic before using it.

Rinse the eggplant very well and pat dry with paper towels. Heat the vegetable oil in a large skillet over medium heat. Place the eggplant in a colander and lightly flour the cubes by sprinkling the flour over and vigorously shaking the colander, letting the excess flour fall through, or lightly flouring the slices.

When the oil is hot, about 375 degrees, add enough eggplant to make just a single layer and fry until lightly golden all over. Line a serving dish with paper towels and use a skimmer to transfer the cooked eggplant to the paper towels to absorb excess fat. Sprinkle with fine salt. Make additional layers in this way until all the eggplant is cooked.

Prepare the pasta with the ingredients and quantities listed above according to the directions on page 3. Roll out the pasta to a thickness of $\frac{1}{16}$ inch (on a manual pasta machine that would be the next to last setting). Cut the pasta sheet into squares. Precook them in a large pot of salted boiling water, then transfer them to a bowl of cold water with the olive or vegetable oil added. Remove from the water and transfer the squares to dampened cotton kitchen towels. Let rest until needed.

Assemble the dish. Preheat the oven to 375 degrees and butter a jelly-roll pan. Line the bottom and sides of the pan with the pasta squares, letting about 2 inches of pasta hang over all around the pan. If the eggplant is cubed, distribute all of it over the pasta. Mix the eggs, Parmigiano, $1\frac{1}{2}$ cups of the prepared tomato sauce, and half of the *balsamella* together and pour it all over the eggplant. If the eggplant is sliced, make three layers of eggplant alternating with two layers of the *balsamella*-tomato sauce. Cover with a final layer of the pasta squares, then fold the overhanging pasta inward. Distribute the remaining *balsamella* over the very top, then drizzle the remaining tomato sauce all over. Bake until bubbling, about 25 minutes. Remove from the oven and, after letting the dish rest for 3 or 4 minutes, cut into squares and serve with the basil leaves.

VARIATION: The *balsamella* may be omitted from the stuffing and the topping.

RUOTE DI PASTA RIPIENE
Stuffed "Wheels"

Makes 8 servings

FOR THE PASTA:

1½ cups unbleached all-purpose flour

2 extra-large egg yolks

3 tablespoons cold water

2 tablespoons olive oil or vegetable oil

Pinch of salt

TO COOK THE PASTA:

Coarse-grained salt

2 tablespoons olive oil or vegetable oil

FOR THE *BALSAMELLA* (BECHAMEL):

6 tablespoons (3 ounces) sweet butter

¼ cup unbleached all-purpose flour

2½ cups milk

Salt and freshly ground black pepper

Freshly grated nutmeg

FOR THE SPINACH FILLING:

3 pounds fresh spinach, well washed and
   large stems removed

Coarse-grained salt

3 tablespoons (1½ ounces) sweet butter

Salt and freshly ground black pepper

Freshly grated nutmeg

1 cup freshly grated Parmigiano cheese

2 extra-large eggs

1 extra-large egg yolk

8 ounces whole-milk ricotta, drained

Salt and freshly ground black pepper

FOR THE MEAT SAUCE:

2 large cloves garlic, peeled

4 ounces prosciutto or pancetta, in one
   piece

8 ounces veal shoulder, trimmed of fat

4 chicken livers, trimmed of fat and
   membranes

¼ cup extra virgin olive oil

2 tablespoons (1 ounce) sweet butter

¼ cup red wine vinegar

2 heaping tablespoons tomato paste,
   preferably imported Italian

2 cups completely defatted chicken broth,
   preferably homemade

Salt and freshly ground black pepper

TO SERVE:

Freshly grated Parmigiano cheese

Prepare the pasta with the ingredients and quantities listed above according to the directions on page 3. Roll it out to a thickness of ¹⁄₁₆ inch (on a manual pasta machine that would be the next to last setting) and cut into 6-inch-wide, 12-inch-long pieces. Precook them in a large pot of boiling salted water, then transfer to a large bowl of cold water with the olive or vegetable oil added. Transfer to dampened cotton kitchen towels and let rest until needed.

Prepare the *balsamella* with the ingredients and quantities listed (see page 4), transfer to a crockery or glass bowl, and cover with a sheet of buttered waxed paper pressed over it for at least half an hour.

Cook the cleaned spinach in a large pot of boiling salted water for 5 minutes, then drain it. Cool the spinach under cold running water and lightly squeeze it. Finely chop the spinach. Place a small saucepan with the butter over medium heat; when it melts, add the spinach and sauté for 2 minutes. Season with salt, pepper, and nutmeg and let cool completely.

Prepare the meat sauce. Use a meat grinder to grind the garlic, prosciutto or pancetta, veal, and chicken livers together. Place a large nonreactive saucepan with the olive oil and butter over medium heat; when the butter is almost melted, add the ground mixture and cook until the pinkness is gone, about 10 minutes, stirring constantly with a wooden spoon. Add the vinegar and let evaporate for 5 minutes. Dissolve the tomato paste in the broth and add it to the pan. Simmer the sauce for 20 minutes, season with salt and pepper, and keep simmering until the sauce has a rather thick consistency, about 1 hour.

Mix the cooled spinach together with the Parmigiano, whole eggs, egg yolk, and ricotta and season with salt and pepper. Preheat the oven to 375 degrees and heavily butter a 13½ × 8¾-inch glass baking dish. Spread a ½-inch-high layer of the spinach stuffing over each piece of pasta, keeping the stuffing about 1 inch away from the pasta sides. Roll up each individual piece of pasta and place the pieces in a row in the prepared baking dish. Distribute the *balsamella* on top of all of them and bake for 20 minutes. It is equally important that the inside and the *balsamella* are completely hot. Remove from the oven, then slice each stuffed pasta roll into 1½-inch-thick *ruote* (wheels). Serve with the reheated meat sauce and Parmigiano sprinkled all over.

VARIATION: Instead of making a single ½-inch-thick layer over the pasta, using up all of the spinach filling, make a layer using half the amount of spinach, about ¼ inch high, cover it with a layer of pasta, then make another spinach layer and cover it with thin slices of boiled ham (*prosciutto cotto*), using ¾ pound ham in all. Then roll it up and slice it the way you do with the *ruote*. This version has its own name, *Rondini nel Nido* (Birds in the Nest).

DRIED PASTA

❖

Dried pasta existed in ancient Roman times. To preserve and not waste the wheat that would not be used for a long period, it was ground, mixed with water, cut, and dried in the sun. This practice started as a means of preserving wheat flour and of more easily shipping it from where it was grown—at that time, largely in Sicily—to other parts of the Roman Empire.

Dried pasta has not always been made from durum wheat, but once hard wheat was developed, it became the flour of choice, particularly in the nineteenth century, when pasta began to be dried by machines rather than in the sun and required harder wheat to survive the tougher handling by the hot machines. It was at this time that dried pasta started to be produced cheaply and in large quantity. And it followed that its use would increase dramatically, such that it replaced *minestre* as the leading type of *primo piatto*, or first course, not only in Southern Italy but throughout the central and northern parts of the peninsula.

The main categories of dried pasta are long pasta and short pasta, both of which may be flat, slightly rounded, or tubular, though most tubular pastas are short. Of the many, many types of long pasta, in this book we use spaghetti, linguine, and perciatelli (also called bucatini). Italians are quite precise about which cut of pasta is appropriate to a particular sauce. But if you can't get a specific cut, try to find another close in shape to the one traditionally used. The thickness of the pasta should be related to the thickness of the sauce. Heavier sauces are those that cook for a long time and are reduced; they may be made with meat, game, or pancetta, among others. Lighter sauces cook for a short time and include those that are vegetable-based, tomato sauces, various pesto sauces and, in general, those sauces that are uncooked. We see specific examples in the individual recipes. We do include a recipe with one long tubular pasta, the true ziti—as opposed to the type that has become well known, which is called cut ziti, or *ziti tagliati*. As for short tubular pastas, the recipes I have included are made with penne (smooth or ridged), *cavatappi*, and *chiocchiole* or shells. Bear in mind that some shapes are called by different names in different regions or by different producers.

Dried pasta is always cooked in a large amount of boiling water, with the salt added after the water boils and just before the pasta is added. The cooking time varies not only for the different shapes but often for different brands. Suggested cooking time is usually printed on the pasta box. But even the term *al dente* can mean different things in different regions of Italy. In Southern Italy people prefer a less cooked pasta, and Neapolitans like dried pasta cooked so little that people from most other places would find it hard to accept. Suggested cooking times are for *al dente* pasta, but not at the extreme end. (Of course, fresh pasta is *never* cooked *al dente*.)

We begin our dried pasta recipes with several combinations of pasta with vegetables.

Bucatini con Peperonata all'Arrabbiata combines the *peperonata* from Rome with this substantial rounded long pasta, much like a thick spaghetti with an almost imperceptible hole running down the center. Because *peperonata* makes a very substantial sauce, you need such a thick pasta. *Peperonata* belongs to a category of bell pepper dishes, of which the Neapolitan, Sicilian, and Roman versions are the most famous. The Roman is the only one of the three that does not contain tomatoes. These peppers may be eaten as a vegetable or combined with pasta as a full-bodied sauce, as they are here.

Pasta col Pesto Invernale alla Trapanese uses one of the Sicilian winter pesto sauces, which means that since basil is not abundantly available in that season, adjustments must be made to normal pesto. There is another version of this in which a small amount of the scarce basil is used, but this one, from the town of Trapani, is made when basil is not to be found. Parsley, onion, and tomato replace it.

The word *pesto* refers to grinding with a mortar and pestle, as all green herb sauces were made in earlier centuries. There are green parsley sauces, which are really the same as a pesto, such as the Tuscan *salsa verde* for boiled meats. And in Sicily we find an uncooked tomato pesto.

The Calabrian *Spaghetti alle Zucchine* combines the pasta and vegetable with a ricotta sauce that is stirred so vigorously that it becomes very creamy, almost an anticipation of a cream sauce in texture. Remember, ricotta is not considered a cheese because it is second curd, made from the whey that is left after the cheese has been produced. In Italy no one would say "ricotta cheese."

Spaghetti in Salsa combines a spicy tomato sauce and almost completely preboiled pasta, then bakes them for a very short time in the oven. From the region of Naples, this procedure is a nod to the baked pasta dishes so loved in Southern Italy.

Cavatappi alla Rucola con Pomodori is an example of the wonderful category of hot pastas dressed with cold sauces. *Cavatappi*, meaning corkscrews, are twisted, ridged tubular short pastas that wrap themselves around the arugula and tomato cubes. Savory scallions and olives are added along with the fresh basil, and lemon juice is used instead of vinegar in the cold sauce.

LAZIO

BUCATINI CON PEPERONATA ALL'ARRABBIATA
Pasta with Spicy Peperonata

Makes 6 to 8 servings

FOR THE SAUCE:

8 large yellow or red bell peppers

4 large cloves garlic, peeled

1 large red onion, cleaned

10 sprigs fresh Italian parsley, leaves only

25 large fresh basil leaves

½ cup extra virgin olive oil

Salt and freshly ground black pepper

Large pinch to ½ teaspoon of hot red pepper flakes, according to your taste

Coarse-grained salt

1 pound dried bucatini or perciatelli, preferably imported Italian

6 tablespoons capers in wine vinegar, drained

TO SERVE:

Sprigs fresh basil

Clean the peppers, removing the stems and seeds, cut them into strips less than 1 inch wide, and let soak in a bowl of cold water for half an hour.

Coarsely chop the garlic, onion, parsley, and five small basil leaves together on a cutting board. Heat the olive oil in a medium-size casserole over medium heat; when the oil is warm, reduce the heat, add the chopped ingredients, and sauté for 15 minutes, stirring every so often with a wooden spoon. Drain the peppers, add them to the casserole, season with salt, black pepper, and the red pepper flakes, and sauté for another 5 minutes, stirring every so often with a wooden spoon. Season again with salt, black pepper, and hot pepper. Reduce the heat even more, cover the casserole, and cook until the peppers are very soft, about 30 minutes, adding some cold water as more liquid is needed.

Pass the contents of the casserole through a food mill fitted with the disk with the smallest holes into a clean casserole and set this over low heat.

Meanwhile, bring a large pot of cold water to a boil over medium heat. Add coarse salt to taste, then the pasta, and cook until *al dente,* 9 to 12 minutes, depending on the brand.

Rinse the capers under cold water and add them to the pepper sauce. Drain the pasta, transfer it to the casserole with the sauce, mix very well over low heat for half a minute, then add the remaining basil leaves torn into thirds.

Transfer the pasta to a large serving platter and serve immediately, topped with sprigs of fresh basil.

PASTA COL PESTO INVERNALE ALLA TRAPANESE
Pasta with Sicilian Winter Pesto

Makes 6 servings

3 large cloves garlic, peeled

½ medium-size red onion, cleaned

10 sprigs fresh Italian parsley, leaves only

1 large ripe tomato (about 6 ounces), cut into large pieces

4 ounces shelled walnuts

1 cup extra virgin olive oil

Salt and freshly ground black pepper

Large pinch of hot red pepper flakes

Coarse-grained salt

1 pound dried pasta, preferably linguine, perciatelli, or bucatini, preferably imported Italian

TO SERVE:

1 large ripe tomato (about 6 ounces), cut into 8 wedges

10 sprigs fresh Italian parsley, leaves only

If using a mortar and pestle, finely chop the garlic and onion together on a cutting board, then transfer to the mortar along with the parsley, tomato pieces, and walnuts. Finely grind all the ingredients together. If using a blender or food processor, process all the solid ingredients together except the onion, then add the onion, cut into large pieces, and process again for only a few seconds so it does not become too watery. Transfer to a crockery or glass bowl, add the olive oil, and season with salt, black pepper, and the hot pepper. Let rest, covered with plastic wrap, in the refrigerator until needed.

Bring a large pot of cold water to a boil, add coarse salt to taste, then the pasta, and cook until *al dente*, 9 to 12 minutes, depending on the brand. Drain the pasta, saving a little of the water. Transfer to a large bowl and toss with the sauce, adding some of the saved cooking water if the sauce does not coat the pasta completely. Transfer to a large serving platter, arrange the tomato wedges on top, sprinkle the parsley leaves over, and serve.

SPAGHETTI ALLE ZUCCHINE
Spaghetti with Sautéed Zucchini

Makes 6 servings

3 large cloves garlic, peeled

15 large sprigs fresh Italian parsley,
   leaves only

2 pounds thin zucchini, but not the
   Japanese type

Coarse-grained salt

½ cup extra virgin olive oil

About 1 cup completely defatted chicken
   broth, preferably homemade

Salt and freshly ground black pepper

15 ounces ricotta, very well drained

5 tablespoons sweet butter (2½ ounces) at
   room temperature, or olive oil

½ cup lukewarm water, or more as needed

FOR THE PASTA:

Coarse-grained salt

1 pound dried pasta such as spaghetti,
   preferably imported Italian

TO SERVE:

Abundant fresh basil leaves

Freshly ground black pepper

Freshly grated Pecorino Romano cheese

Coarsely chop the garlic and parsley together on a cutting board. Trim the ends of the zucchini, quarter them lengthwise, then cut each quarter into 1½-inch pieces. Soak the zucchini in a bowl of cold water with a little coarse salt for half an hour. Set a large stockpot with cold water to boil over medium heat.

When ready, drain the zucchini and rinse under cold running water to remove excess salt and the bitter taste from the zucchini. Heat the olive oil in a medium-size skillet over medium heat; when the oil is warm, add the garlic mixture and sauté for 2 minutes. Add the zucchini and sauté until cooked but not mushy, about 20 minutes, adding a little of the broth as needed. Season with salt and abundant pepper.

Meanwhile, place the ricotta in a large serving bowl, season with salt and pepper, and add the butter or olive oil. Mix very well, add the lukewarm water, and mix again until very smooth and creamy, adding more water if necessary.

When the zucchini is ready and the water reaches a boil, add coarse salt to the stockpot, then the pasta, and cook until *al dente,* 9 to 12 minutes, depending on the brand. Drain the pasta, transfer it to the bowl containing the ricotta, and mix very well, then add the zucchini and abundant basil leaves, and mix again. Serve hot with black pepper and the Pecorino Romano sprinkled over.

SPAGHETTI IN SALSA
Baked Pasta in Tomato Sauce

Makes 6 servings

15 sprigs fresh Italian parsley, leaves only

10 large fresh basil leaves

2 large cloves garlic, peeled

¾ cup extra virgin olive oil

2½ pounds very ripe tomatoes or canned
  tomatoes, preferably imported Italian,
  undrained

Salt and freshly ground black pepper

TO COOK THE PASTA:

Coarse-grained salt

1 pound dried spaghetti, preferably
  imported Italian

TO BAKE THE PASTA:

2 tablespoons (1 ounce) sweet butter

6 ounces Pecorino Romano cheese, cut into
  slivers

TO SERVE:

Fresh basil leaves

Coarsely chop the parsley, basil, and garlic together on a cutting board. Place a medium-size non-reactive casserole with the olive oil over medium heat; when the oil is lukewarm, add the chopped ingredients and sauté for 2 minutes, stirring several times with a wooden spoon. If using fresh tomatoes, cut them into pieces. Pass the tomatoes through a food mill fitted with the disk with the smallest holes into a crockery or glass bowl. Add the tomatoes to the casserole, cover, and cook for 25 minutes, stirring every so often with a wooden spoon. When the sauce is almost ready (it will be rather thick), add salt and pepper to taste.

Bring a large pot of cold water to a boil, add coarse salt to taste, then the pasta, and cook it for 8 to 11 minutes, that is, 1 minute less than normal for *al dente*. Drain the pasta, transfer to a crockery or glass bowl, and toss it with half of the tomato sauce.

Preheat the oven to 375 degrees and heavily butter a glass baking casserole. Place half of the pasta in the casserole, pour half the remaining sauce over, then distribute half of the cheese over the sauce. Make one more layer of pasta, arrange the remaining cheese over that, and then the remaining tomato sauce. Cover the casserole and bake for 20 minutes; the cheese should be completely melted. Remove from the oven. Once the pasta has absorbed the sauce, gently mix the pasta and cheese together. Serve hot with the basil leaves.

CAVATAPPI ALLA RUCOLA CON POMODORI
Pasta with Uncooked Arugula and Tomatoes

Makes 4 to 6 servings

2 large bunches arugula (*rucola* or *ruchetta*),
  cleaned and cut horizontally into
  1-inch-wide strips

1½ pounds ripe tomatoes, cut into 1-inch
  cubes

6 medium-size scallions, white part only,
  cut into ½-inch-thick slices

10 large black olives in brine, pitted

Salt and freshly ground black pepper

Large pinch of hot red pepper flakes
  (optional)

2 anchovy fillets packed in olive oil
  (optional), drained and finely chopped

1 medium-size clove garlic (optional),
  peeled and finely chopped

5 tablespoons extra virgin olive oil

1 tablespoon fresh lemon juice

TO COOK THE PASTA:

Coarse-grained salt

1 pound dried pasta such as *cavatappi* or
  penne, preferably imported Italian

TO SERVE:

30 large fresh basil leaves

Place the arugula in a bowl of cold water and let rest until needed. Put the tomatoes, scallions, and olives in a crockery or glass bowl. Sprinkle over with salt and black pepper and, if desired, the hot pepper, anchovy fillets, and garlic. Pour the olive oil and lemon juice over everything. Refrigerate, covered with plastic wrap, until needed.

Leave the arugula in the bowl of cold water until the pasta is to be cooked; at that point, drain it and dry in a vegetable spinner.

When ready, bring a large pot of cold water to a boil, add coarse salt to taste, then the pasta, and cook until *al dente,* 9 to 12 minutes, depending on the brand. Drain the pasta, transfer it to a large bowl, pour the tomato mixture over, then add the arugula and mix again. Transfer everything to a large serving platter and scatter the basil leaves all over. Serve immediately; the still hot pasta should be mixed together with the cold seasonings.

Dried Pasta with
Olive Oil and Garlic

Dried pasta with olive oil and garlic, and often some hot red pepper flakes, is one of the great standbys for a fast but delicious first course or late-night snack like the famous Roman *spaghettata* (a full-bodied snack based on spaghetti) at midnight. Everyone in most regions of Italy has good olive oil, some garlic, and dried pasta in the house, so no shopping is necessary. Any kind of dried pasta may be used in *aglio/olio* dishes. I suggest two short pastas in these recipes, but you may substitute spaghetti or anything else you prefer. Fresh pasta is never used in *aglio/olio* dishes.

Because the *aglio/olio* combination is so popular, and eaten so often, some variants have arisen in which a few other staple ingredients are added. *Aglio, Olio, ed Erbe* adds four of the most common Italian fresh herbs—basil, mint, parsley, and marjoram. It is rare that Italians do not have these fresh herbs on hand and not usual for them to use dried herbs for anything.

Another favorite variation is to add fresh bread crumbs and fresh rosemary leaves to the oil and garlic. Bread crumbs are often made at home from leftover bread, but since there is always a bread bakery, called a *forno,* in every neighborhood, it is easy to obtain them. Flavored bread crumbs do not exist in Italy; you add the fresh flavorings to the dish.

AGLIO, OLIO, ED ERBE

Pasta with Garlic, Oil, and Aromatic Herbs

Makes 4 to 6 servings

Coarse-grained salt

1 pound dried short tubular pasta, such as
  penne, preferably imported Italian

½ cup extra virgin olive oil

3 large cloves garlic, peeled

Salt and freshly ground black pepper

Hot red pepper flakes (optional)

15 fresh basil leaves, any small stems
  removed

15 fresh mint leaves, any small stems
  removed

10 sprigs fresh Italian parsley, leaves only,
  any small stems removed

20 fresh marjoram leaves, any small stems
  removed

Bring a large pot of cold water to a boil over medium heat. When the water reaches a boil, add coarse salt to taste, then the pasta, and cook until *al dente,* 9 to 12 minutes, depending on the brand.

Meanwhile, heat the olive oil in a small saucepan over low heat. Add the garlic cloves and season with salt, black pepper, and hot pepper if desired, and cook, stirring. When the garlic is golden and the pasta is ready to be drained, discard the garlic, drain the pasta, and transfer it to a large serving platter. Pour the hot olive oil over, mix, then immediately sprinkle the aromatic herbs all over, mix again, and serve hot.

PANGRATTATO, AGLIO, OLIO, E ROSMARINO
Pasta with Bread Crumbs and Rosemary

Makes 6 servings

1 cup very fine unseasoned bread crumbs, preferably homemade, lightly toasted

4 large cloves garlic, peeled

2 tablespoons rosemary leaves, fresh or preserved in salt (page 2)

1 teaspoon fine salt

¼ teaspoon freshly ground black pepper

Large pinch of hot red pepper flakes (optional)

1 cup extra virgin olive oil

TO COOK THE PASTA:

Coarse-grained salt

1 pound dried short tubular pasta, such as penne, penne rigate, *chiocchiole,* or *denti di cavallo,* preferably imported Italian

Finely chop the bread crumbs, garlic, and rosemary together on a cutting board. Transfer to a small bowl and add the salt, black pepper, and hot pepper, if desired. Pour in the olive oil and mix very well.

Bring a large pot of cold water to a boil, add coarse salt to taste, then the pasta, and cook until *al dente,* 9 to 12 minutes, depending on the brand. As the pasta cooks, transfer the contents of the bowl to a small saucepan set over medium heat. Constantly mix with a wooden spoon and remove the pan from the heat just before the bread crumbs become deep golden in color.

Drain the pasta, saving 1 cup of the boiling water, and transfer it to a large bowl. Immediately pour the sauce over the pasta, using some of the cup of water if the pasta is too dry. Mix very well and serve hot with no cheese added.

Dried Pasta with Meat

Egg pasta also appears in the dried form. Especially popular is egg tagliatelle, which is used in combination with both vegetables and meat, with some especially interesting examples of the latter. Preserved duck, which you are shown how to make on page 15, is delicious used as a dressing for dried tagliatelle.

Tagliatelle al Sugo also utilizes dried tagliatelle, together with one of Emilia-Romagna's famous ragù sauces. This one is notable for omitting the usual heavy cream that is so typical of this part of Italy. The sauce is also atypical of the region in that it contains cinnamon and rosemary, in itself an unusual combination. The ragù sauces in general are also famously employed to dress Emilia's celebrated fresh egg pasta, including fresh tagliatelle.

Dried trenette, like fresh trenette, is from Liguria, and also like fresh, contains no eggs at all. Trenette is a little wider than tagliatelle and has one serrated edge. Eggless fresh trenette is the classic pasta for Genoese pesto.

Rich meat extract, without any bits of meat in it, is the typical Ligurian meat sauce. The cut of meat is cooked for several hours, and only the juices are used. Like so many Ligurian sauces, it is called *tocco,* "a touch of."

VENETO

TAGLIATELLE CON L'ANITRA
Pasta with Preserved Duck

Makes 6 servings

FOR THE SAUCE:

Anitra al Coccio (page15)

TO COOK THE PASTA:

Coarse-grained salt

1 pound dried egg tagliatelle, preferably
    imported Italian

TO SERVE (OPTIONAL):

15 sprigs fresh Italian parsley, leaves only

1 small clove garlic, peeled

Salt and freshly ground black pepper

¼ cup extra virgin olive oil

If the preserved duck has been prepared and is ready to be used, bone it and strain off all the fat. Place all the meat pieces in a glass baking dish and pour ¼ cup of the duck juices over (the duck juices are at the bottom of the jar, under the fat). Cover the dish and preheat the oven to 375 degrees.

Bring a large pot of cold water to a boil, add coarse salt to taste, then the pasta, and cook until *al dente,* 6 to 9 minutes, depending on the brand. Place the baking dish in the oven and place 5 more tablespoons of the duck juices in a large bowl. Set the bowl over the pot of boiling pasta to warm it. Drain the pasta, transfer to the bowl with the juices, mix very well, then serve with some of the reheated duck and juices in each portion. If you wish to add the optional sauce, chop the parsley and garlic together very finely, season with salt and pepper, mix together well with the olive oil, and drizzle it over the duck pieces on each individual plate.

TAGLIATELLE AL SUGO
Tagliatelle in Veal Sauce

Makes 4 to 6 servings

FOR THE MEAT SAUCE:

4 ounces prosciutto, with the fat left on, or
    pancetta, in one piece

2 medium-size cloves garlic, peeled

1 tablespoon rosemary leaves, fresh or
    preserved in salt (page 2)

2 tablespoons extra virgin olive oil

2 tablespoons (1 ounce) sweet butter

1 pound veal stew meat, trimmed of fat and
    cut into large pieces

Salt and freshly ground black pepper

Pinch of freshly grated nutmeg

Pinch of ground cinnamon

1 cup dry red wine

3 tablespoons tomato paste, preferably
    imported Italian

2 cups completely defatted chicken or meat
    broth, preferably homemade

TO COOK THE PASTA:

Coarse-grained salt

1 pound dried egg tagliatelle, preferably
    imported Italian

TO SERVE:

About 2 tablespoons (1 ounce) sweet butter

Freshly grated Parmigiano cheese

Prepare the sauce. Cut the prosciutto or pancetta into tiny pieces and finely chop the garlic and rosemary together on a cutting board. Heat the olive oil and butter in a medium-size casserole over medium heat; when the oil is warm, add the butter, almost melted, and the prosciutto and garlic mixture and sauté for 3 minutes, stirring constantly. Add the veal and sauté until lightly golden on all sides, about 5 minutes. Season with salt and pepper and add the nutmeg and cinnamon. Mix very well, then add the wine and cook for another 9 minutes. Strain the contents of the casserole, pour the liquid back into the casserole, and use a meat grinder to finely grind all the solids together into a crockery or glass bowl. Transfer the ground mixture back to the casserole and set it over medium heat. Dissolve the tomato paste in 1 cup of the broth and add it to the casserole. Cover the casserole and simmer for at least 1 hour, adding more broth as needed. The texture of the sauce should be quite thick. Taste for salt and pepper.

Bring a large pot of cold water to a boil, add coarse salt to taste, then the pasta, and cook until *al dente,* 6 to 9 minutes, depending on the brand. Drain the pasta, transfer to a large bowl with the butter, mix very well, then pour the sauce over and mix again. Transfer to a large serving platter and serve hot with the reheated meat sauce and Parmigiano.

LIGURIA

TRENETTE AL SUGO DI CARNE
Trenette Pasta with Meat Sauce Ligurian Style

Makes 6 servings

Fresh trenette is the most classic Genoese and Ligurian pasta type and should be made without eggs. It is traditionally paired with the Genoese basil pesto. The width is similar to that of the pappardelle, ½ inch, and one side is jagged while the other is straight.

With the popularity of dried pasta in this last century, even trenette has appeared in a dried pasta version, keeping the shape of the fresh trenette, and the dried pasta has acquired its own preferred sauces.

FOR THE SAUCE:

1 pound boneless top sirloin, in one piece,
    extra fat removed

2 tablespoons extra virgin olive oil

¼ cup (2 ounces) sweet butter

1 medium-size red onion, cleaned

1 medium-size carrot, scraped

15 sprigs fresh Italian parsley, leaves only

1 cup dry red wine

1 tablespoon unbleached all-purpose flour

Salt and freshly ground black pepper

1 pound drained canned tomatoes,
    preferably imported Italian

Completely defatted chicken or meat broth,
    preferably homemade, as needed

TO COOK PASTA:

Coarse-grained salt

1 pound dried trenette, preferably
    imported Italian

TO SERVE:

Freshly grated Parmigiano cheese

Tie the meat like a salami (see page 5) if the butcher has not done so. Place a medium-size nonreactive casserole with the olive oil and butter over medium heat; when the butter is melted, add the meat and lightly brown it on all sides, about 5 minutes. Finely chop the onion, carrot, and parsley together on a cutting board and add to the casserole. Add the wine and let evaporate for 10 minutes, turning the meat over two or three times. Sprinkle the flour and salt and pepper over the sautéed vegetables and mix very well. Cut the tomatoes in half without removing the seeds and add them to the casserole. Add enough broth to cover the meat completely. Cover the casserole and simmer for 2 hours.

When ready, remove the meat (save it for a different meal or preparation) and pass the sauce through a food mill fitted with the disk with the smallest holes into a clean saucepan. Place over medium heat, and reduce to a rather thick sauce.

Bring a large pot of cold water to a boil, add coarse salt to taste, then the pasta, and cook for 8 to 11 minutes depending on the brand; that is, one minute less than *al dente*. Drain the pasta, transfer it to a large nonreactive skillet, add half of the sauce, and sauté for 2 minutes, mixing very well. Transfer to a large serving platter, pour over more sauce, mix again, and serve hot with the Parmigiano.

Dried Pasta with Fish

The only pasta native to Venice is bigoli. It is a long pasta, longer even than spaghetti, as it was known before it was cut short to fit into boxes. In fact, traditional bigoli is probably the longest of all pastas. In one of Goldoni's plays, a character complains that he has been served only one bigolo, that is, one strand of pasta, and it turns out the bigolo is so long that when curled up it fills the entire bowl. Bigoli are made with a special machine, called, unsurprisingly, *bigolo,* which is really the original extrusion machine—manual, of course, rather than electric. Bigoli are made with both white and whole-wheat flours and are now more available as dried pasta than as fresh.

When Venetians say "bigoli in sauce," without specifying, they mean only one sauce, made with anchovies and, specifically and classically, whole anchovies preserved in salt, cleaned and filleted under cold running water. Venice's *cucina* still retains dishes prepared with preserved ingredients. Because Venice is a port and a series of islands, Venetians lived under threat of blockade and had to store food that could be kept for long periods should Venice be cut off from the inland farms or even from its usual fishing. Bigoli in its salted anchovy sauce is in the life's blood of the old Venetians, delicious even without a siege. This version of the recipe also uses Venice's so-called *dorate,* golden onions. The sauce may be made authentically with or without the onions. In this recipe, they are prepared with Venice's famous painfully slow sautéing of the chopped onions, their "sofrito," over the lowest possible heat, for a very long time. The Venetians are proud of their patience in cooking them and feel that the longer and more slowly they sauté, the more succulent the "sofrito" becomes.

Perciatelli all'Acciuga alla Sorrentina uses the heavier perciatelli and, appropriately for Sorrento, a tomato sauce flavored with anchovies and capers in wine vinegar, parsley, and basil. Sorrento doesn't "produce" capers, they just naturally grow there because of climactic and other conditions. Capers generally grow wild. Because of this gift of nature, Sorrento cooking is able to employ an abundance of capers.

Spaghetti alle Vongole e Basilico from the Naples area is a version of Spaghetti with Clams, with no tomatoes, but with the unusual juxtaposition of abundant fresh basil and hot red pepper, with the added, almost Sicilian, touch of bread crumbs.

BIGOLI SCURI IN SALSA
Whole-Wheat Bigoli with an Onion Anchovy Sauce

Makes 6 servings

1 pound yellow onions (*dorate*), cleaned
    and finely chopped or sliced

2 small cloves garlic, peeled

¾ cup extra virgin olive oil

1 cup cold water

15 sprigs fresh Italian parsley (optional),
    leaves only, coarsely chopped

Freshly ground black pepper

8 whole anchovies preserved in salt
    (see Note on page 10) or 16 anchovy
    fillets packed in oil, drained

TO COOK THE PASTA:

Coarse-grained salt

1 pound dried whole-wheat bigoli or
    spaghetti, preferably imported Italian,
    or fresh bigoli (below)

TO SERVE:

Fresh Italian parsley leaves

Mix the onions together with the garlic, but do not chop the garlic. Place a medium-size saucepan with the olive oil and water over low heat and, after a few seconds, add the onion mixture, parsley, and the black pepper. Slowly sauté until the onions are translucent and soft, 15 minutes or more. Remove the garlic. Finely chop the anchovies on a cutting board, add them to the pan, mix well, and slowly cook for 10 minutes more.

Bring a large pot of cold water to a boil over medium heat, add coarse salt to taste, then the pasta, and cook until *al dente,* 9 to 12 minutes, depending on the brand. Drain the pasta, transfer to a large bowl, pour the sauce over, mix very well, then transfer to a large serving platter. Sprinkle the parsley over and serve immediately. No cheese is added.

VARIATION: For fresh bigoli, prepared with the classic Venetian pasta machine, called a *bigolo,* here are the ingredient proportions. Follow the directions for making pasta on page 3, cutting it as you would for spaghetti, but at least double in length.

2 cups unbleached all-purpose flour

1 cup whole-wheat flour, sifted to remove
    the large bran pieces

3 extra-large eggs (the traditional recipe
    calls for duck eggs)

3 tablespoons (1½ ounces) sweet butter,
    melted and cooled to room temperature

3 tablespoons milk

Large pinch of salt

PERCIATELLI ALL'ACCIUGA ALLA SORRENTINA
Perciatelli Pasta Sorrento Style

Makes 4 to 6 servings

¼ cup extra virgin olive oil

6 whole anchovies preserved in salt
(see Note on page 10) or 12 anchovy
fillets packed in oil, drained

1½ pounds ripe tomatoes or drained canned
tomatoes, preferably imported Italian

Salt and freshly ground black pepper

15 sprigs fresh Italian parsley, leaves only,
coarsely chopped

3 tablespoons capers in wine vinegar,
drained

TO COOK THE PASTA:

Coarse-grained salt

1 pound dried perciatelli or linguine,
preferably imported Italian

TO SERVE:

Fresh basil leaves

Place a large nonreactive casserole with the olive oil over low heat; when the oil is barely luke-warm, add the anchovies and mash them with a fork. Don't let the oil get any hotter than that or the anchovies will crumble and become very fishy in taste. When ready, add the tomatoes (if fresh, cut into large pieces), raise the heat to medium, and cook for 10 minutes, mixing every so often with a wooden spoon. The tomatoes do not dissolve into a homogeneous sauce and are barely cooked.

Bring a large pot of cold water to a boil, add coarse salt to taste, then the pasta, and cook until *al dente,* 9 to 12 minutes, depending on the brand. Meanwhile, finish the sauce. Add some of the pasta water if the tomato sauce is too thick, season with salt and pepper, and keep it simmering until the pasta is ready.

Drain the pasta, transfer it to a large bowl, add the parsley and capers to the sauce, stir, and pour it over the pasta. Mix very well, then transfer to a serving platter and serve with the basil leaves.

SPAGHETTI ALLE VONGOLE E BASILICO
Spaghetti with Clams and Basil

Makes 4 to 6 servings

2 pounds very small clams in their shells,
  such as Manila clams

Coarse-grained salt

3 large cloves garlic, peeled

25 sprigs fresh Italian parsley, leaves only

½ cup extra virgin olive oil

Salt and freshly ground black pepper

Large pinch of hot red pepper flakes

1 cup dry white wine

3 tablespoons very fine unseasoned bread
  crumbs, preferably homemade, lightly
  toasted

30 large fresh basil leaves, torn into thirds

TO COOK THE PASTA:

Coarse-grained salt

1 pound dried long pasta such as spaghetti,
  preferably imported Italian

TO SERVE:

Abundant fresh basil leaves

Scrub the clams very well and soak them in a bowl of cold water with a little coarse salt added for a half hour.

Finely chop the garlic and parsley together on a cutting board. Set a pot of cold water over medium heat and place a large skillet with the olive oil over low heat. When the oil is lukewarm, add the garlic mixture and sauté for 1 minute. Drain the clams, rinse them two or three times under cold water to be sure all the sand has been removed, and discard any that won't close. Add the clams to the skillet, season with salt, black pepper, and hot pepper, and mix very well. Raise the heat to medium and cover the skillet. Cook until the clams are all opened, shaking the skillet several times.

By then the water in the pot should be boiling. Add coarse salt to taste, then the pasta, and cook until *al dente,* 9 to 12 minutes, depending on the brand.

Remove and discard any clams that do not open and transfer the remaining ones to a large crockery or glass bowl. Raise the heat under the skillet to high, add the wine, and let it reduce by half, then add the bread crumbs and basil and mix very well. Add the reserved clams and all their juices. Mix well for less than 1 minute. By that time the pasta should be ready. Drain the pasta, transfer it to a large bowl, and pour the contents of the skillet over and mix very well. Transfer everything to a large serving platter, sprinkle the basil leaves on top, and serve hot.

PASTA NELL'ALVEARE
Cut Ziti Baked in a Beehive of Pasta
Makes 8 servings

This is a special form of *timballo* or, as they sometimes call it in Southern Italy, *timpano*. Both words mean "drum," and we are talking about a pastry drum as a container for a stuffing. There are sweet *timballi*, usually made from *pasta frolla*, sugar pastry, which may contain pears poached in wine or some other sweet.

A *timballo* may also be constructed of a savory crust filled with *maccheroni* and other ingredients. Some *timballi* have a rice crust, others a lighter pastry, usually reserved for dishes called *pasticci* rather than *timballi*. These *pasticci* are stuffed with many ingredients, such as the Florentine Renaissance *Pasticcio di Caccia*, which contains layers of stuffed pasta, sausages, quail, and chicken.

The present dish makes a crust of dried long ziti, shaped into a beehive. The stuffing is dried cut ziti or even fresh pasta in a rich meat sauce. In most of these stuffed dishes, as in the beehive, the crust is really not supposed to be eaten, but merely serves as a container to hold in the flavor of the stuffing.

FOR THE SAUCE:

1 pound boneless beef sirloin, in one piece

4 ounces prosciutto or pancetta, in one piece

3 sweet Italian sausages without fennel seeds (about 9 ounces), casings removed, or 9 ounces finely ground pork

1 large carrot, scraped

1 medium-size red onion, cleaned

1 medium-size leek, white part only, well washed, or 1 additional red onion, cleaned

1 stalk celery

1 large clove garlic, peeled

10 sprigs fresh Italian parsley, leaves only

Small piece of lemon rind

¼ cup extra virgin olive oil

¼ cup (2 ounces) sweet butter

1 cup dry red wine

1 pound very ripe tomatoes, blanched for 1 minute, peeled, and seeded, or drained canned tomatoes, preferably imported Italian, seeded

Salt and freshly ground black pepper

Pinch of ground cinnamon

2 to 3 cups completely defatted chicken or meat broth, preferably homemade

FOR THE BEEHIVE:

2 tablespoons vegetable oil or olive oil

Coarse-grained salt

¾ pound dried long ziti, preferably
    imported Italian

TO COOK THE STUFFED ZITI:

2 tablespoons vegetable oil or olive oil

Coarse-grained salt

1 pound dried cut ziti (*ziti tagliati*),

preferably imported Italian, or fresh
    spaghetti (recipe follows)

TO ASSEMBLE THE DISH:

6 tablespoons (3 ounces) sweet butter, cut
    into pats, plus enough to butter
    the mold

¾ cup freshly grated Pecorino Romano
    cheese

Prepare the sauce. In a meat grinder finely grind the beef, then finely grind the prosciutto or pancetta along with the sausage meat. Finely chop the carrot, onion, leek, celery, garlic, parsley, and lemon rind together on a cutting board.

Place a medium-size nonreactive casserole with the olive oil and butter over medium heat; when the butter is almost melted, add the ground prosciutto/sausage mixture and sauté for 2 minutes, mixing continuously with a wooden spoon. Add the ground sirloin and cook, stirring, until no longer pink, about 2 minutes more. Add the chopped vegetable mixture and cook, stirring occasionally, until the onion is translucent, about 15 minutes. Pour in the wine and let evaporate very slowly over low heat, about 10 minutes. Add the tomatoes, season with salt, pepper, and the cinnamon, and simmer, covered, until you have quite a thick sauce, 1½ hours, adding the broth as needed.

Bring a medium-size pot full of cold water to a boil over medium heat. Fill a large bowl with cold water and add the vegetable or olive oil. Wet several kitchen towels with cold water. When the water reaches a boil, add coarse salt to taste, then cook the long ziti. Remove the ziti from the water with a skimmer and cool them in the bowl of cold water, then transfer to the wet towels. The cooking time for the ziti is about 11 minutes, leaving it a little bit undercooked as it will be baked afterward. Be very careful not to break the long ziti; they must be laid out evenly on the towel. Then follow the same procedure for the cut ziti or fresh spaghetti to be used in the stuffing. If using fresh spaghetti, parboil them for 30 seconds to 1 minute, depending on their dryness.

Preheat the oven to 400 degrees. Heavily butter a 4-quart round overproof glass bowl or casserole and line it with the long ziti, arranged horizontally to make the beehive. Start lining the bowl from the bottom, leaving a small hole in the center. Once the sides of the bowl are lined, take two or three of the leftover ziti and cut them into ½-inch pieces. With these pieces, all standing up, fill the hole in the bottom of the bowl; they will function as the chimney for the mold.

Mix the cut ziti or fresh spaghetti with the sauce and add the grated Pecorino Romano. Fill the bowl with the sauced pasta. The stuffing and beehive should end at the same point. Arrange the pats of butter on top, then cover everything with a sheet of parchment paper. On top of the parchment paper place an ovenproof dinner plate as a weight. Bake for 45 minutes. Remove from the oven and let rest for about 10 minutes before unmolding onto a large round serving dish.

Remove all the pieces of the cut-up long ziti "chimney." Then remove the long ziti one by one and serve only the cut-up ziti or fresh spaghetti stuffing with its sauce. Sprinkle cheese over each serving.

PASTA FRESCA

Fresh Spaghetti

2¼ cups unbleached all-purpose flour

¼ cup very fine semolina flour

4 extra-large eggs

1 tablespoon vegetable oil or olive oil

1 tablespoon cold water

Pinch of salt

Prepare the pasta dough and cut into fresh spaghetti following the directions on page 47. Use the fresh spaghetti in place of the cut ziti as described in the recipe above.

MINESTRE, MINESTRONI, E ZUPPE (SOUPS)

❖

Soups are served as the *primo piatto,* or first course, after the antipasto, if there is one, in an Italian meal. You never have a sauced pasta *and* a soup in the same meal; it's one or the other. In the Renaissance, before dried pasta was used in most of Italy, most first courses were called *minestre* and were spicy soups containing "ravioli," dumplings made of meat, fish, fowl, cheese, or mushrooms. Even some types of stuffed fresh pasta, such as lasagne, were called *minestre* in those times.

In making a *minestra,* you start with a light broth, that is, one that is not thickened with pureed beans, riced potatoes, or cornmeal. It may be a vegetable or meat broth, and may contain small amounts of cut-up vegetables or some pasta or rice. *Minestroni* are based on a thicker broth, containing pureed legumes, and/or on a higher ratio of solid vegetables and pasta to broth. The word *zuppa* is restricted to those soups that are served over bread slices or croutons.

STRACCIATELLA AI CARDI
Roman "Egg Drop" Soup with Cardoons

Makes 8 servings

Stracciatella, the Italian soup in which eggs are beaten into the broth, is usually called *alla romana.* In this interesting version, the very intriguing vegetable cardoon, first cousin to the artichoke, is introduced. It is the long, thick stem of the vegetable that is eaten, and the authentic way of cooking cardoons is described below. They have a slightly bitter but very satisfying taste. Cardoons are normally green, like artichokes. They are sometimes covered while growing in order to keep them white, in much the same way that white asparagus are produced. White cardoons are the original vegetable for dipping in the celebrated *bagna cauda,* the hot anchovy dip so loved in the Piedmont region. The vegetable is called *cardi* or *cardoni,* and in Tuscany has its own name, *gobbi.*

1 bunch fresh cardoons

1 lemon, cut in half

Coarse-grained salt

1 tablespoon unbleached all-purpose flour

1 cup cold water

9 cups completely defatted chicken or meat broth, preferably homemade

Salt and freshly ground black pepper

3 extra-large eggs

6 tablespoons freshly grated Parmigiano cheese

5 sprigs fresh Italian parsley, leaves only, finely chopped

Freshly grated nutmeg

TO SERVE:

Fresh basil leaves

Before cleaning the cardoons, rub them with the lemon halves and immediately put them in a bowl of cold water and the juice squeezed from the lemon halves. Clean the cardoons, removing the tough outer leaves, and cut the remaining whitish stalks into 3-inch-long pieces. Let the cardoons rest in the acidulated water until needed.

Bring a medium-size casserole with cold water to a boil over medium heat. Add coarse salt to taste, then dissolve the flour in the cup of cold water and add the mixture to the boiling water. This will prevent the cardoons from discoloring. Mix very well. Drain the cardoons and add them to the casserole. Reduce the heat to medium-low and let simmer for about 35 minutes. The cooking time may vary a lot with cardoons. If they grew in a place with very cold weather, they are at their softest and may cook in the minimum of 35 minutes. Otherwise the cooking time is difficult to predict; after 35 minutes you must keep testing them. The cardoons are cooked when they rather soft but still retain their shape. When ready, transfer them onto paper towels to absorb excess liquid.

Bring 8 cups of the broth to a boil and add salt and pepper to taste, then add the cardoons, reduce the heat to medium-low, and simmer for 20 minutes. Mix the eggs, Parmigiano, parsley, nutmeg, and the remaining cup broth together in a small bowl with a fork. Add the egg mixture to the broth and stir vigorously so the eggs break up very well. Simmer for 2 minutes, then serve with the basil leaves.

VARIATIONS

- One heaping tablespoon of very fine semolina flour may be added to the egg mixture to make a thicker soup.
- The cardoons can be cut into pieces less than 2 inches long.

PASTA E FAGIOLI ALLA VENETA
Pasta and Beans Venetian Style

Makes 6 to 8 servings

Each region of Italy has its own version or versions of pasta and beans. The beans vary from cannellini (white kidney beans) to borlotti ("Roman" beans—see Note), lentils, fava beans, and so on.

The versions from Veneto are among the most celebrated. Venice uses the Lamon bean, pancetta, and a dried egg pasta such as tagliatelle. Lamon beans are the finest type of borlotti beans and they grow in Lamon. They are difficult to obtain anywhere but in Venice: borlotti make a very close substitute. Venetians do, however, consider Lamon beans to be their special treasure and superior to all others.

continued

1 cup dried Lamon or borlotti (Roman) beans, picked over

2 medium-size carrots, scraped

1 stalk celery

4 sage leaves, fresh or preserved in salt (page 2)

½ tablespoon rosemary leaves, fresh or preserved in salt (page 2)

2 cloves garlic, peeled

5 sprigs fresh Italian parsley, leaves only

3 quarts cold water

Coarse-grained salt

Freshly ground black pepper

5 tablespoons extra virgin olive oil

6 ounces pancetta, ground

8 ounces dried egg tagliatelle

TO SERVE:

A few drops extra virgin olive oil for each serving

Freshly grated Grana Padano cheese

Soak the beans in a bowl of cold water overnight. The next morning, drain and rinse the beans and put them in a medium-size stockpot. Coarsely chop the carrots, celery, sage, rosemary, garlic, and parsley together on a cutting board and add to the stockpot. Pour in the cold water and set the pot over medium heat. When it reaches a boil, reduce the heat to medium-low and simmer until the beans are almost cooked and soft, about 45 minutes. Season with coarse salt and pepper and cook for another 10 minutes.

Pass one-third of the cooked beans through a food mill fitted with the disk with the smallest holes directly back into the pot set over medium heat. When the bean broth returns to a boil, heat the olive oil in a small skillet over low heat, then add the pancetta and cook, stirring, until very crisp, about 10 minutes. Season with salt and pepper. Meanwhile, add the pasta to the stockpot and cook until *al dente,* about 9 minutes, depending on the brand. Add the pancetta and any rendered fat to the soup and mix very well. The consistency of the soup should be rather thick. Let the soup rest for 5 minutes before serving it, with a few drops of olive oil and the grated Grana Padano for each serving.

NOTE: The translation "Roman" beans is generally used in English, but it is not really accurate, because these beans are used all over Italy and are associated more with Northern Italy than with Rome. And in Rome other types of beans are used just as frequently.

FAGIOLI E FARRO ALL'ELBANA
Beans and Farro Elba Style

Makes 6 to 8 servings

Farro, the ancient soft wheat, is especially popular in Tuscany, and most sections of Tuscany have their own farro soups. Especially appreciated are the ones from Lucca and from the island of Elba, famous as the place of exile for Napoleon. Farro combines well with beans (either whole or pureed) as well as the seasonings that are so often used with beans—garlic, pancetta, prosciutto, and the aromatic vegetables.

Here farro is used in the form of whole soft wheatberries, as it usually is in desserts such as the farro tart of Lucca. Farro may also be used ground into flour or cracked into pieces.

Since farro has become better known outside of Italy, a misconception has arisen regarding the famous Neapolitan Easter Cake called *pastiera*. That pastry is made with wheatberries, left whole, not from farro, but from the soft spring wheat that is a symbol of spring and rebirth in Naples; this wheat, wonderful as it is, is not farro.

Abruzzi also has traditional farro dishes, including its own version of farro and beans, different from this one from Elba because in Abruzzi they use the farro cracked up, which is called *farretto*.

1½ cups dried cannellini (white kidney)
    beans, picked over
2 tablespoons extra virgin olive oil
1 large clove garlic, peeled
Coarse-grained salt

FOR THE FARRO:
6 ounces (1 scant cup) raw farro
Coarse-grained salt

TO FINISH THE SOUP:
1 medium-size carrot, scraped
3 medium-size stalks celery

6 large fresh basil leaves
2 cloves garlic, peeled
3 ounces pancetta or prosciutto, ground
6 tablespoons extra virgin olive oil
1½ tablespoons tomato paste, preferably
    imported Italian
Salt and freshly ground black pepper
¼ cup water, as needed

TO SERVE:
8 teaspoons extra virgin olive oil
Freshly ground black pepper
1 or 2 fresh basil leaves, shredded

continued

Soak the beans in a bowl of cold water overnight. The next morning, place a medium-size stock-pot of cold water over medium heat; when the water reaches a boil, drain the beans and add them to the pot along with the olive oil and garlic. Simmer until the beans are almost cooked but still retain their shape, about 45 minutes. Season with salt and simmer for another 2 minutes.

Meanwhile, soak the farro in a bowl of cold water for about 45 minutes, or according to cooking instructions on the package (see page 19). Cook the farro in a large amount of salted, already boiling water for about 45 minutes. Drain the farro, cover with plastic wrap, punching some holes in it, and let cool for at least half an hour.

Drain the beans, discarding the garlic and saving 8 cups of the cooking water. Pour this water back into the stockpot. Pass 2 cups of the beans (you may change the quantity of beans according to your taste) through a food mill fitted with the disk with the smallest holes directly into the stock-pot containing the bean broth. Set the rest of the beans aside. Set the pot over medium heat; when the water reaches a boil, add the cooled farro and simmer until the wheatberries are completely open and quite soft, at least 20 minutes.

Coarsely chop the carrot, celery, basil, garlic, and pancetta or prosciutto together on a cut-ting board. Put the olive oil in a medium-size saucepan over medium heat; when the oil is warm, add the chopped mixture and sauté over low heat for 5 minutes. Add the tomato paste and season with salt and pepper. All the vegetables should be cooked at this point, but if not, add the water and cook until done.

When the farro is ready, add the reserved beans to the stockpot along with the sautéed veg-etables and cook for 10 minutes more. Add salt and pepper to taste. Let the soup rest for at least 10 minutes before serving. Drizzle 1 teaspoon of olive oil over each portion, with a little freshly ground black pepper and the shredded basil leaves.

FAGIOLI ED ORZO ALLA FRIULANA
Beans and Barley Friuli Style
Makes 6 to 8 servings

Friuli, after centuries of being ruled by Venice, acquired some Venetian dishes but adapted them to its own ingredients. The Venetian pasta and beans became an extraordinary barley and beans, as barley was actively cultivated in the highlands of Friuli. Barley in earlier centuries was used much more frequently and was even ground into flour for bread and cereals. Before corn was brought to Italy from the New World, barley was one of the grains used for polenta, as it had been since Roman times. Cornmeal triumphed so completely that I have not been able to find a single surviving barley polenta at the present time.

1 cup pearl barley

1 cup dried borlotti (Roman) beans,
    picked over

3 quarts cold water

1 medium-size stalk celery

1 medium-size carrot, scraped

1 medium-size red onion, cleaned

4 large fresh basil leaves

5 sprigs fresh Italian parsley, leaves only

2 sage leaves, fresh or preserved in salt
    (page 2)

3 ounces pancetta or prosciutto, in one
    piece

1 medium-size boiling potato
    (about 7 ounces)

Coarse-grained salt

5 tablespoons extra virgin olive oil

1 bay leaf

Salt and freshly ground black pepper

Soak the barley and beans in two different bowls of cold water to cover overnight. The next morning, drain the beans but leave the barley in its bowl of water until needed. Place a heavy casserole with the 3 quarts cold water and the beans over medium heat. Coarsely chop the celery, carrot, onion, basil, parsley, and sage together on a cutting board. Cut the pancetta or prosciutto into squares of less than ½ inch. Peel the potato, cut into 1-inch square pieces, and put in a bowl of cold water.

When the water with the beans reaches a boil, add coarse salt to taste, cover, and simmer for 10 minutes. Meanwhile, heat the olive oil in a small saucepan over medium heat; when the oil is warm, add the chopped ingredients, pancetta or prosciutto, and bay leaf. Sauté for 5 minutes, then add the contents of the saucepan, together with the drained cut-up potatoes, to the beans. Cover and simmer for 1 hour. Remove the bay leaf, then pass the contents of the casserole through a food mill fitted with the disk with medium-size holes into another casserole. Set that casserole over medium heat, season with salt and pepper, and simmer, uncovered, for 10 minutes.

Drain the barley, rinse it under cold running water, then add it to the simmering broth. Stir and let cook until the barley is very soft, about 25 minutes, mixing often. Remove from the heat and let the soup rest for 10 minutes before serving with freshly ground black pepper.

LATTUGHE RIPIENE ALLA GENOVESE
Soup of Stuffed Romaine Lettuce Leaves

Makes 5 servings

Lettuces are, of course, primarily utilized for salads in Italy as elsewhere, but in addition they are used in cooked dishes, perhaps more than in some countries. Shredded lettuce is not unknown as an ingredient in vegetable soups, but more often you find it as a lighter alternative to cabbage for wrappings. Indeed, stuffed lettuce leaves are found in a number of highly traditional forms in Rome, Liguria, and Livorno.

Here the stuffed lettuce leaves are eaten in soup. The stuffing includes sweetbreads, which in Italy are eaten most often as an ingredient in stuffing. There are also such popular dishes as *Fritto alla Fiorentina*, in which sweetbreads or brains are cleaned, cut into cubes, and deep-fried along with artichokes cut into similar shapes, as well as a small number of other dishes. In these recipes, brains and sweetbreads are treated interchangeably. But it is really in stuffings, especially in Liguria, that sweetbreads find their main role. It is a very important ingredient in such stuffed classics as *Cima alla Genovese* (Boned Stuffed Pressed Veal Breast), *Polpettone alla Genovese*, and this dish.

20 large Romaine lettuce leaves

Coarse-grained salt

FOR THE STUFFING:

2 ounces white bread, crusts removed

1 cup milk

4 ounces sweetbreads or boneless skinless
chicken breast

20 sprigs fresh Italian parsley, leaves only

5 large fresh basil leaves

5 large fresh mint leaves

8 ounces boneless skinless chicken breast,
cut into pieces

Salt and freshly ground black pepper

Large pinch of freshly grated nutmeg

1 or 2 extra-large eggs, depending on the
size of the lettuce leaves

2 tablespoons (1 ounce) sweet butter,
melted and cooled

1 quart completely defatted chicken broth,
preferably homemade

1½ quarts completely defatted meat broth,
preferably homemade

TO SERVE:

Fresh basil and Italian parsley leaves

Blanch the lettuce leaves in salted boiling water for 30 seconds, then transfer them to a large bowl of cold water. Carefully remove them, one after the other, and spread them out very well on paper towels. Cover the leaves with additional paper towels until needed.

Prepare the stuffing. Place the bread in a small saucepan, pour the milk over, and set the pan over low heat. Mix the bread with the milk, using a wooden spoon, until a rather smooth, thick paste forms. Transfer to a crockery or glass bowl and let rest until cool, about half an hour.

If sweetbreads are used, place in a small bowl and clean by pouring boiling water over them. Then remove the membranes and rinse under cold running water. Place the parsley, basil, mint, cut-up chicken breast, and sweetbreads in a medium-size crockery or glass bowl. Season with salt, pepper, and the nutmeg and mix very well. Add the cooled bread paste and mix again. In a meat grinder fitted with the disk with the smallest holes, grind the contents of the bowl into a clean crockery or glass bowl. The texture of the ground ingredients should be rather smooth; this is the reason for adding the eggs. Add either one or two eggs, whichever better achieves the desired smoothness, together with the melted butter, and mix very well.

Place a heaping tablespoon of this stuffing on each leaf. Carefully wrap the stuffing in the leaves and transfer each package, seam side down, to a large casserole in a single layer. Mix the two broths together and add enough broth to the casserole to completely cover the stuffed leaves. Set the casserole over medium heat, cover, and simmer for 10 to 12 minutes.

Meanwhile, heat the remaining broth to a boil, then transfer it to a soup tureen. When ready, with a slotted spoon transfer each package to the tureen. Each serving will consist of 4 *lattughe ripiene*, some of the broth, and the basil and parsley leaves sprinkled over.

TAGLIATELLE E FIORI DI ZUCCA
Tagliatelle and Zucchini Blossoms

Makes 8 to 10 servings

Because zucchini grow so beautifully in the Roman countryside, and because they are so abundant, the blossoms from the vegetable are utilized by the Romans in many different types of dishes, from appetizers to desserts. Romans love to see the displays of large baskets of these blossoms arranged just as carefully and attractively as if they were decorative flowers.

This minestrone made with beans and potatoes is flavored with a favorite herb, the wild mint that the Romans call *mentuccia* and the Tuscans call *nepitella,* which combines so well with the zucchini blossom. It is stronger and more pungent than the mint used in the United States, which is also used in Italy.

1 cup dried cannellini (white kidney) beans, picked over

2 tablespoons extra virgin olive oil

2 medium-size cloves garlic, peeled

1 medium-size baking potato (about 8 ounces), peeled

5 fresh *nepitella* leaves, or as the Romans call it, *mentuccia*, or 3 fresh mint leaves and 3 fresh basil leaves

4 ounces pancetta, coarsely ground

Coarse-grained salt

About 7 cups completely defatted chicken or meat broth, preferably homemade

FOR THE ZUCCHINI BLOSSOMS:

5 tablespoons extra virgin olive oil

4 ounces pancetta, coarsely ground

20 large zucchini blossoms (see Note on page 157), cleaned, with pistils removed and cut into thirds

Salt and freshly ground black pepper

Hot red pepper flakes

1 cup completely defatted chicken or meat broth, preferably homemade

FOR THE PASTA:

8 ounces dried egg tagliatelle, preferably imported Italian, or fresh tagliatelle (page 3) prepared with 2 cups unbleached all-purpose flour, 3 extra-large eggs, and pinch of salt

TO SERVE:

Fresh basil leaves

Soak the beans overnight in a bowl of cold water. The next morning, drain the beans and put them in a stockpot. Add the olive oil, garlic, potato, *mentuccia* (*nepitella*) or mint with basil, and pancetta, then enough cold water to reach 2 inches above the level of the ingredients. Simmer for about 45 minutes. By then the beans and potato should be rather soft. Add coarse salt to taste and simmer for 10 minutes more. Discard the pancetta and pass the solids from the stockpot through a food mill fitted with the disk with the smallest holes into a clean stockpot. Add enough cold broth to yield 10 cups of liquid. Place the stockpot back over medium heat.

Meanwhile, set a medium-size skillet with the olive oil over medium heat and when the oil is warm, add the pancetta and the zucchini blossoms and season with salt, black pepper, and hot pepper flakes. Sauté for 2 minutes, then add the broth and cook for 3 to 4 minutes.

Add the pasta, dried or fresh, to the stockpot and cook until completely done but not mushy. Add the contents of the skillet and mix very well. Taste for salt and pepper. Transfer to a soup tureen and let rest for a few minutes before serving with the basil leaves.

SICILY

MINESTRA CON CAVOLO E PASTA

Cabbage Minestrone

Makes 8 to 10 servings

In Italian, this dish retains its old name of *minestra*, even though it is what we call nowadays a minestrone.

Pancetta is often the only meat ingredient in a basically vegetable soup, but here the broth itself is of chicken or meat. An unusual touch is the inclusion of cut-up black olives. Most *minestroni* from Sicily use a large quantity of cabbage, and the type of cabbage normally utilized in Italian soups is the wrinkled Savoy cabbage, rather than the smooth-leaved *lasagnino*, the type normally found abroad. In Italy *lasagnino* is generally used uncooked, as it is more tender; Savoy cabbage is best used cooked, for its fuller flavor.

continued

1 head Savoy cabbage (about 1½ pounds)

Coarse-grained salt

4 ounces pancetta, in one piece

6 tablespoons extra virgin olive oil

1 large red onion, cleaned

1 small clove garlic, peeled

15 sprigs fresh Italian parsley, leaves only

5 large fresh basil leaves

10 large black olives in brine, pitted and cut
  into small pieces

Salt and freshly ground black pepper

2 large ripe tomatoes, blanched for 1
  minute, peeled, and seeded, or 1 pound
  drained canned tomatoes, preferably
  imported Italian, seeded

2 quarts completely defatted chicken or
  meat broth, preferably homemade

1 pound dried short tubular pasta, such as
  elbow macaroni or ditalini, preferably
  imported Italian

TO SERVE:

Extra virgin olive oil as needed

Clean the cabbage, discarding the very tough outer leaves. Save the inside part of the core. Slice the leaves horizontally into 1-inch strips. Remove the green part of the core and cut it into small cubes. Place the cabbage and cut-up core in a large bowl of cold water for half an hour. Bring a large pot of cold water to a boil, add coarse salt to taste, then drain the cabbage and add it to the boiling water. Cook for 10 minutes.

Meanwhile, cut the pancetta into small pieces. Place a medium-size stockpot with the olive oil over low heat. Add the pancetta and sauté for 5 minutes until golden. Finely chop the onion, garlic, parsley, and basil together on a cutting board. Add the chopped mixture to the stockpot; drain the cabbage. Once the pancetta and onion mixture have been sautéing for 10 minutes, add the cabbage along with the olives and season with salt and pepper. Mix very well and cook, stirring a few times, for another 10 minutes. Add the tomatoes and cook for another 10 minutes. Pour in the broth and cook until the cabbage is very soft, about another 25 minutes. Taste for salt and pepper. Add the pasta and boil until *al dente,* 9 to 12 minutes, depending on the brand.

Transfer the soup to a large tureen and let rest for a few minutes before ladling it into individual bowls. Drizzle a "C" of olive oil over each portion and serve.

MINESTRONE DI CECI ALLA MARCHIGIANA
Chick-Pea Soup in the Style of the Marches

Makes 8 to 10 servings

The food of Marche is warm and rich, and its chick-pea minestrone, instead of using only simple pancetta or prosciutto, is enriched with the flavor of pork spareribs. Among its vegetables we find the strong-flavored escarole. This vegetable becomes even more strong-flavored when it is cooked and is especially characteristic of the soups of Abruzzo as well as of Marche.

1½ cups dried chick peas, picked over

20 sprigs fresh Italian parsley, leaves only

2 medium-size stalks celery

1 medium-size red onion, cleaned

2 medium-size cloves garlic, peeled

3 or 4 escarole leaves

3 ounces prosciutto, in one piece

4 medium-size ripe tomatoes, blanched for
    1 minute, peeled, and seeded,
    or 4 canned tomatoes, preferably
    imported Italian, seeded

4 very small pork spareribs

¼ cup extra virgin olive oil

3 quarts cold water

Salt and freshly ground black pepper

TO SERVE:

8 to 10 large slices country-style bread

Freshly grated Pecorino Romano cheese

Soak the chick peas in a bowl of cold water overnight. The next morning, rinse them under cold running water and place in a nonreactive stockpot, preferably made of terra-cotta. Coarsely chop the parsley, celery, onion, garlic, and escarole together on a cutting board, and coarsely grind the prosciutto. Add the chopped mixture and prosciutto to the stockpot along with the tomatoes cut into pieces, the spareribs, and olive oil. Add the cold water, cover the pot, and place over medium heat. Let simmer until the chick peas are cooked and soft but still whole, about 1 hour. Season with salt and pepper. Remove 1 cup of the chick peas and pass them through a food mill fitted with the disk with the smallest holes directly back into the pot, then season with salt and pepper and simmer for another 15 minutes, stirring every so often with a wooden spoon. The chick peas should be very soft.

Meanwhile, toast the bread in the oven or over a fire. Place one slice of bread in each soup bowl, ladle some of the soup over, and serve with the grated Pecorino Romano.

VARIATION: The toasted bread may be rubbed with a clove of garlic.

QUADRUCCI E CECI
Quadrucci Pasta with Chick Peas

Makes 8 to 10 servings

Though the word *minestrone* does not appear in its title, this is a minestrone, because the broth has a large quantity of boiled whole chick peas in it. The distinguishing element of the dish, however, is the special pasta, with whole parsley leaves incorporated into the pasta dough itself. This parsley pasta, which has become rare even in its native Puglia, I am proud to have resurrected and popularized once again over a wider area. This is one of several soups employing parsley pasta. One uses a clear turkey broth with the pasta, which also contains grated cheese. *Quadrucci* means a square pasta.

FOR THE SOUP:

1 cup dried chick peas, picked over

2 stalks celery

1 medium-size red onion, cleaned

10 sprigs fresh Italian parsley, leaves only

1 large clove garlic, peeled

2 bay leaves

1 tablespoon extra virgin olive oil

4 quarts completely defatted cold chicken
    or meat broth, preferably homemade,
    or cold water

Coarse-grained salt

Freshly ground black pepper

FOR THE PASTA:

2 cups unbleached all-purpose flour

¼ cup very fine semolina flour

1 tablespoon extra virgin olive oil

3 extra-large eggs

Pinch of salt

Freshly ground black pepper

15 sprigs fresh Italian parsley, leaves only,
    with even the tiny stems attached to
    each leaf removed

TO COOK THE PASTA:

3 quarts completely defatted chicken or
    meat broth, preferably homemade, or
    water

¼ cup extra virgin olive oil

10 sprigs fresh Italian parsley, leaves only

Salt and freshly ground black pepper

Soak the chick peas in a bowl of cold water overnight. The next morning, drain the beans, rinse them under cold running water, and put them in a medium-size stockpot. Coarsely chop the celery, onion, and parsley together on a cutting board and finely chop the garlic. Add the chopped veg-etables to the stockpot along with the bay leaves and olive oil. Pour in the cold broth or water and set the pot over medium heat. When it reaches a boil, reduce the heat to medium-low and simmer until the chick peas are almost cooked and soft, about 45 minutes. Season with coarse salt and pep-per and simmer for another 10 minutes.

Meanwhile, prepare the pasta with the ingredients and quantities listed above according to the directions on page 3, placing the semolina flour, together with the other ingredients, in the well of the all-purpose flour. Roll the pasta out to a thickness of ⅛ inch (on a manual pasta machine that would be two settings before the last one). Place the parsley leaves over half of the pasta sheet, then fold the other half over. Press together very well, then roll the double layer of pasta with the pars-ley leaves between through the last setting of the pasta machine. (If the stems of the parsley have not been removed completely, you could end up with many holes in your pasta.) Use a scalloped pastry wheel to cut the pasta sheet into 2-inch squares. Let the pasta rest on paper towels or kitchen towels until needed.

When you are ready to cook the pasta, you have three options: You may cook it in the boiling broth, in boiling water, or in the broth with the chick peas. The pasta must be cooked completely, 30 seconds to 1 minute, depending on its dryness. As the pasta cooks, heat the olive oil in a small skillet, add the parsley, and cook, stirring, for 1 minute. Season with salt and pepper, add to the stockpot, mix very well, taste for salt and pepper, and discard the bay leaves. Transfer the soup to a tureen and let rest for a few minutes before serving.

CREMA DI CECI AI FUNGHI

Pureed Chick-Pea Soup with Mushrooms

Makes 8 servings

From Umbria we have a *crema* of chick peas. The term *crema* is used for pureed soups and really does not imply the inclusion of heavy cream as an ingredient. A significant difference between French and Italian cooking is that Italians almost never add small amounts of cream to a dish in which it is not featured as one of the primary ingredients, as is true of French cooking. One could almost say that in Italian cooking olive oil takes the place that heavy cream has in French cuisine.

Dried porcini mushrooms, soaked, provide the dominant flavor here and it is intensified by adding some of the mushroom soaking water to the soup. Dried porcini have a much more intense flavor than fresh ones, and they are an important ingredient in their own right. And fortunately they are plentiful, especially under the chestnut trees that grow in Tuscany and elsewhere.

2 cups dried chick peas, picked over

3 quarts cold water

1 large carrot, scraped and cut into large pieces

1 medium-size red onion, cleaned and quartered

1 large clove garlic, plus 1 small clove garlic, both peeled

1 bay leaf

¼ cup extra virgin olive oil

2 ounces pancetta or prosciutto, in one piece

Coarse-grained salt

1 ounce dried porcini mushrooms

15 sprigs fresh Italian parsley, leaves only

1 cup strained mushroom soaking water

1 tablespoon tomato paste (optional), preferably imported Italian, dissolved in the strained mushroom water

Salt and freshly ground black pepper

TO SERVE:

Fresh Italian parsley leaves

Extra virgin olive oil to drizzle all over

Soak the chick peas in a large bowl of cold water overnight. The next morning, drain and rinse the peas and place them in a medium-size stockpot. Add the cold water, carrot, onion, large garlic clove, and bay leaf, then 2 tablespoons of the olive oil and the pancetta or prosciutto. Set the pot over medium heat and boil the chick peas for at least 50 minutes or until soft. Add coarse salt to taste and cook for another 5 minutes. Discard the bay leaf and pancetta and pass the contents of the pot through a food mill fitted with the disk with the smallest holes into a clean medium-size stockpot. Set over medium heat and reduce for 10 minutes.

Soak the mushrooms in a bowl of lukewarm water for half an hour. Finely chop the parsley and small garlic clove together on a cutting board. Clean the soaked mushrooms very well, removing all the sand attached to the stems, and coarsely chop them. Remove the sand from the soaking water by pouring it through paper towels or a coffee filter several times. Save 1 cup of this water for this recipe and freeze the remaining water to be used when you prepare a meat sauce and want to enhance its taste.

Place the remaining 2 tablespoons olive oil in a small nonreactive saucepan set over low heat. When the oil is warm, add the garlic mixture and very lightly sauté for 2 minutes. Add the mushrooms and sauté for another 2 minutes. Add the cup of mushroom soaking water containing the dissolved tomato paste if desired, season with salt and pepper, and simmer for 15 minutes. Pour the contents of the saucepan into the stockpot, mix very well, and let simmer over low heat for at least 15 minutes, stirring every so often with a wooden spoon to prevent the *crema* from sticking to the bottom of the pot.

Serve hot or at room temperature, sprinkling the parsley leaves and olive oil over each serving. This soup may be prepared up to a day before and reheated at the last moment before serving.

GNOCCHI IN BRODO
Gnocchi in Broth

Makes 8 servings

The squash gnocchi on page 129 are also eaten, in a smaller quantity, in broth. Gnocchi in broth survives from the old days, before dried pasta became the omnipresent *primo piatto*, and the old ravioli made without pasta were all eaten in a thick spicy broth.

The gnocchi must first be cooked in salted water, not directly in the broth; they are then added to the chicken/meat broth. Because they are lightly cooked a second time, they require less flour when being made, and are even more tender than when eaten with sauce.

FOR THE GNOCCHI:

1 small Butternut squash (about 2 pounds)

¾ pound baking potatoes, such as Idahos

Coarse-grained salt

Pinch of ground saffron

1 scant tablespoon finely ground amaretti (bitter almond cookies), preferably imported Italian

1 extra-large egg

Salt and freshly ground black pepper

Pinch of freshly grated nutmeg

Scant ¼ cup unbleached all-purpose flour

¼ cup freshly grated Grana Padano cheese

About ½ cup unbleached all-purpose flour for coating

TO FINISH THE DISH:

10 cups completely defatted chicken or meat broth, preferably homemade

Coarse-grained salt

½ cup freshly grated Grana Padano cheese

24 fresh basil leaves

Prepare the gnocchi with the above ingredients according to the directions on page 130.

Bring a large pot of cold water to a boil and heat the broth as well in a separate pot. Add coarse salt to taste to the boiling water, then add the gnocchi and as they rise to the surface of the water, transfer them to the pot of hot broth. Do not let the gnocchi boil in the broth. Serve hot with the grated Grana Padano and basil leaves.

RISOTTI AND RISI E BISI

❖

Italy's most celebrated way of cooking rice is the risotto method, in which the unwashed raw rice is first sautéed in oil or butter, a combination of both, or even a small amount of sauce, then boiling liquid is added, little by little, while the rice is constantly stirred as it absorbs the liquid. This process takes time—up to twenty minutes—but you must be patient if you want real risotto; it is worth the wait. This technique is most associated with Milan and Lombardy, and probably the most celebrated risotto is *Risotto alla Milanese,* using saffron and veal marrow.

The main regions that grow rice are Lombardy, Piedmont, and Veneto. But each of the three, when making veal risotto (i.e., Milanese), though using the same technique, ends up with final textures that differ slightly from one to the other.

There are many varieties of *risotti,* made with sauces from vegetables, meat, fish, fowl, aromatic herbs, mushrooms, etc. We begin with three vegetable *risotti*—one with asparagus tips, another with peppers, and finally one with leeks and potatoes. We follow with *risotti* made with duck, pheasant, or chicken livers, with pancetta or prosciutto, with duck meat, and finally with fresh white truffles.

But Italy also has other methods of cooking rice, the most famous of which is probably Venice's *Risi e Bisi,* in which pancetta or prosciutto, onion, and garlic are sautéed in butter and olive oil, then peas and parsley are added. When everything is quite hot, boiling broth made from the pea pods is added, at first just one cup and then, after a few minutes, the bulk of the broth. The rice is then added and boiled in the abundant broth.

The Veneto region consumes a lot of rice, but has relatively few real *risotti.* Most of these dishes combine vegetables with rice, cooked using a technique close to that of a pilaf. The pilaf technique sautés the rice, pours in the broth all at once, and lets it finish cooking in the oven.

It's interesting to note that the three northern regions have great savory rice dishes, but it is Tuscany in Central Italy and Sicily, neither of which grows rice, that have created the outstanding rice desserts.

RISOTTO CON PUNTE DI ASPARAGI

Risotto with Asparagus Tips

Makes 8 servings

In Italy it is still possible to find wild asparagus and an even more special type called "snow asparagus," which, wild of course, peeps out from under the spring snows on the mountains. White asparagus is cultivated, and is called *Bassano* because that town in the Veneto first developed the Italian white type and still specializes in it. Green asparagus is popular and most common, but Italians prefer it as thin as possible, like the so-called "pencil" asparagus. All of these are available in season, and you rarely find even the cultivated types at other times of the year. And because of its rarity, asparagus is considered a special treat and prepared in relatively few different ways. Butter and grated Grana Padano or Parmigiano cheese most often form the dressing, and different regions have versions with a fried egg on top. Several green herb sauces are also used. Asparagus tips are considered rare and fancy enough in Italy to be added as a final embellishing touch to some dishes, much like a few shavings of truffle.

2 pounds fresh white or green asparagus

3 quarts cold water

Coarse-grained salt

4 ounces prosciutto or pancetta, in one piece

6 tablespoons (3 ounces) sweet butter

2 tablespoons extra virgin olive oil

Salt and freshly ground black pepper

3 cups completely defatted chicken or beef broth, preferably homemade

3 cups raw rice, preferably Italian Arborio

¼ cup freshly grated Parmigiano cheese

Leaves from 20 sprigs fresh Italian parsley, coarsely chopped

TO SERVE:

Freshly grated Parmigiano cheese

Clean the asparagus, removing the woody bottom part, and place in a bowl of cold water for half an hour.

Meanwhile, place a medium-size casserole with the water over medium heat; when the water reaches a boil, add the coarse-grained salt, drain the asparagus, and add it to the pot to let boil for 2 minutes. Remove the asparagus from the water, cut off the tips, and place the tips on a plate until needed. Put the rest of the asparagus back in the boiling water and let simmer for a half hour longer. By that time, the asparagus should be very soft and tender. Remove from the water and pass through a food mill, using the disk with the smallest holes, into a crockery or glass bowl. Be sure there are no threads from the asparagus; otherwise, pass the puree through a very thick sieve.

Add enough cooking water from the asparagus to make 4 cups of liquid and let stand until needed.

Cut the proscuitto into small pieces, then place a medium-size casserole, preferably made of terra-cotta, with the butter and oil over medium heat; when the butter is completely melted, add the prosciutto and sauté for 2 minutes. Then add the asparagus tips, season with salt and pepper, and let cook, covered, for 1 minute more.

Combine the broth and the asparagus liquid in a medium-size saucepan and bring to a boil over medium heat. Remove the asparagus tips from the casserole with a slotted spoon to a crockery or glass bowl, cover, and let stand until needed. Be sure that no proscuitto pieces have been removed. Sauté the proscuitto for 2 more minutes, then add the rice and sauté for 4 minutes, constantly stirring with a wooden spoon. Start adding the boiling liquid 1/2 cup at a time, continuously stirring, and do not add additional broth until the previous broth is completely absorbed by the rice. When all the liquid but the 1/2 cup has been absorbed and the rice is almost ready (about 15 minutes from the first 1/2 cup of broth), add the cheese, mix very sell, taste for salt and pepper, and add the last 1/2 cup of broth. When almost absorbed, add the asparagus tips and the parsley and mix thoroughly but gently, letting cook for a few seconds more. Transfer to a large warmed serving dish and serve immediately with additional grated Parmigiano.

❖

RISOTTO AI PEPERONI

Risotto with Red and Yellow Peppers

Makes 6 servings

2 yellow bell peppers

2 red bell peppers

2 medium-size cloves garlic, peeled

Leaves from 10 sprigs fresh Italian parsley

6 tablespoons extra virgin olive oil

Salt and freshly ground black pepper

2 cups raw rice, preferably Italian Arborio

¾ cup dry white wine

Large pinch of ground saffron

About 4 cups completely defatted chicken
broth, preferably homemade

TO SERVE:

Sprigs fresh Italian parsley

Skin the peppers (page 176), seed them, and cut them lengthwise into ½-inch-wide strips. Soak the peppers in a bowl of cold water for half an hour, then transfer them to paper towels.

Meanwhile, finely chop the garlic and parsley together on a cutting board. Heat the oil in a medium-size casserole over low heat; when the oil is warm, add the chopped ingredients and sauté for 1 minute.

Add the peppers to the casserole. Sauté for 5 minutes, stirring constantly with a wooden spoon. Season with salt and pepper. Use a slotted spoon to transfer the peppers to a cockery or glass bowl, leaving the juices from the peppers in the casserole. Cover the bowl and let stand until needed.

Add the rice to the casserole containing the juices from the peppers and heat over medium heat. Sauté the rice, stirring constantly for 3 minutes, then add the wine and, still stirring, let the wine evaporate for 2 minutes. Shake the saffron into the heated broth. When the rice is ready, start pouring in the broth ½ cup at a time, constantly stirring, and do not add more broth until the broth is completely absorbed by the rice. When all the broth but ½ cup is used up, season the rice with salt and pepper and transfer the peppers from the bowl to the casserole. Add the remaining ½ cup broth and mix very well but gently, until the rice is cooked, but still has a "bite." Transfer the contents of the casserole to a large warm serving platter, sprinkle the parsley sprigs all over, and serve hot.

RISOTTO CON PORRI E PATATE

Leek Risotto with Potatoes

Makes 6 to 8 servings

2 pounds leeks

1 pound all-purpose potatoes, peeled and
    cut into 1-inch cubes

4 tablespoons (2 ounces) sweet butter

2 tablespoons extra virgin olive oil

Salt and freshly ground black pepper

FOR THE RISOTTO:

4 cups completely defatted chicken broth,
    preferably homemade

5 tablespoons (2½ ounces) sweet butter

1 tablespoon extra virgin olive oil

2 cups raw rice, preferably Italian Arborio

1 cup dry white wine

2 small sprigs fresh majoram or 1 teaspoon
    dried marjoram

Salt and freshly ground black pepper

¼ cup heavy cream

¼ cup freshly grated Parmigiano cheese

TO SERVE:

3 tablespoons freshly grated Parmigiano
    cheese

6 to 8 sprigs fresh marjoram

Clean the leeks, removing all the green leaves, and cut them into quarters vertically. Let soak in a bowl of cold water for half an hour. You should have a yield of about 1 pound of cleaned leeks.

Place the potato cubes in another bowl of cold water to avoid discoloring.

When you are ready, drain and rinse the leeks several times to be sure all the sand is removed, then finely chop them on a cutting board. Place the butter and olive oil in a heavy, medium-size casserole and set it over medium heat. When the butter is melted, put in the leeks and sauté until they are translucent, 2 to 3 minutes. Then drain the potatoes and put them in the casserole, cooking for 3 minutes more. Season with salt and pepper. Meanwhile, heat the chicken broth to a boil.

Use a slotted spoon to transfer the sautéed leeks and potatoes from the casserole to a bowl. Using the same casserole, add 4 tablespoons of the butter and the olive oil for the risotto and when the butter is melted, add the rice and sauté, constantly stirring with a wooden spoon, for 3 minutes. Pour in half the wine and let it evaporate for about 2 minutes. Then add the marjoram leaves and the remaining wine. When the rice is quite dry, return the leeks and potatoes to the casserole. Start adding the boiling broth ½ cup at a time, constantly stirring with a wooden spoon. Do not add more broth until what was previously added is absorbed. Season with salt and pepper when all but ½ cup of the broth has been used up. The cooking time of the rice should be 18 to 19 minutes.

continued

When the risotto is almost ready, taste for salt and pepper and pour in the heavy cream. Stir very well, remove the casserole from the heat, and add the remaining tablespoon butter and the Parmigiano. Mix very well in a "churning" motion. Transfer the risotto to a warm serving platter.

Serve immediately with more cheese sprinkled all over and a sprig of fresh marjoram on top of each serving.

RISOTTO ALLE CICCHE
Risotto with Duck, Pheasant, or Chicken Livers

Makes 6 servings

6 large duck livers (or 8 pheasant or chicken livers), cleaned, with all the fat removed

6 tablespoons extra virgin olive oil

1 cup dry white wine

Salt and freshly ground black pepper

1 medium-size red onion, cleaned

2 cups raw rice, preferably Italian Arborio

4 cups completely defatted chicken or meat broth, preferably homemade

2 tablespoons (1 ounce) sweet butter

Freshly grated Parmigiano cheese

Cut the livers into quarters and wash them very well. Heat the olive oil in a medium-size casserole over medium heat. When the oil is warm, add the livers, sauté for 1 minute, then add the wine and let evaporate for 1 minute more. Season with salt and pepper. Transfer the livers, using a slotted spoon, to a small bowl, cover, and let rest until needed. Let the wine simmer in the casserole for 5 minutes more.

Meanwhile, finely chop the onion on a cutting board, add it to the casserole, and sauté until the onion is translucent, about 4 minutes. Add the rice and sauté for 4 minutes, stirring constantly with a wooden spoon. Bring the broth to a boil. When the rice is ready, start adding the boiling broth 1/2 cup at a time, constantly stirring, and do not add extra broth until what was previously added is completely absorbed by the rice. When all the broth but 1/2 cup is used up, add the livers and the remaining broth. By that time the rice should be cooked, but with a "bite," as risotto should be. Remove the casserole from the heat, add the butter and mix very well until it is completely amalgamated. Serve immediately with freshly grated Parmigiano.

RISOTTO ALL'ANITRA
Duck Risotto

Makes 12 servings

FOR THE BROTH:

1 duck (about 5 pounds), Long Island type,
    its liver reserved

1 stalk celery

1 carrot, scraped

1 small red onion, cleaned

1 clove garlic, peeled

5 sprigs fresh Italian parsley, leaves only

Coarse-grained salt

FOR THE SAUCE:

2 large stalks celery

3 large cloves garlic, peeled

1 medium-size red onion, cleaned

1½ tablespoons rosemary leaves, fresh or
    preserved in salt (page 2)

2 sage leaves, fresh or preserved in salt
    (page 2)

15 sprigs fresh Italian parsley, leaves only

⅓ cup extra virgin olive oil or ¼ cup
    (2 ounces) sweet butter

Salt and freshly ground black pepper

½ cup red wine vinegar

2 heaping tablespoons tomato paste,
    preferably imported Italian

FOR THE RISOTTO:

5 cups raw short-grain rice, preferably
    Italian Arborio

Salt and freshly ground black pepper

TO SERVE:

6 tablespoons freshly grated Parmigiano
    cheese

Sprigs fresh rosemary

Carefully wash the duck, removing the extra fat and saving its liver. Pat dry with paper towels. Place a medium-size stockpot of cold water over medium heat. When the water reaches a boil, add the celery, carrot, onion, garlic, parsley, and coarse salt to taste and cook for 20 minutes. Add the whole duck, bring to a boil, and let boil for 30 minutes, skimming the surface of foam. Transfer the duck to a large serving platter and let cool for about half an hour. Strain the broth, discarding all the vegetables, and let the broth cool completely, about 1 hour.

Prepare the sauce. Finely chop the celery, garlic, onion, rosemary, sage, and parsley together on a cutting board. Place a large casserole with the olive oil or butter over medium heat; when the oil or butter is warm, add the duck. Season with salt and pepper and brown on both sides until golden, about 10 minutes. Add the chopped mixture and sauté for another 15 minutes, turning the duck over several times.

continued

Skim all the fat from the surface of the duck broth, then measure out about 4 cups of it, reserving the rest. Heat this broth in a small saucepan over medium heat. Add the vinegar to the casserole and cook, stirring for 5 minutes more. Dissolve the tomato paste in the warmed broth. Add this broth to the casserole 1 cup at a time, not adding the next cup until the first addition is almost entirely absorbed. Turn the duck every time you add the broth. Cook for about 1 hour total. By that time the broth should be incorporated into the duck and vegetables, the duck cooked, and a very rich sauce formed.

Transfer the duck to a cutting board and let cool for 10 minutes. Remove the breast from the duck, discard the skin, and cut the meat into ½-inch squares. Skim some of the fat off the top of the duck sauce. (All these steps may be done up to one day in advance.)

Start the risotto. Finely chop the reserved duck liver, heat the remaining broth (should be about 10 cups) to boiling, and reheat the sauce. When the duck sauce is well heated, add the rice and sauté for 4 minutes, stirring constantly with a wooden spoon. Start adding the boiling broth ½ cup at a time, stirring constantly, without adding any more broth until what you've added is completely absorbed by the rice. After 5 cups of the broth have been incorporated, add the chopped liver and the pieces of duck breast and season with salt and pepper. Keep adding broth until the rice is cooked but still *al dente*; it should be creamy, but have a "bite" (it should take about 18 minutes from the time the first broth is added). Remove the risotto from the heat, add the Parmigiano, and mix very well. Transfer to a warmed serving platter and serve hot with the sprigs of rosemary.

RISOTTO ALL'AMATRICIANA
Risotto Amatrice Style

Makes 6 servings

4 ounces guanciale (the cured meat of the cheek of a pig), pancetta, or prosciutto, in one piece

¼ cup extra virgin olive oil

1 large red onion, cleaned

1½ pounds ripe tomatoes or drained canned tomatoes, preferably imported Italian

3 cups completely defatted chicken or beef broth, preferably homemade

½ to ¾ teaspoon hot red pepper flakes, to your taste

Salt and freshly ground black pepper

2 cups raw short-grain rice, preferably Italian Arborio

TO SERVE:

6 tablespoons freshly grated Pecorino Romano cheese

Cut the guanciale, pancetta, or prosciutto into tiny cubes. Place a heavy medium-size nonreactive casserole, preferably made of terra-cotta, with the olive oil over medium heat; when the oil is warm, add the meat and sauté for 10 minutes, stirring every so often.

Meanwhile, coarsely chop the onion on a cutting board. If the tomatoes are fresh, cut them into small pieces. Whether using fresh or canned tomatoes, pass them through a food mill, using the disk with the smallest holes, into a small crockery or glass bowl. When the meat is crisp, use a slotted spoon to transfer the pieces from the casserole to a plate. Add the onion to the casserole and sauté until translucent, about 5 minutes.

Heat the broth in a small saucepan. Add the tomatoes and red pepper flakes to the onion, and season with salt and pepper. Let simmer for 15 minutes, stirring every so often with a wooden spoon. Remove half of the tomato sauce and let it stand in a small crockery or glass bowl until needed. Add the rice to the casserole, stir very well with the remaining sauce, and sauté for 4 minutes. Start adding the hot broth ½ cup at a time, constantly mixing with a wooden spoon; do not add any extra broth until what has been added is completely absorbed by the rice. Before adding the last ½ cup of broth, add the tomato sauce from the small bowl. Taste for salt and pepper. Add the last ½ cup broth and let the rice absorb it. By that time the rice should be cooked but still retain a "bite" (it should take about 18 minutes from the time the first broth is added). Add the meat, mix very well, and transfer to a large warmed serving platter. Serve immediately with the Pecorino Romano sprinkled over.

VARIATION: Add the Pecorino Romano cheese to the casserole along with the reserved meat and mix with the rice.

RISI E BISI
Rice and Peas Venetian Style

Makes 6 servings

FOR THE BROTH:

1 pound snow peas or, if using fresh peas
    for the dish, 1 pound of the pods
    of the peas
15 cups cold water
1 medium-size carrot, scraped and cut into
    2-inch pieces
1 medium-size stalk celery, cut into large
    pieces
1 very small clove garlic, peeled
5 sprigs fresh Italian parsley, leaves only
Coarse-grained salt

FOR THE RICE:

4 ounces pancetta or prosciutto, in one
    piece
1 medium-size cipollotto (Venetian white
    onion) or yellow onion, cleaned

¼ cup (2 ounces) sweet butter
2 tablespoons extra virgin olive oil
1 medium-size clove garlic (optional),
    peeled
15 sprigs fresh Italian parsley, leaves only
1 pound very small, sweet fresh peas or
    frozen "tiny tender" peas, not defrosted
Salt and freshly ground black pepper
1 cup raw short-grain rice, preferably
    Vialone or Italian Arborio

TO SERVE:

2 tablespoons (1 ounce) sweet butter
6 tablespoons freshly grated Grana Padano
    cheese
Sprigs fresh Italian parsley

Wash the snow peas or pea pods very well under cold running water. In a large pot bring the cold water to a boil with the snow peas or pods, carrot, celery, garlic, and parsley over medium heat. While boiling, add coarse salt to taste, reduce the heat to medium-low, and simmer for 50 minutes. Strain the broth and discard all the vegetables.

Finely grind the pancetta or prosciutto in a meat grinder and coarsely chop the onion on a cutting board. Place the butter and olive oil in a medium-size casserole set over low heat. When the butter is melted, add the pancetta or prosciutto, onion, and garlic clove, if used. Sauté slowly for about 15 minutes, then add the parsley and mix very well, then add the fresh or still frozen peas. Season with salt and pepper. Raise the heat to medium, add 1 cup of the vegetable broth, cover, and cook for 5 minutes. Remove the garlic and discard. Pour in 5 cups of the broth and when it reaches a boil, add the rice. Mix very well, reduce the heat to medium-low, and simmer for 18 minutes. Be sure to have enough broth in the casserole for the rice to absorb to cook completely, with a tiny amount of liquid left; the final texture should be something between a real risotto and a thick bean soup. Remove the casserole from the heat, add the butter and cheese, and mix very well. (*Mantecare*—to churn—is the word used to describe the movement of absorbing the butter and the cheese into the rice.) Serve with the Italian parsley.

PIEDMONT

RISOTTO AL TARTUFO
Risotto with Fresh White Truffle

Makes 6 to 8 servings

1 medium-size yellow onion, cleaned

8 tablespoons (4 ounces) sweet butter

1 tablespoon olive oil

3 cups raw rice, preferably Italian Arborio

5 to 6 cups very light chicken broth, preferably homemade

1 cup dry white wine

Salt and freshly ground black pepper

6 tablespoons freshly grated Parmigiano cheese

TO SERVE:

Slivers of fresh white truffle (about ½ ounce) or 1 ounce white truffle paste

Finely chop the onion on a cutting board. Place a heavy medium-size casserole with 6 tablespoons of the butter and the oil over medium heat. When the butter is melted, put in the onion and lightly sauté for 10 minutes. By that time the onion should be translucent and still white, not yet golden. Add the rice to the casserole and sauté for 3 minutes, stirring constantly with a wooden spoon.

Meanwhile, heat the broth to boiling in a saucepan. Pour the wine into the casserole and, still stirring constantly, let the wine evaporate, about 3 minutes. Season with salt and pepper and add the broth ¾ cup at a time, still stirring constantly, and adding more broth as that previously added is completely absorbed by the rice. Within 16 to 18 minutes the broth should be all used up and the rice cooked, but still with a "bite."

Remove the casserole from the heat, add the remaining 2 tablespoons butter and cheese and mix very well. Transfer the risotto to a warmed serving platter and serve hot, shaving some of the fresh truffles on top of each serving

If using truffle paste, add it to the risotto along with the last of butter and the cheese when the casserole is removed from heat.

GNOCCHI

❖

Gnocchi are found in the oldest Italian cookbooks, from the 1300s; interestingly, they were called *ravioli*, after *robiola*, the rounded root of a type of turnip, the greens of which we now call rape or broccolirab. Seeds have recently been developed abroad for broccolirab turnips that no longer have the round root, but the traditional type is the one that has always been used in Italy. Through the Renaissance and into the early nineteenth century, these "ravioli" without pasta were eaten in the spicy soups or *minestre* that were the usual first course of Italian meals before the swift spread of dried pasta in the middle of the nineteenth century. Ravioli wrapped in pasta were a less employed alternative, but acquired different shapes through the centuries. One version kept the name and the original shape, the ravioli *nudi* that are still traditional in Florence, made from spinach and ricotta. We ate them often in my family, and our family name for them is "naked ravioli." It much amuses me to see recipes called *ravioli nudi* in English-language cookbooks that appeared after the publication of the recipe in my *Fine Art of Italian Cooking*, pretending that the authors found the dish in Florence and that they never heard of my book. Mary McCarthy in *The Stones of Florence* called them "Green Gnocchi," but they are always called simply "ravioli" in Florence, and have no flour in them; green gnocchi are quite another thing.

Gnocchi as we know them in modern times are based on potatoes, alone or in combination with another vegetable or even other starches. And potatoes are a late arrival in Italian cooking, although they arrived earlier than when Parmentier popularized them in France.

Gnocchi made from potatoes alone should be very tender, and as little flour as possible should be added to help hold them together. The more flour added, the easier it is to hold them together, but the tougher they get. Eggs and grated cheese should not be added to the "dough" for potato gnocchi, as they make them tougher still. Authentic gnocchi often come as a surprise to people who have eaten only the commercial type, because they are not chewy and really do, as they say, "melt in your mouth." The toughness of badly made gnocchi is a standing joke in Italy, and the slang word *gnocco* is used to describe a dense person.

To achieve the lightness required, the potatoes should be prepared so they absorb the least liquid: the older the potatoes, the better for gnocchi, because they have less liquid-absorbing starch. Potatoes with "eyes" popping out of the skin are ideal. They should be peeled while still very hot, without running any water over them, then riced and left to become cold before mixing in the flour, as the cold potatoes will absorb less flour than when warm or even lukewarm.

We begin with a Ligurian version of pure potato gnocchi, dressed with an interesting combination of two sauces, one a basil-and-parsley pesto and the other a tomato sauce. From Piedmont, we have gnocchi made with a combination of potatoes and beets. When gnocchi are made with potatoes in combination with another vegetable, we do add eggs and grated cheese to hold together the more watery combination created by the second vegetable. The beet-and-potato gnocchi may be dressed with some butter and additional cheese, in Piedmont most often grated Grana Padano, as in other far north regions, or with typically Piemonte truffle sauce.

The wonderful squash-and-potato gnocchi are from Mantua in Lombardy. Flavored with saffron, nutmeg, and crushed bitter-almond amaretti, they are topped only with thinly shaved slivers of Grana Padano. The carrot-and-potato gnocchi, also from Liguria, are served with a superb *agliata*, a sauce made from many cloves of crushed raw garlic combined with white wine and vinegar. Gnocchi from Padua, near Venice, combine potatoes, cornmeal, and the very interesting addition of bread crumbs. These slightly chewy gnocchi are baked with a savory meat sauce.

GNOCCHI DI PATATE AL PESTO

Potato Gnocchi with Ligurian Pesto and Tomatoes

Makes 8 to 10 servings

FOR THE GNOCCHI:

3 pounds all-purpose potatoes

Coarse-grained salt

1¼ cups unbleached all-purpose flour

Salt to taste

FOR THE PESTO:

1 cup lightly packed fresh basil leaves

15 sprigs fresh Italian parsley, leaves only

1 medium-size clove garlic, peeled

½ cup freshly grated Parmigiano cheese

½ cup pine nuts (*pignoli*)

Salt and freshly ground black pepper

½ to ¾ cup extra virgin olive oil, as needed

FOR THE TOMATO SAUCE:

1½ pounds ripe tomatoes or drained canned
  tomatoes, preferably imported Italian

5 tablespoons extra virgin olive oil

3 large cloves garlic, peeled and cut into
  small slivers

Salt and freshly ground black pepper

10 large fresh basil leaves

TO COOK THE GNOCCHI:

Coarse-grained salt

TO SERVE:

Fresh basil leaves

Place the potatoes in a stockpot and add coarse salt to taste and enough cold water to cover the potatoes completely. Set the pot, uncovered, over medium heat and cook until the potatoes are very soft, about 35 minutes, depending on their size. Drain, then peel the potatoes while still very hot and pass them through a potato ricer fitted with the disk with the smallest holes onto a board. Let them rest until cool.

Meanwhile, prepare the pesto sauce. Place the basil, parsley, garlic, Parmigiano, and pine nuts in a blender or food processor and process until quite smooth. Transfer to a crockery or glass bowl. Season with salt and pepper, add the olive oil to a thick consistency, and mix very well. Refrigerate, covered, until needed.

Bring a large pot of cold water to a boil over medium heat. Knead 1 cup of the flour into the riced potatoes and season with salt. Cut the potato mixture into several pieces and, using your fingers and the heavily floured palms of your hands, roll them out into "ropes" about 1 inch in diameter. Cut each "rope" into ½-inch pieces.

Prepare the tomato sauce. If fresh tomatoes are used, cut them into large pieces. Place a large nonreactive skillet with the olive oil over medium heat; when the oil is warm, add the garlic and lightly sauté for 20 seconds. Add the tomatoes, fresh or canned, and cook for 15 minutes, stirring every so often with a wooden spoon. Season with salt and pepper. Warm a serving platter.

When the water in the pot reaches a boil, add coarse salt to taste, then the gnocchi, 10 to 15 at a time. When they float to the surface of the water, use a skimmer to transfer them to the warmed platter. As you cook the gnocchi, finish the tomato sauce. Add the basil leaves and cook for 1 minute more. Add the pesto sauce to the tomato sauce, mix very well, and immediately remove the skillet from the heat. When all the gnocchi are cooked and on the serving platter, pour the sauce over them. Serve with the basil leaves. No extra cheese should be added.

PIEDMONT

GNOCCHI DI BARBE ROSSE
Red Beet Gnocchi

Makes 6 to 8 servings

1½ pounds all-purpose potatoes

Coarse-grained salt

¾ pound red beets, leaves removed, leaving
    1 inch of the stalks

2 extra-large eggs

¼ cup unbleached all-purpose flour

½ cup freshly grated Grana Padano cheese

Large pinch of freshly grated nutmeg

Salt and freshly ground black pepper

TO COOK AND SERVE THE
GNOCCHI:

Coarse-grained salt

½ cup (4 ounces) sweet butter

1 cup unbleached all-purpose flour for
    coating

½ cup freshly grated Grana Padano cheese,
    or more to taste

Place the potatoes in a medium-size pot of cold water, add coarse salt to taste, and set over medium heat. Let cook, uncovered, until the potatoes are very soft, about 35 minutes, depending on their size.

Meanwhile, boil the red beets in a large saucepan of salted water until very soft, about 40 minutes, the time depending on the size.

Drain, then peel the potatoes while still very hot and rice them, using a potato ricer fitted with the disk with the smallest holes, into a large crockery or glass bowl. Let rest until completely cool. Peel the beets under cold running water; the skins will come off very easily. Place the beets in a blender or a food processor and process until smooth. Let rest until completely cool, about half an hour. When the riced potatoes are cool, add the eggs and flour to them and mix very well.

continued

Add the Grana Padano, nutmeg, and pureed beets, season with salt and pepper, and mix together very well.

Place two pots of cold water over medium heat, one a stockpot to be used to cook the gnocchi, the second a saucepan with a serving dish placed over it. When the water in the stockpot reaches a boil, add coarse salt to taste. Then melt 2 tablespoons of the butter on the warmed serving dish over the the saucepan of boiling water. Heavily flour the palms of your hands. Take a heaping tablespoon of the beet mixture between your two palms and fashion into ball-shaped gnocchi, pressing each ball tight so that no air remains inside. Once you have shaped them, gently drop the gnocchi, as many as seven or eight at a time, into the boiling water and, when they float to the surface, transfer them with a strainer-skimmer onto the melted butter in the warmed serving platter. As you cook the gnocchi, melt the remaining 6 tablespoons butter in a small bowl placed over simmering water. When all the gnocchi are on the serving dish, pour the melted butter over and serve immediately with the grated Grana Padano.

VARIATION: Serve with White Truffle Sauce (*Salsa di Tartufo Bianco*) instead of the butter and cheese.

¼ cup (2 ounces) sweet butter	Salt and freshly ground black pepper
1 medium-size clove garlic, peeled	1 heaping tablespoon white truffle paste
¼ cup unbleached all-purpose flour	(available at specialty food stores)
2 cups whole milk	

Melt the butter in a small saucepan over medium heat. Add the garlic and flour and stir very well. When the flour is well incorporated and starts sizzling, remove the pan from the heat and let rest. Bring the milk just to a boil in a second saucepan. Place the pan with the butter back over medium heat, pour in all the hot milk at once, and stir very well. Season with salt and pepper and simmer for 3 to 4 minutes. By that time the sauce should be very smooth and like a thin paste. Add the truffle paste, mix very well, and simmer for a few seconds more. Discard the garlic clove and serve.

GNOCCHI DI CAROTE CON AGLIATA
Carrot Gnocchi with Ligurian Garlic Sauce
Makes 6 to 8 servings

FOR THE GNOCCHI:

1½ pounds baking potatoes such as Idaho potatoes

Coarse-grained salt

1 pound scrubbed fresh carrots, with the skins left on

1 large clove garlic, peeled

3 extra-large eggs

Salt and freshly ground black pepper

Large pinch of freshly grated nutmeg

½ cup freshly grated Grana Padano cheese

½ cup unbleached all-purpose flour

FOR THE SAUCE (LIGURIAN AGLIATA):

½ cup white dry wine

½ cup white wine vinegar

3 ounces white bread, crusts removed

6 to 8 medium-size cloves garlic, to your taste, peeled

15 sprigs fresh Italian parsley, leaves only

5 fresh basil leaves

1 small potato (about 3 ounces), boiled until tender and peeled

Salt and freshly ground black pepper

½ cup extra virgin olive oil

TO COOK THE GNOCCHI:

Coarse-grained salt

1 tablespoon (½ ounce) sweet butter

1 cup unbleached all-purpose flour for coating

TO SERVE:

Fresh basil leaves

Put the potatoes in a medium-size pot of cold water, add coarse salt, and set the pot over medium heat. Let cook, uncovered, until the potatoes are very soft, about 35 minutes, depending on size.

Meanwhile, place the carrots in a large bowl of cold water and soak for 30 minutes, then boil them in a medium-size pot of salted boiling water with the clove of garlic, until very soft. Discard the garlic clove.

Peel the potatoes while still very hot and rice them, using a potato ricer with the disk with smallest holes, into a crockery or glass bowl. Let rest until completely cool.

Drain the carrots and peel under cold running water; the skins will come off very easily and the carrots retain their full flavor. If carrots are young and thin, when cooked weigh out ¾ pound of them and process them to a paste. If you have large carrots, first remove the lighter colored woody inside part before measuring out the correct amount.

continued

Combine the pureed carrots with the riced potatoes and mix very well. When ready, add the eggs, season with salt, pepper, and nutmeg, and add the cheese and flour. Mix very well with a wooden spoon. Place two pots of cold water over medium heat, one a stockpot to be used for boiling the gnocchi, the second a saucepan with a serving dish placed over it.

Meanwhile, prepare the sauce. Mix the wine with the vinegar and soak the bread in it for 10 minutes. Then lightly squeeze the bread to remove excess liquid and place the soaked bread together with garlic, parsley, basil, and the potato in a blender or food processor and blend until a very smooth paste forms. Transfer the sauce to a crockery or glass bowl, season with salt and pepper, and mix very well. Slowly pour in the oil, constantly stirring with a wooden spoon.

When the water in the stockpot reaches a boil, add coarse salt to taste. Melt the butter on the warmed serving platter over the saucepan of boiling water.

Heavily flour the palms of your hands. Use a heaping tablespoon of the carrot mixture to make ball-shaped gnocchi between your two palms, pressing the balls tight so that no air remains inside. Gently drop the gnocchi, as many as 7 or 8 at a time, into the boiling water; when they come up to the surface, transfer them with a strainer-skimmer onto the melted butter in the warmed serving platter. When all the gnocchi are on the serving dish, immediately place them on individual plates with some of the *agliata* sauce on one side and basil leaves on top.

VARIATION: Some may find the *agliata*, the classic sauce for these gnocchi, too strong for their taste. I offer as an alternative the following sauce.

4 ounces white bread, crusts removed

½ cup red wine vinegar

25 sprigs fresh Italian parsley, leaves only

10 fresh basil leaves

1 teaspoon fresh marjoram leaves or a pinch
    of dried marjoram

2 medium-size cloves garlic, peeled

2 tablespoons capers in wine vinegar,
    drained

5 tablespoons shelled walnuts

2 hard-boiled eggs, shelled

Salt and freshly ground black pepper

2 whole anchovies preserved in salt (see
    Note on page 10) or 4 anchovy fillets
    packed in oil (optional), drained

¾ cup to 1 cup extra virgin olive oil, to
    your taste

TO SERVE:

Fresh basil leaves

Soak the bread in the vinegar for 10 minutes. Squeeze the bread and discard the liquid. Place the bread, parsley, basil, marjoram, garlic, capers, walnuts, and eggs in a blender or food processor and blend until a very smooth sauce forms. Season with salt and pepper and, if using the anchovies, blend again. Transfer the sauce to a crockery or glass bowl, add the oil, and stir very well. Cover the bowl and refrigerate until needed.

When the gnocchi are cooked and sitting in the serving dish, remove the sauce from the refrigerator, add ¾ cup of the hot water left in the pot in which you cooked the gnocchi, and mix very well. Pour the sauce all over the gnocchi and serve with fresh basil leaves.

MANTUA

GNOCCHI DI ZUCCA AL GRANA
Squash Gnocchi

Makes 6 to 8 servings

1 medium-size Butternut squash (about
    3 pounds), or 3 pounds Acorn squash
1½ pounds baking potatoes such as Idaho
    potatoes
Coarse-grained salt
Large pinch of ground saffron
1½ tablespoons finely ground amaretti
    cookies (bitter almond cookies)
2 extra-large eggs
Salt and freshly ground black pepper
Large pinch of freshly grated nutmeg

½ cup unbleached all-purpose flour
½ cup freshly grated Grana Padano cheese

TO COOK THE GNOCCHI:

Coarse-grained salt
½ cup (4 ounces) sweet butter
1 cup unbleached all-purpose flour
    for coating

TO SERVE:

8 ounces Grana Padano cheese, shaved
    into thin slivers

Preheat the oven to 400 degrees.

Wash the squash very well and dry with paper towels. Place the squash on a jelly-roll pan and bake until very soft, about 2 hours. Meanwhile put the potatoes in a medium-size pot of cold water, add coarse salt to taste, and set pot over medium heat. Let cook, uncovered, until potatoes are very soft, about 35 minutes, depending on their size. Peel the potatoes, still very hot, and rice them, using a potato ricer with the disk with smallest holes, into a crockery or glass bowl. Let rest until completely cool, about 1 hour.

continued

When the squash is ready, transfer it to a cutting board and cut it into pieces. Scoop up the pulp and use a fork to mash it completely. Weigh out 3/4 pound and add it to the potatoes. Let cool completely. When ready, add the saffron, ground amaretti cookies, and eggs. Season with salt, pepper, and nutmeg, then add the flour and cheese and mix very well with a wooden spoon.

Set two pots of cold water over medium heat, one a stockpot to be used to boil the gnocchi, the second a saucepan with a large serving platter over it. When the water in the stockpot reaches a boil, add coarse salt to taste. Melt the butter on the warmed serving platter over the saucepan of boiling water.

Heavily flour the palms of your hands. Use a heaping tablespoon of the squash mixture to make ball-shaped gnocchi between your two palms, pressing the balls tightly so that no air remains inside. Gently drop the gnocchi, as many as 7 or 8 at a time, into the boiling water; when they come up to the surface, transfer them with a strainer-skimmer to the melted butter in the warmed serving platter.

When all the gnocchi are on the serving platter, immediately shave the cheese over and serve very hot.

GNOCCHI ALLA PADOVANA
Bread Crumb Gnocchi

Makes 6 to 8 servings

1 pound all-purpose potatoes

Coarse-grained salt

⅔ cup unbleached all-purpose flour

½ cup very fine stone-ground yellow
cornmeal, preferably imported Italian

¼ cup very fine unseasoned bread crumbs,
preferably homemade, lightly toasted

3 extra-large eggs

¼ cup (2 ounces) sweet butter, melted

Salt and freshly ground black pepper

Freshly grated nutmeg

FOR THE SAUCE:

1 large carrot, scraped

1 large stalk celery

1 small red onion, cleaned

1 clove garlic, peeled

15 sprigs fresh Italian parsley, leaves only

8 fresh sage leaves

1 heaping tablespoon fresh rosemary leaves

¼ cup extra virgin olive oil

¼ cup (2 ounces) sweet butter

1 pound ground beef

1 cup dry white wine

Salt and freshly ground black pepper

2 pounds ripe tomatoes or undrained
canned tomatoes, preferably imported
Italian

TO COOK THE GNOCCHI:

Coarse-grained salt

TO SERVE:

Freshly grated Grana Padano cheese
(optional)

Place the potatoes in a medium-size saucepan of cold water, add coarse salt to taste, and set the pan over medium heat. Bring to a boil and cook until the potatoes are very soft, about 35 minutes, depending on their size. Immediately peel the potatoes and rice them with a potato ricer, using the disk with smallest holes, into a crockery or glass bowl. Let rest until completely cool, about 1 hour.

Meanwhile, prepare the sauce. Finely chop the carrot, celery, onion, garlic, parsley, sage, and rosemary all together on a cutting board. Place a large nonreactive skillet with the oil and butter over medium heat; when the butter is melted, add the chopped vegetables and aromatic herbs. Sauté for 2 minutes, mixing with a wooden spoon. Add the ground meat and sauté until the meat is not reddish anymore, about 2 minutes more. Pour in the wine and let evaporate for 2 to 3 minutes. Season with salt and pepper. If using fresh tomatoes, cut them into large pieces. Add the tomatoes, whether fresh or canned, to the skillet and cook for 20 minutes, still over medium heat. Pass the contents of the skillet through a food mill fitted with the disk with the smallest holes into a crockery or glass bowl. Return the sauce to the skillet and reduce it, over medium heat, until a rather thick sauce forms, about 5 minutes. Taste for salt and pepper.

Transfer the sauce to a glass baking dish and preheat the oven to 375 degrees. Place a large stockpot of cold water over medium heat.

Add the flour, cornmeal, bread crumbs, eggs, and the melted butter to the potatoes, season with salt, pepper, and nutmeg and mix very well. Be sure to add enough seasonings because the potatoes, cornmeal, and bread crumbs absorb a lot of the flavors.

Add coarse salt to taste to the boiling water, then start shaping the gnocchi. Use a heaping tablespoon of the potato mixture, shape it into a small ball between the palms of your hands, lightly flour it all over, and gently drop it into the boiling water, cooking 7 to 8 at a time. As they come to the surface, transfer them with a skimmer to the baking dish containing the sauce. When all the gnocchi are in the baking dish, cover the dish and bake for 15 minutes.

Serve hot with or without grated cheese.

❖

VEGETABLES

Vegetables are rarely served in Italy as side dishes on the same plate with the main course. They are treated as full-fledged courses in themselves, served not only on a separate plate but often as a separate course. In a normal family meal, vegetables usually occupy a larger percentage of the whole than the meat. Aside from the vegetable course, you may find them as an antipasto. If there is a separate salad course, it comes at the end, before the fruit or dessert, and it always consists of uncooked greens alone or with tomato, sometimes with the addition of a fresh herb such as basil, with the one exception of *insalata composta,* which is a combination of several boiled vegetables. All are dressed simply with good olive oil and wine vinegar. There is no cheese or cream dressing or croutons.

Cold or room-temperature cooked vegetable dishes are often called *insalate* and may have more elaborate dressings. These are usually eaten as a vegetable course. We begin this chapter with a large variety of cold vegetable *insalate* recipes. Then we follow with a variety of Roman vegetable dishes, because Roman vegetables are so prized in Italy and also because vegetable dishes form such a large percentage of authentic dishes from the Eternal City. The rest of the chapter ("More Vegetables") is arranged according to the individual vegetables, with recipes from different regions. Italians eat a greater variety of vegetables in their everyday meals than many other nations, and the preparations involve an equally great variety of ways of cooking and saucing.

ITALIAN VEGETABLE SALADS

❖

The fourteen *insalate* that follow are cold vegetable courses. Two, *Insalata alla Milanese* and *Insalata del Bersagliere*, are each made from a combination of vegetables. There are two *insalate* of tomatoes, and one treatment each for ten other vegetables.

SICILY

CAROTE IN INSALATA
Carrot Salad

Makes 6 to 8 servings

In Sicily, very thinly sliced lemons and citrons are often eaten with their skins. Citrons look like much larger lemons, with much thicker skins. These skins are candied and used in many savory and sweet dishes. In this carrot salad, the lemon pieces combine magically with the parsley and capers in vinegar to provide the slightly sour taste that, against the carrots, makes a "sweet-and-sour" dish.

2 pounds carrots

Coarse-grained salt

1 medium-size lemon

15 sprigs fresh Italian parsley, leaves only

2 large cloves garlic, peeled

2 tablespoons capers in wine vinegar, drained

½ cup extra virgin olive oil

Salt and freshly ground black pepper

TO SERVE:

Fresh Italian parsley leaves

Boil the carrots, with the skins on, in salted boiling water for 10 minutes or more, depending on their size; the carrots must be cooked—not mushy—but not undercooked. Remove the skins under cold running water and cut the carrots into disks about ¼ inch thick.

Cut the lemon into quarters and each quarter into very thin slices. Coarsely chop the parsley and finely chop the garlic, then combine them. Place the carrots, lemon slices, and capers together in a large crockery or glass bowl. Add the garlic mixture and olive oil and season with salt and pepper. Mix very well and transfer to a serving dish. Serve at room temperature with a few leaves of the parsley on each portion.

RADICCHIO ALLA VICENTINA
Radicchio Salad Vicenza Style

Makes 6 servings

Of the several types of red radicchio—the bitter salad leaf—two are most prominent. The type from Treviso in Veneto is somewhat fragile and appears only seasonally. It has long stems and leaves, resembling a bit the shape of a bunch of celery; it is this type that is most prized in Italy and is what Italians are referring to when they say "red radicchio." Another type, from Chioggia, another town in Veneto, is less fragile, can be found all year round, and has more the shape of a cabbage. While the tops of the leaves are red, the bottoms are white and thicker and there is no stem. Both types are eaten cooked or grilled as well as uncooked, but Treviso radicchio is more delicate and less bitter when cooked.

This salad can also be served as an appetizer.

3 bunches red radicchio from Treviso or
  3 heads red radicchio from Chioggia
  (the Treviso type of radicchio is found
  in fancier gourmet shops)

FOR THE SAUCE:

4 ounces pancetta, in one piece

¼ cup (2 ounces) sweet butter

2 tablespoons extra virgin olive oil

Salt and freshly ground black pepper

3 tablespoons red wine vinegar

Clean the radicchio and rinse it many times under cold running water, then pat dry. Cut the bunches or heads into quarters or eighths, depending on their size, and arrange them on a large serving platter.

To make the sauce, finely chop or grind the pancetta. Place a medium-size saucepan with the butter and olive oil over low heat; when the butter is completely melted, add the pancetta and slowly sauté until golden and very crisp, about 10 minutes. Season with salt and pepper, keeping in mind that the pancetta may be rather salty. Mix very well and add the vinegar. Let the vinegar evaporate for 1 or 2 minutes, mix well again, and pour the sauce over the radicchio. Serve immediately. The sauce should be very warm.

VARIATION: The radicchio can be coarsely shredded and 2 to 3 tablespoons red wine vinegar or balsamic vinegar may be added to the saucepan with the sautéed pancetta just before removing it from the heat.

INSALATA DI ARANCE E CARCIOFI
Orange and Artichoke Salad

Makes 6 servings

Most artichokes in Italy have very tender leaves, and after removing a few outer leaves the whole artichoke may be eaten raw. Normal-size artichokes have little or no choke to remove. Raw, the artichoke is a favorite dipping vegetable for the *pinzimonio* dip of olive oil and salt.

The orange salads of Sicily are dressed with the usual oil and wine vinegar or lemon juice. Because the Sicilian lemons are sweeter than most, they combine quite well with oranges. These "salads" are used both as an appetizer and as a vegetable course. The combination of orange and tender raw artichoke is quite popular. If you make the dish carefully following the directions below, it can be successful even with less tender artichokes.

4 large juicy oranges, carefully peeled and cut into ½-inch-thick slices	1 large lemon, cut in half
4 stalks celery from the heart, thinly sliced	¼ cup extra virgin olive oil
2 artichokes hearts with stems attached, from 2 large artichokes	1 teaspoon fresh lemon juice
	Salt
	3 or 4 twists black pepper

Arrange the orange slices and celery on a plate. Use a mandoline or truffle cutter to thinly slice the artichoke hearts, holding them by their stems. Discard the stems when the hearts are sliced. Soak these uncooked artichoke slices in a bowl of cold water with the juices from the lemon halves for half an hour. This will tenderize them so they may be eaten raw; the lemon juices will keep them from discoloring.

When ready to serve, drain the artichoke slices, pat them dry, and arrange them with the orange slices and celery on the plate. Mix together the olive oil, 1 teaspoon lemon juice, salt, and pepper in a small bowl and pour it over all the ingredients on the plate. Serve at room temperature.

SEDANO E FINOCCHIO IN INSALATA
Celery and Fennel Bulb Salad

Makes 6 servings

Both celery and fennel are much used with the traditional "dip" of good olive oil and salt in the *pinzimonio* appetizer so common in Tuscany and other regions. Both vegetables, when eaten raw, are generally cut into large strips. In this "salad," they appear in a much more delicate form, sliced paper thin using a mandoline or even a truffle cutter, with a more elaborate sauce of garlic, wine vinegar, anchovies, and black pepper. Sliced so thin, the vegetables are almost marinated in the sauce.

1 large bunch celery

3 medium-size fennel bulbs

2 tablespoons extra virgin olive oil

FOR THE SAUCE:

1 large clove garlic, peeled

2 whole anchovies preserved in salt (see Note on page 10) or 4 anchovy fillets packed in oil, drained

2 tablespoons red wine vinegar

½ cup extra virgin olive oil

Salt and freshly ground black pepper

TO SERVE:

Fresh Italian parsley leaves

Discard all the green outer stalks from the celery. Remove the leaves from the white inner stalks and put them in a large bowl of cold water for half an hour. Clean the fennel bulbs very well, cutting off the stalks and removing the tough outer leaves. Cut each fennel bulb into quarters and put them in the bowl with the celery.

Prepare the sauce. The classic way is to use a marble mortar and pestle to mash the garlic, then add the anchovy fillets. If you do not use the mortar, finely chop the garlic and anchovy fillets together on a cutting board. Transfer the paste to a small crockery or glass bowl, add the vinegar, and mix very well. Then add the olive oil, season with salt and pepper, and mix thoroughly. Refrigerate the sauce, covered, until needed.

When ready, drain the celery and fennel, pat dry, and finely slice them using a mandoline or truffle cutter. Transfer to a bowl, add the 2 tablespoons olive oil, and mix well. Refrigerate, covered, for at least half an hour.

Remove the sauce and vegetables from the refrigerator and combine them. Mix thoroughly and transfer to a serving platter. Serve cold with the Italian parsley leaves sprinkled over.

INSALATA DI BARBABIETOLE
Beet Salad Roman Style
Makes 6 servings

The remarkable flavor of beets cooked in the Roman style comes from baking them between two layers of their own leaves until soft, then discarding the leaves. There are Italian dishes in which the leaves of the beets are eaten, but they are boiled and dressed or sautéed rather than baked.

2 pounds beets with the stems and leaves on	2 tablespoons red wine vinegar
1 medium-size clove garlic, peeled	Salt
Coarse-grained salt	Fresh basil leaves
6 tablespoons extra virgin olive oil	

Cut the stems off about an inch from the beets. This way the color will not bleed from the beets while they are cooking. Clean and wash the beets and the stems with the leaves very well and soak everything in a bowl of cold water for half an hour. Preheat the oven to 400 degrees. Drain everything. Place half the stems with the leaves in the bottom of a baking pan to improve the taste. Distribute the beets over them, then place the remaining stems and leaves on top. Pour in enough cold water to cover. Add the garlic and coarse salt to taste. Cover and bake until very tender, about 2 hours if the beets are medium-size or longer if they are larger. After cooking, discard the stems with the leaves and remove the skin from the beets under cold running water, then pat dry. Cut the beets into ½-inch-thick slices and arrange them on a platter. Drizzle the olive oil all over, then the vinegar, and add a little salt. Serve with the basil leaves.

VARIATIONS: One medium-size onion, cleaned and thinly sliced, may be added to the beets just before serving. Combine the following ingredients for an alternative way to dress the beets instead of the oil and vinegar: 15 sprigs fresh Italian parsley, leaves only, very finely chopped; 1 small clove garlic, peeled and finely chopped, or 6 scallion whites, very thinly sliced; 3 tablespoons fresh lemon juice; salt and freshly ground black pepper to taste.

LASAGNINO
Italian Cabbage Salad

Makes 6 servings

This *lasagnino* preparation is the Italian counterpart of coleslaw, in which the shredded raw cabbage is dressed not with *maionese* but with a dressing made from olive oil and wine vinegar, ground herbs, garlic, capers, and hard-boiled egg, thickened with bread and soaked in vinegar.

The wrinkled Savoy cabbage is most often used in cooked Italian cabbage dishes, but exceptionally, in this salad, the more tender smooth type is used because it remains uncooked.

1½ pounds cabbage (*lasagnino*), cored

FOR THE DRESSING:

2 slices white bread

½ cup red wine vinegar plus 1 to 2 tablespoons, to your taste

15 sprigs fresh Italian parsley, leaves only

5 fresh basil leaves

2 tablespoons capers in wine vinegar, drained

1 small clove garlic, peeled

1 extra-large egg, hard-boiled and shelled

¾ cup extra virgin olive oil

Salt and freshly ground black pepper

Large pinch of hot red pepper flakes

TO SERVE:

Fresh basil leaves

Soak the cabbage in a bowl of cold water for half an hour (this freshens the cabbage). Remove the crusts from the bread and soak it in ½ cup vinegar for 5 minutes. Drain the bread, squeeze very well, and set aside.

Drain the cabbage, pat dry, and thinly slice it with a sharp knife or mandoline. Transfer the cabbage to a bowl and refrigerate, covered with plastic wrap, until needed.

Finely chop together on a cutting board or in a food processor the parsley, basil, capers, garlic, egg, and bread. Transfer to a small crockery or glass bowl, add the olive oil and 1 to 2 tablespoons vinegar, and season with salt, black pepper, and the hot pepper. Mix very well and refrigerate, covered, for at least half an hour before serving.

When ready, remove the cabbage and sauce from the refrigerator and mix together. Transfer to a serving platter, sprinkle on the basil leaves, and serve.

INSALATA DEL BERSAGLIERE
"Sharpshooter's" Salad

Makes 12 servings

In Italy there are three explanations for the recipe title "Sharpshooter's" Salad. All refer to the *Carabinieri,* one of the two Italian police forces—the sharpshooters. The first is that the *Carabinieri* have a reputation as being very precise, and in this dish the vegetables must be sliced very precisely. Second, the speed with which the *Carabinieri* march resembles the speed with which the vegetables must be sliced. Third, the shape of their hats is echoed in the cheese slivers on top of the salad.

This is an unusual and delicious salad of uncooked fennel, celery, cabbage, and escarole, all very finely sliced with a mandoline or knife, the vegetables first soaked in lemon juice and cold water and then dressed with wine vinegar and olive oil. The salad is topped with slivers of Parmigiano and a *crostino,* smeared with truffle butter on each serving.

1 fennel bulb

6 inner white stalks celery

¾ pound cored cabbage

1 bunch escarole (about 6 ounces), dark green leaves discarded

2 lemons, cut in half

Salt and freshly ground black pepper

¾ cup extra virgin olive oil

¼ cup red wine vinegar

TO SERVE:

12 *crostini* (country-style bread cut into 4-inch-square slices ½ inch thick)

1 tube white truffle paste, about 1⅖ ounces (available in specialty food stores)

¼ cup (2 ounces) sweet butter, at room temperature

Salt and freshly ground black pepper

4 ounces Parmigiano cheese, cut into slivers

Rinse the fennel, cutting off the stalks and removing the tough outer leaves, cut into quarters, and put in a bowl of cold water for half an hour. Place the celery, cabbage, and escarole each in its own bowl of cold water for half an hour. This will keep the vegetables from wilting. Drain and pat dry, then thinly slice all the vegetables with a knife or a mandoline, place them together in a large crockery or glass bowl of cold water, and squeeze over the lemon halves. Let rest for half an hour—*no longer,* or else the vegetables will wilt.

When ready to serve, drain the vegetables and season them with salt and pepper, then add the olive oil and vinegar and mix very well.

Lightly toast the slices of bread on both sides. Mix the truffle paste with the butter and season with a little salt and pepper. Spread some of this topping on each *crostino*. Each serving will consist of a small mound of the mixed vegetables, some slivers of Parmigiano arranged over the mound, and the *crostino* on top.

INSALATA DI POMODORI
Tomato Salad

Makes 6 servings

In Italy tomatoes used for salad are traditionally still a little green, not extremely red and ripe. These still slightly green tomatoes are quite sweet, though a little firmer than the ripe ones, and their complex taste is preferred for salads. In recent times, restaurants in Italy with many tourists as clientele have begun to use riper tomatoes in the salads to please these visitors who are not familiar with green tomatoes.

In salads, the tomatoes are cut without removing skin or seeds. This Roman dressing, combining both parsley and basil with garlic, is slightly more complex than that of some other regions. The Neapolitan version of this salad (page 142) has still more ingredients in the dressing: capers, olives, tuna, and, in addition to the basil and parsley, a third herb, oregano.

2 pounds ripe but not overripe tomatoes	½ cup extra virgin olive oil
1 large clove garlic, peeled	Salt and freshly ground black pepper
15 sprigs fresh Italian parsley, leaves only	10 large fresh basil leaves, torn into thirds

Wash the tomatoes very well and cut them into 1½-inch cubes. Cut the garlic in half and rub the inside of a crockery or glass serving bowl with the cut sides. Place the tomato cubes in the bowl. Finely chop the parsley, transfer it to a small bowl, add the olive oil, season with salt and pepper, and mix very well. Pour this sauce over the tomatoes and mix thoroughly. Sprinkle the torn basil leaves over and serve. The salad may be prepared up to several hours in advance and refrigerated, covered, until needed, but the basil should be added only at the last moment before serving.

VARIATION: The garlic may be finely chopped along with the parsley.

INSALATA DI POMODORI ALLA NAPOLETANA
Tomato Salad Neapolitan Style

Makes 6 servings

The tomatoes grown around Naples may perhaps be equaled, but are probably unexcelled, in the world. The San Marzano type, grown nearby, are excellent canned and exported everywhere.

Tomatoes are used, cooked, a great deal in Neapolitan *cucina*, but they are also utilized uncooked in salads and added to cooked dishes just before serving. This tomato salad has many of the most typical Italian ingredients: basil, capers, Gaeta olives, and oregano; the oregano is most commonly used in the southern half of Italy.

As mentioned elsewhere, the tuna canned in Italy is of especially high quality, always preserved in good full-bodied olive oil and cut into substantial slices, *trance,* rather than broken up. It is not considered a substitute for fresh tuna, which is plentiful, but rather the basis for its own group of dishes.

1½ pounds ripe but not overripe tomatoes (see the headnote on page 141)

10 sprigs fresh Italian parsley, leaves only, finely chopped

1 large clove garlic, peeled and finely chopped

2 heaping tablespoons capers in wine vinegar, drained

4 ounces Gaeta olives, pitted or left whole

Salt and freshly ground black pepper

6 tablespoons extra virgin olive oil

One 3½-ounce can tuna packed in olive oil, preferably imported Italian, drained

10 fresh basil leaves, torn into thirds

A few fresh oregano leaves or pinch of dried oregano

Wash the tomatoes very well, then cut them into slices about ½ inch thick and place them in a large crockery or glass bowl. Add the parsley, garlic, capers, and olives and mix very well. Season with salt and pepper and add the olive oil. Mix again, then arrange on a large serving platter. Distribute the tuna, roughly broken up, over the tomatoes, then sprinkle with the basil and oregano and serve at room temperature. The tomatoes with their dressing may be prepared several hours in advance and kept in the refrigerator, covered, and the tuna, basil, and oregano added at the very last moment before serving.

- Four anchovy fillets may be very finely chopped with the parsley.
- A red onion (preferably the sweet Tropea onion) may be thinly sliced and added with or without the garlic.

TUSCANY

PATATE E CAPPERI
Potatoes in a Caper Sauce

Makes 6 servings

Caper bushes grow out of the walls of ancient stone buildings in Italy where the seeds have embedded themselves. Capers traditionally grow wild, as they still do in Tuscany and some other regions, but in parts of Southern Italy there has been some success in creating an environment friendly to their cultivation. The capers themselves are the unopened flower buds of the plant. In medieval times, the opened flowers were used along with the buds in salad-type dishes. Italian capers are very large; the small French ones are not considered preferable. Since capers are fresh, they must be preserved in brine, salt, or wine vinegar. It is possible to find them preserved in vinegar with no salt, a boon for those who are searching for flavor in salt-free diets.

Tuscany has several wonderful potato salads, none of which is dressed with *maionese*, and certainly not commercial *maionese*. Olive oil, wine vinegar, garlic, and herbs do the job in a healthier and lighter way. (Note: *Maionese* is the Italian spelling for a sauce that probably has existed in Italy as long as or longer than it has in France. Hence there is no need to use the French word for it.)

2 pounds all-purpose potatoes

8 cups cold water

2 cups red wine vinegar

Coarse-grained salt

FOR THE SAUCE:

3 tablespoons capers in wine vinegar, drained

15 sprigs fresh Italian parsley, leaves only

5 fresh basil leaves

1 medium-size clove garlic, peeled

½ cup extra virgin olive oil

5 scallions, white part only, very thinly sliced

Salt and freshly ground black pepper

TO SERVE:

5 large fresh basil leaves, torn into thirds

continued

Peel the potatoes and cut them into 1½-inch cubes. Soak the potatoes in a bowl of cold water for half an hour to remove some of the starch and keep them from discoloring.

Bring a medium-size pot with the 8 cups cold water to a boil over medium heat. Add the vinegar and coarse salt to taste, then drain the potatoes and add them to the pot. Simmer until the potatoes are perfectly cooked but retain their shape, about 10 minutes. Drain the potatoes, transfer them to a crockery or glass bowl and let cool, covered with a wet paper or kitchen towel, until needed.

Prepare the sauce. Finely chop the capers, parsley, basil, and garlic together on a cutting board. Transfer to a small bowl, add the olive oil and scallions, and season with salt and pepper. Pour the sauce over the potatoes, mix gently but thoroughly, and transfer to a serving platter. Sprinkle the torn basil leaves all over and serve at room temperature.

INSALATA ALLA MILANESE
Milanese Vegetable Salad

Makes 6 servings

The four vegetables used for this salad are cooked in separate pots and dressed separately, though with the same sauce. The dressing contains mustard powder, used rarely in modern times in Italy, but sometimes found in Lombardy or other parts of the far North. The mustard seed disappeared in Central Italy several centuries ago along with the once popular mustard greens. This salad has an attractive presentation, with its differently colored vegetables and chopped eggs sprinkled over. The optional bed of lettuce adds to the visual appeal.

½ pound trimmed string beans, left whole and placed in a bowl of cold water

½ pound peeled all-purpose potatoes, cut into 1½-inch cubes and placed in a bowl of cold water

½ pound scraped carrots, cut into strips the size of the string beans and placed in a bowl of cold water

½ pound trimmed celery hearts, cut into strips the size of the string beans and placed in a bowl of cold water

Coarse-grained salt

FOR THE DRESSING:

½ cup extra virgin olive oil

2 tablespoons red wine vinegar

3 tablespoons capers in wine vinegar, drained

Salt and freshly ground black pepper

Large pinch of mustard powder or more to taste

1 tablespoon cold water

TO SERVE:

A bed of Boston lettuce leaves on the serving platter (optional)

3 extra-large eggs, hard-boiled, shelled, and very coarsely chopped

Fresh basil leaves and Italian parsley leaves

Let all the vegetables soak in their separate bowls of cold water for half an hour. Boil the different vegetables in separate pots of salted water until cooked but still firm. Drain, then let all the vegetables cool for about half an hour between wet paper towels.

Prepare the dressing. Pour the olive oil and vinegar into a small crockery or glass bowl. Add the capers and season with salt and black pepper. Dissolve the mustard powder in the tablespoon cold water and add it to the bowl. Mix very well. If the lettuce leaves are used, line a serving platter with them. Place one of the cooked vegetables in a bowl, toss it with 1 tablespoon of the dressing, and transfer it onto the serving platter. Repeat with the other vegetables. When all the vegetables are on the dish, arranged by type, sprinkle the chopped hard-boiled eggs all over, then pour the remaining dressing over. Serve with the basil and parsley leaves.

VARIATION: Four anchovy fillets and/or a small clove of garlic, peeled, may be chopped very finely and added to the dressing.

INSALATA DI CAVOLFIORE
Cauliflower Salad

Makes 6 servings

Cauliflower is one of the vegetables that was developed from cabbage in the Mediterranean area, probably in Italy. It is considered to be in the category of *broccoli*, which means "hard flower," and is often called by that name in Southern Italy, where there are several different types of cauliflower alone. Italians generally cook it whole and like it still with a little bite, though they don't eat it raw. It is preferred dressed with a savory sauce, not with cheese or cream. None of the broccoli family is used in vegetable soups, though Savoy cabbage often is.

2 medium-size heads cauliflower

2 tablespoons red wine vinegar

Coarse-grained salt

FOR THE SAUCE:

4 ounces large black Greek olives in brine, pitted

4 ounces green olives in brine, pitted

2 tablespoons capers in wine vinegar, drained

1 bell pepper preserved in wine vinegar (available in gourmet shops), drained

2 whole anchovies preserved in salt (see Note on page 10) or 4 anchovy fillets packed in oil, drained

4 ounces gherkins, drained and cut into small pieces

½ cup extra virgin olive oil

Salt and freshly ground black pepper

TO SERVE:

Fresh Italian parsley leaves

Clean the cauliflower heads, removing the green outer leaves, and soak them in a bowl of cold water for half an hour. Bring a large pot of cold water to a boil, add the vinegar and salt to taste, then drain the cauliflower and add it to the pot. Cook for about 15 minutes. By that time the cauliflower heads should be cooked but still retain their shape; transfer them to a serving platter with a strainer-skimmer, cover with a wet kitchen towel, and let rest until needed.

Prepare the sauce. Finely chop or process together in a food processor or blender the olives, capers, bell pepper, and anchovies. Transfer the olive mixture to a crockery or glass bowl, add the gherkins, then the olive oil, season with salt and pepper, and mix very well.

Detach the florets from the cauliflower and arrange them on a serving platter. Sprinkle the parsley leaves all over and serve with the sauce on the side.

SARDINIA

INSALATA DI ZUCCHINE
Zucchini Salad

Makes 6 servings

1 pound very thin zucchini, but not the
    Japanese type

Coarse-grained salt

Juice of 1 large lemon

6 tablespoons extra virgin olive oil

Salt and freshly ground black pepper

12 large slivers Parmigiano or aged
    Pecorino Romano or Sardo cheese

Fresh Italian parsley leaves

Remove their ends and soak the zucchini in a bowl of cold water with a little coarse salt added for half an hour to remove the bitter taste. Drain the zucchini, rinse them under cold running water, pat dry with paper towels, and use a mandoline or truffle cutter to thinly slice them. Place the zucchini in a crockery or glass bowl and season with the lemon juice, olive oil, salt, and pepper. Mix well. Refrigerate, covered, for at least half an hour.

When ready, transfer the thinly sliced zucchini to a serving platter, arrange the cheese slivers on top, and serve with the Italian parsley leaves.

❖

INSALATA DI CECI ALLA SICILIANA
Sicilian Chick-Pea Salad

Makes 6 servings

The very Sicilian raisins, *pignoli,* olive oil, and lemon juice as well as wine vinegar, anchovies, and scallions form the sauce for chick peas, which are then arranged on a plate with tuna pieces in the center, hard-boiled egg quarters placed all around, and basil leaves on top. This makes a substantial course by itself or even a nice light lunch.

1 cup dried chick peas, picked over

3 quarts cold water

1 tablespoon extra virgin olive oil

Coarse-grained salt

FOR THE SAUCE:

½ cup extra virgin olive oil

1 tablespoon fresh lemon juice

1 tablespoon red wine vinegar

1 tablespoon raisins

1 tablespoon pine nuts (*pignoli*)

6 scallions, white part only, sliced ¼ inch thick

2 whole anchovies preserved in salt (see Note on page 10) or 4 anchovy fillets packed in oil, drained and coarsely chopped

Salt and freshly ground black pepper

TO SERVE:

2 extra-large eggs, hard-boiled, shelled, and cut into quarters

One 7-ounce can tuna packed in olive oil, preferably imported Italian, drained

Fresh basil leaves

Soak the chick peas in a bowl of cold water overnight. The next morning drain the chick peas, and place them in a medium-size casserole over medium heat with the 3 quarts cold water and the olive oil. When it reaches a boil, reduce the heat to medium-low and simmer for about 50 minutes. By that time the peas should be almost cooked. Add coarse salt to taste and cook until the peas are soft but still retain their shape, about 10 minutes more. Drain the peas, transfer to a crockery or glass bowl, cover with a wet kitchen towel, and let rest until cool, about 1 hour.

Prepare the sauce. Place the olive oil, lemon juice, vinegar, raisins, pine nuts, scallions, and anchovies in a crockery or glass bowl. Mix well and season with salt and pepper. Pour the sauce over the cooled chick peas, mix very well, then transfer everything to a serving platter. Place the hard-boiled eggs all around and the tuna, cut into pieces, in the center. Serve with the basil leaves.

ROMAN VEGETABLES

❖

The area around Rome is celebrated for the excellence and variety of its vegetables. Wonderful vegetable dishes are a real specialty of Roman cooking. Certain vegetables, such as *puntarelle* and the Roman green cauliflower, are not easily available away from the Eternal City and one should certainly take the opportunity to eat them when in Rome. Others, such as artichokes, fennel, zucchini, and especially zucchini blossoms, chard, spinach, button onions, and peas, are of unique quality in the area and have outstanding, specifically Roman preparations. Some of these recipes *alla Romana* have spread all over Italy and are included in other parts of this chapter, but I include here a gathering of dishes that really are specialties of Rome and Lazio.

FINOCCHI IN FRICASSEA ALLA ROMANA
Fennel Fricassee Roman Style

Makes 6 to 8 servings

6 large fennel bulbs

1 large lemon, cut in half

Coarse-grained salt

3 tablespoons (1½ ounces) sweet butter

1 tablespoon extra virgin olive oil

Salt and freshly ground black pepper

FOR THE FRICASSEE:

2 extra-large egg yolks

6 tablespoons fresh lemon juice

¼ cup heavy cream

Salt and freshly ground black pepper

10 sprigs fresh Italian parsley, leaves only, finely chopped

6 large fresh basil leaves, finely chopped

Remove the stalks and tough outer leaves from the fennel bulbs. Cut each fennel bulb into quarters and place in a crockery or glass bowl of cold water. Squeeze over the lemon halves and let soak for half an hour.

Bring a medium-size pot of cold water to a boil over medium heat and add coarse salt to taste. Drain the fennel and add it to the pot. Boil until they are cooked but still a little crunchy, as they will be sautéed later. Drain the fennel, saving ½ cup of the cooking water, and let cool for at least 5 minutes.

Place a large skillet with the butter and olive oil over low heat. When the butter is almost melted, distribute the fennel all over the skillet and lightly sauté for 3 or 4 minutes on each side. Season with salt and pepper.

Meanwhile, mix the egg yolks with the 6 tablespoons lemon juice and the heavy cream in a small crockery or glass bowl. Transfer the fennel to a warmed serving platter. Add the still warm fennel cooking water to the egg mixture and stir very well in order to temper the yolks, which will prevent them from curdling. Add the egg/lemon mixture to the juices in the skillet, stirring constantly until the sauce is about to simmer. *Absolutely do not allow it to boil.* Taste for salt and pepper. At that moment the sauce should be rather thick. Add the parsley and basil, mix well, and immediately pour the sauce over the fennel in the serving dish. Serve still very hot with more basil leaves if desired.

CIPOLLINE ALLA ROMANA
Pearl or Button Onions Roman Style

Makes 6 servings

2 pounds pearl or button onions, cleaned

Coarse-grained salt

2 tablespoons (1 ounce) sweet butter

2 tablespoons extra virgin olive oil

4 ounces prosciutto, with fat left on, cut
　　into very small pieces

3 heaping tablespoons granulated sugar

¾ cup red wine vinegar

Salt and freshly ground black pepper

About ¾ cup vegetable or completely
　　defatted meat broth, preferably
　　homemade

TO SERVE:

12 slices country-style bread about 3 × 2
　　inches and 1 inch thick, lightly toasted
　　on both sides

Soak the onions in a bowl of cold water for half an hour. Bring a medium-size pot of cold water to a boil, add coarse salt to taste, then drain the onions and add them to the pot. Simmer until the onions are half cooked, about 5 minutes. Use a skimmer to transfer the onions onto a serving platter lined with paper towels to absorb excess water.

Place a large skillet with the butter and olive oil over medium heat; when the butter is melted, add the prosciutto and mix very well, then add the sugar. Constantly stirring with a wooden spoon, little by little add the vinegar. Then put in the onions and season with salt and pepper. Add the broth a few tablespoons at a time and gently mix with the onions. Cook for about 15 minutes. By that time the onions should be soft and completely coated with a rather thick sauce. Serve with the toasted slices of bread.

VARIATION: One tablespoon of unbleached all-purpose flour can be added with the sugar to give you a thicker sauce. In this case you would need more than 1 cup of broth.

PISELLI ALLA ROMANA
Peas Roman Style

Makes 6 servings

Peas made in the Roman style share the raisins and *pignoli* also used in Genoese-style peas. This unlikely sharing may mean that these ingredients were more universal in Italian medieval and Renaissance *cucine,* and their common appearance in Sicilian dishes may also be a survival from earlier periods. Another interesting survival in Rome is the use of puree of pea pods, quite common in Italy in earlier periods, seen here in the recipe on page 153.

6 ounces guanciale (the cured meat of the cheek of a pig), or pancetta, or prosciutto, in one piece

2 large cloves garlic, peeled and finely chopped

15 sprigs fresh Italian parsley, leaves only, coarsely chopped

¼ cup (2 ounces) sweet butter

2 tablespoons extra virgin olive oil

2 pounds shelled fresh peas or 2 pounds "tiny tender" frozen peas, not defrosted

1 to 1½ cups completely defatted chicken or meat broth, preferably homemade

Salt

A few fresh mint leaves and/or 1 tablespoon granulated sugar (optional)

TO SERVE:

Fresh Italian parsley leaves

Small *crostini* (country-style bread cut into small squares ½ inch thick) fried in butter

Cut out the fat part of the guanciale, pancetta, or prosciutto and finely chop it. Cut the lean part into small pieces or thin strips or coarsely grind it. Mix the garlic and parsley together. Place a large skillet with the butter and olive oil over medium heat, add the chopped-up fat, and lightly sauté it for 1 minute. Add the garlic mixture and cook for a few seconds, then add the fresh or still frozen peas. After a few minutes, add the lean meat. Start adding the broth ½ cup at a time. Simmer, adding more broth as needed. If fresh peas are used and they are very large, cover the skillet while simmering. Season with salt. The peas are ready when they are soft and their sauce is not very thin. Add the mint and/or sugar if you wish at this point. Mix very well and transfer to a serving platter. Serve with the Italian parsley leaves and fried crostini on the side.

VARIATION: Add 1 small red onion, finely chopped, instead of the garlic.

The *Gubana* Cake. This ancient pastry is probably the granddaddy of all Viennese pastry types and coffee cakes, including Danish, which is of Viennese origin. Cividale (Friuli)

Udine (Friuli region): White celery in an Udine market in the Friuli region. Stalks of this celery are quite thick, with a lot of pulp. It is used mainly as a vegetable, not as an aromatic herb.

Cherry tarts in the gardens of the famous Villa Manin
in Friuli. This area is celebrated for its cherries.

The famous latteria cheeses of the
Friuli region, both fresh and aged.

Buying very fresh zucchini with the blossom still attached.
The blossom of the female *zucchino,* which is not eaten in
Italy, is attached to the *zucchino* itself, which is the fruit.
The blossom of the male *zucchino,* which is cooked and
eaten, is attached to a very long stem, and there is no fruit.

The fish soup shown here in one of Trieste's main squares is similar to Venetian-Style Fish Soup.

The fish market on Canal Grande in Trieste.

Scallops in their shells with the pink roe, which, according to the Italians, is the fish's greatest delicacy.

Eel fishing in Comacchio on the coast of Romagna, close to Ravenna. It is said that all the world's eels pass through here at some point in their lives. Eels have been fished here since Roman times.

(*Opposite page*) Tricesimo in Friuli: *Frittata alle Erbe,* a frittata flavored with a variety of the region's fresh herbs.

Farmers still using the old implements to cut the grass in Carnia, in the northern part of the Friuli region.

A classic brick oven for bread in Tuscany.

Fagottini di San Daniele: A very rare instance of the San Daniele prosciutto used in cooking. I found this dish in a little local trattoria in town. The very small production of this prosciutto is jealously reserved to be eaten uncooked.

Crema Fritta from Venice: This ancient dessert has evolved over the centuries but is possibly still the favorite traditional dessert of the "Queen of the Adriatic."

Pasta nell'Alveare: The *timballo* of pasta from the South, sometimes called *timpano,* does not have a fresh pastry covering but is contained in a traditional beehive-shaped container made with long uncut ziti.

Pasta nell'Alveare opened so that the short ziti may be served. The crust is usually not eaten.

Sformatini di Ricotta, if left in the molds, are small soufflés;
if unmolded, as Italians prefer, they become very light cheesecakes.

Puddica, the pizza with pockets from Puglia.

Peperoni Arrotalati, skinned peppers, stuffed and rolled up, may be eaten as an appetizer or a vegetable course.

Coda alla Vaccinara, Oxtail Roman-Style with Celery, is usually served with a soft polenta.

Gnocchi in Brodo, sweet-and-savory dumplings of yellow squash, from Lombardy.

Nidi di Rondine, a sheet of fresh pasta, stuffed with vegetables and rolled up, then sliced
through to resemble the bird's nest to which it refers and served with a rich meat sauce on the side.

Tiella di Riso e Vongole: Tiella is the name of the Pugliese terra-cotta or iron pot used to bake this type of dish, which can include a variety of ingredients. Most contain rice, and they may also include meat, fish, tomatoes, and/or vegetables, together with aromatic herbs. This *tiella* of clams is one of the most characteristic.

Strucolo di Mele: The *strucolo* from Friuli, like the strudel of Trento, shares characteristics with the Viennese apple strudel, as both regions border Austria.

Spiedino di Gamberi al Marsala: Sicilian shrimp wrapped in pancetta, flavored with the famous Marsala wine from the island.

A typical Tuscan landscape.

Fishermen in Friuli.

An old Friuli kitchen, transferred intact to the Museum of Tolmezzo in Friuli.

The classic open grill used in restaurants or at home in Friuli.

TIMBALLINI DI BUCCE DI PISELLI

Little Drums of Snow Peas

Makes 6 servings

1 pound snow peas

Coarse-grained salt

1 small clove garlic, peeled

3 extra-large eggs

½ cup freshly grated Parmigiano cheese

Salt and freshly ground black pepper

Freshly grated nutmeg

2 tablespoons (1 ounce) sweet butter, at
    room temperature

TO SERVE:

Fresh Italian parsley leaves

Soak the snow peas in a bowl of cold water for half an hour. Bring a large saucepan of cold water to a boil, add coarse salt to taste, then drain the peas and add them to the pot along with the garlic. Cook until very soft, about 25 minutes. Drain the snow peas and pass them with the garlic through a food mill fitted with the disk with smallest holes into a crockery or glass bowl. Add the eggs and Parmigiano and mix very well, then season with salt, pepper, and nutmeg. Add the butter and mix very well.

Preheat the oven to 375 degrees and lightly butter six custard cups. Line a baking dish with paper towels or a kitchen towel to be used later for the water bath (*bagno Maria*). Pour a scant ½ cup of the mixture into each custard cup and place the cups in the prepared baking dish. Pour in enough lukewarm water to almost reach the level of the mixture in the custard cups. Bake until golden on top, resistant to the touch, and puffy, about 45 minutes. Remove from the oven, let rest for a few seconds, then unmold onto the individual plates. Serve warm, with fresh Italian parsley leaves.

COSTE DI BIETOLE SALTATE
Sautéed Swiss Chard Stems

Makes 4 to 6 servings

1½ pounds large white Swiss chard stems,
    strings removed

Coarse-grained salt

15 sprigs fresh Italian parsley, leaves only

2 large fresh basil leaves

2 cloves garlic, peeled

6 tablespoons extra virgin olive oil

1 tablespoon (½ ounce) sweet butter

Salt and freshly ground black pepper

2 tablespoons red wine vinegar

2 tablespoons pine nuts (*pignoli*)

TO SERVE:

Fresh Italian parsley leaves

Soak the chard stems in a bowl of cold water for half an hour. Bring a large pot of cold water to a boil, add coarse salt to taste, then drain the stems, cut them into 2-inch pieces, and add them to the pot. Cook for 5 minutes. They should be almost completely cooked, not mushy at all. Transfer the cooked chard to a dish lined with paper towels to absorb excess water.

Finely chop the parsley, basil, and garlic together on a cutting board. Place a large skillet with the olive oil and butter over medium heat; when the butter is melted, add the garlic mixture and, after a few seconds, the chard and lightly sauté for 1 minute, constantly mixing with a wooden spoon. Season with salt and pepper. At this point the chard should be completely cooked. Add the vinegar and pine nuts and mix again. Transfer to a serving platter and season with pepper. Serve warm or at room temperature, with the Italian parsley leaves sprinkled over.

SPINACI ALLA ROMANA
Spinach Roman Style

Makes 4 to 6 servings

4 pounds fresh spinach

Coarse-grained salt

6 tablespoons (3 ounces) sweet butter

1 tablespoon extra virgin olive oil

¼ cup raisins

1 cup lukewarm water

2 large cloves garlic, peeled

Salt

2 tablespoons pine nuts (*pignoli*)

Clean the spinach, removing the large stems. Soak the spinach in a large bowl of cold water for half an hour.

Bring a large pot of cold water to a boil over medium heat, add coarse salt to taste, then drain the spinach and add to the pot. Simmer for 5 minutes from the moment the water returns to a boil. Drain the spinach and cool under cold running water. Lightly squeeze the spinach and coarsely chop on a cutting board.

Put the butter and olive oil in a skillet and set over medium heat. Meanwhile, soak the raisins in the lukewarm water. When the butter is melted, add the whole cloves of garlic and lightly sauté for 30 seconds. Discard the garlic, add the spinach, season with salt to taste, and cook for 5 to 6 minutes, frequently mixing with a wooden spoon. Drain the raisins, pat them dry with paper towels, and add them to the skillet along with the pine nuts. Mix very well, then transfer to a serving platter and serve hot.

FIORI DI ZUCCA IMBOTTITI
Stuffed Zucchini Blossoms

Makes 6 servings

18 large zucchini blossoms (see Note)

FOR THE BATTER:

2¼ cups unbleached all-purpose flour

½ teaspoon fine salt

Freshly ground black pepper

Large pinch of freshly grated nutmeg

¼ cup extra virgin olive oil

3 extra-large eggs, separated

½ cup dry white wine

1 tablespoon unflavored vodka

1 cup cold water

FOR THE STUFFING:

15 sprigs fresh Italian parsley, leaves only

5 whole anchovies preserved in salt
   (see Note on page 10) or 10 anchovy
   fillets packed in oil, drained

¼ cup very fine unseasoned bread crumbs,
   preferably homemade, lightly toasted

¼ cup extra virgin olive oil

Salt and freshly ground black pepper

TO FRY:

3 cups vegetable oil (½ corn oil and
   ½ sunflower oil)

½ cup extra virgin olive oil

TO SERVE:

2 large lemons

Fine salt

Clean the zucchini blossoms very well, leaving some of the stems on. Remove the pistils from the inside, trying not to break the blossoms. Lightly wash the blossoms, gently pat them dry, and let them rest between paper towels.

Prepare the batter. Mix the flour with the salt, pepper, and nutmeg and sift it into a large bowl. Make a well in the center of the flour, then add the olive oil a tablespoon at a time, mixing very well and incorporating just a little of the flour from the rim of the well. Add the egg yolks one at a time. Then add the wine and vodka and incorporate more flour. Finally, add the water and mix everything together very well. The batter should be very smooth with no lumps at all. Let it rest in a cool place for at least 1 hour before using it.

Prepare the stuffing. Finely chop the parsley and anchovies together on a cutting board. Transfer to a bowl, add the bread crumbs and olive oil, and season with salt and pepper. Insert a little stuffing into each blossom.

When ready, heat the vegetable oil and olive oil together in a fryer or large, heavy, deep-sided skillet over medium heat. Meanwhile, with a wire whisk, beat the egg whites in a copper bowl until stiff peaks form. Gently fold the whites into the batter, using a rubber spatula in a rotating motion. When the oil is hot, about 400 degrees, dip the stuffed blossoms into the batter a few at a time, add to the oil, and cook until golden all over, turning them over several times. Transfer from the oil to a serving platter lined with paper towels to absorb excess oil or to a *scolafritto* (a special Italian dish used for fried ingredients to remove excess oil). Repeat with the remaining blossoms and batter.

Cut one of the lemons into thin wedges and the other in half. When all the blossoms are on the platter, remove the paper towels, squeeze the juice of the lemon halves over, sprinkle on a little salt, and serve hot with the lemon wedges.

VARIATIONS

- Instead of using a very puffy batter, you can lightly flour the stuffed blossoms, then dip them into two whole eggs, lightly beaten with a fork and seasoned with a little salt and pepper.
- In the old days some granulated sugar would be sprinkled over the blossoms when ready to serve, in which case salt and lemon juice were omitted.
- The stuffing can be prepared with or without anchovies.
- A small piece of mozzarella may be added to the stuffing for each blossom.

Note: A zucchini plant has both male and female blossoms. Only the male blossoms, which sit on a long stem, are used for cooking. The female blossom sits on the fruit, which we know as zucchini. In Italy we do not eat that blossom.

LATTUGHE RIPIENE
Stuffed Heads of Lettuce

Makes 6 servings

This is an example of the cooked lettuce dishes common in Italy.

6 medium-size heads Boston lettuce, but not Bibb lettuce

6 ounces pitted black olives

6 whole anchovies preserved in salt (see Note on page 10) or 12 anchovy fillets packed in oil, drained

4 ounces capers in wine vinegar, drained and rinsed under cold running water

¼ cup very fine unseasoned bread crumbs, preferably homemade, lightly toasted

½ cup extra virgin olive oil

Fine salt

¼ cup cold water, as needed

TO SERVE:

1 pound ripe tomatoes, seeded and diced

¼ cup extra virgin olive oil

Salt and freshly ground black pepper

Remove a little from the bottoms of the lettuce heads to make them flat enough to stand up. In this way the outer layer of leaves also become detached; discard them. The green leaves that are left will help to prevent the white inner leaves from turning very dark when cooked. Wash the lettuce heads very well, being careful not to detach any more outer leaves. Let the lettuce heads soak in a bowl of cold water for half an hour.

Finely chop the olives, anchovies, and capers together on a cutting board. Transfer the olive mixture to a small crockery or glass bowl and add the bread crumbs and 2 tablespoons of the olive oil. Mix very well. Drain the lettuce, leaving the leaves lightly dampened. Arrange one-sixth of the stuffing between the leaves of each lettuce head.

Pour ¼ cup of the olive oil into a casserole large enough to hold all six heads and put them in, standing up. Drizzle the remaining 2 tablespoons oil all over and sprinkle with a little salt. Set the casserole over medium heat; when the oil is lukewarm, cover, and cook for about 30 minutes, making sure the lettuce does not stick to the bottom. If the lettuce does not shed enough liquid to prevent this, add the cold water. Once cooked, the head of lettuce becomes small enough to be a portion for one person.

Meanwhile, toss the diced tomatoes with the olive oil and season with salt and pepper. Transfer the *lattughe ripiene* to a serving platter or individual plates, sprinkle the diced tomatoes over, and serve.

FRITTATA DI FIORI DI ZUCCA
Zucchini Blossom Frittata

Makes 6 servings

About 30 large zucchini blossoms
(see Note on page 157)

1 cup unbleached all-purpose flour

1 cup plus 3 tablespoons extra virgin
olive oil

6 extra-large eggs

Salt and freshly ground black pepper

10 sprigs fresh Italian parsley, leaves only

1 medium-size clove garlic, peeled

TO SERVE:

Fresh Italian parsley leaves

Clean the zucchini blossoms, removing or keeping the pistils as you prefer. Wash the blossoms very well and pat them dry with paper towels. Lightly flour the blossoms.

Place a skillet with 1 cup of the olive oil over medium heat; when the oil is hot, about 400 degrees, fry the blossoms a few at a time until lightly golden all over. Transfer the fried blossoms to a serving dish lined with paper towels to remove excess oil. Lightly beat the eggs with a fork and season with salt and pepper. Finely chop the parsley and garlic together on a cutting board.

Place a 9-inch omelet pan with the remaining 3 tablespoons oil over medium heat; when the oil is warm, arrange all the blossoms in the pan, then add the eggs. After a few seconds, sprinkle the garlic mixture over the top. When the eggs are set, place a plate over the pan and flip both over, then slide the frittata back into the pan, cooked side up. Cook for a few seconds more. The frittata should be completely cooked but still very soft inside. Transfer the frittata to a serving platter and serve with the parsley leaves.

PATATE IN FORMA
Potato Timbales

Makes 6 servings

3 ounces prosciutto or pancetta, in one
    piece

1 clove garlic, peeled

10 sprigs fresh Italian parsley, leaves only

1½ pounds all-purpose potatoes

2 tablespoons (1 ounce) sweet butter, at
    room temperature

4 extra-large eggs, separated

6 tablespoons heavy cream

Salt and freshly ground black pepper

Six ¼-tablespoon pats sweet butter

TO SERVE:

Fresh Italian parsley leaves

Cut the prosciutto or pancetta into small pieces. Finely chop or grind the meat, garlic, and parsley together and place in a crockery or glass bowl. Peel the potatoes and coarsely grate them. Rinse the potatoes in a colander under cold running water and pat them dry with paper towels. Let the potatoes rest between paper towels until needed. Preheat the oven to 400 degrees and heavily butter six custard cups.

Place paper towels or a kitchen towel on the bottom of a baking dish to be used later as a water bath (*bagno Maria*). Transfer the potatoes to a crockery or glass bowl, add the prosciutto or pancetta mixture, egg yolks, and heavy cream, and season with salt and pepper. Mix very well. Let the potato mixture rest for 15 minutes, covered, to get some liquid from the potatoes. When ready, use a copper bowl and wire whisk to beat the egg whites until soft peaks form. Gently fold the whites into the potato mixture, using a rubber spatula.

Divide the potato mixture among the six custard cups, about a scant ½ cup each, and put a pat of butter on top of the potato mixture in each custard cup. Place the cups in the baking dish, add enough warm water to almost reach the level of the potato mixture in the cups, and bake until golden on top, resistant to the touch, and puffy, about 50 minutes. If the tops of the timbales start to get too brown, cover with a sheet of aluminum foil. Transfer the custard cups to a board. Let them rest for several seconds in order that the timbales detach a bit from the sides before unmolding and reversing again onto individual plates. The golden top should face up. Serve with parsley leaves sprinkled over.

MORE VEGETABLES

❖

Artichokes, grown in many parts of Italy, are among the most popular vegetables. Not available year-round, during the colder weather they are to be found in many dishes. Italian artichokes, whether large or small, are more tender than most and usually do not have much of a choke, if any, so they are easy to clean and are often tender enough to be eaten raw *in pinzimonio* (dipped in good olive oil with salt).

The dark outer artichoke leaves are removed and those on the inside are torn at the point at which the green gets lighter. The light inside part of the stem is retained and eaten with the "heart" and much of the leafy part.

The Sicilian and Tuscan artichoke dishes that follow all cling strongly to their own regional approach. The "sweet-and-sour" contrast in the Sicilian dish of that name is achieved simply by combining red wine vinegar with sugar, with both flavors reinforced by other ingredients.

Pancetta or prosciutto flavors the Tuscan artichokes stewed in tomato sauce. In Tuscany one finds the normal variety of the vegetable, but also very large artichokes called *mamme* that were developed around Pistoia in the eighteenth century. These large artichokes are just as tender as the smaller variety.

CARCIOFI IN AGRO DOLCE
Sweet-and-Sour Artichokes

Makes 6 to 8 servings

1 large lemon, cut in half

6 large artichokes

Coarse-grained salt

TO FRY THE ARTICHOKES:

2 cups vegetable oil (½ corn oil and
 ½ sunflower oil)

1 cup olive oil

1 cup unbleached all-purpose flour

FOR THE SAUCE:

1 large white or red onion, cleaned

6 tablespoons extra virgin olive oil

1 heaping tablespoon capers in wine
 vinegar, drained

20 large green olives in brine, pitted and
 coarsely chopped

1 large stalk celery, coarsely chopped

2 medium-size carrots, scraped and finely
 chopped

½ to 1 cup cold water, as needed

20 sprigs fresh Italian parsley, leaves only,
 coarsely chopped

10 fresh basil leaves, torn into thirds

½ pound ripe tomatoes or drained
 canned plum tomatoes, preferably
 imported Italian

2 whole anchovies preserved in salt
 (see Note on page 10) or 4 anchovy
 fillets packed in oil, drained

1 cup lukewarm water

Salt and freshly ground black pepper

2 teaspoons granulated sugar

½ cup very light red wine vinegar

TO SERVE:

Fresh basil leaves

Squeeze the lemon halves into a bowl of cold water and add the artichokes. Let rest for half an hour. Remove the artichokes from the water and clean them (see technique on page 4), removing the outer green leaves and choke. Cut them into quarters and place them back in the acidulated water.

Bring a medium-size casserole with cold water to a boil. Add coarse salt to taste, then the artichokes, and cook them for 4 minutes. Transfer the artichokes to paper towels to absorb excess water.

Heat the vegetable oil and olive oil in a large, heavy, deep-sided skillet over medium heat. When the oil is hot, about 375 degrees, lightly flour the artichoke pieces and fry them until lightly golden all over. Transfer the cooked artichokes to a serving platter lined with paper towels to absorb the excess oil.

Prepare the sauce. Finely chop the onion on a cutting board. Heat the olive oil in a medium-size nonreactive casserole over medium heat; when the oil is warm, add the onion and sauté for 5 minutes, stirring every so often with a wooden spoon. Then add the capers, olives, celery, and carrots and cook, stirring, for 15 minutes, adding the cold water as needed if the mixture needs more liquid. Arrange the cooked artichokes in one layer on top of the vegetables and sprinkle the parsley and basil all over.

Meanwhile, if using fresh tomatoes, cut them into small pieces. Whether using fresh or canned tomatoes, pass them through a food mill fitted with the disk with the smallest holes into a crockery or glass bowl. Cut the anchovies into small pieces and add them to the casserole along with the strained tomatoes. Cover the casserole and cook for 5 minutes, then add the lukewarm water and season with salt and pepper. Let cook, uncovered, for about 15 minutes, until soft, shaking the casserole to prevent the sauce from sticking to the bottom. Taste again for salt and pepper. Dissolve the sugar in the vinegar, add it to the casserole, and cook for another 5 minutes.

Transfer the contents of the casserole to a large serving platter, trying to keep all the artichokes on top. Serve hot or at room temperature with the basil leaves sprinkled all over.

NOTE: This same sauce may be used for poached or deep-fried fish. Pour the sauce over when the fish is already on the serving platter.

CARCIOFI IN UMIDO O STUFATI

Artichokes Stewed in Tomato Sauce

Makes 6 servings

1 lemon, cut in half

6 large artichokes

Coarse-grained salt

FOR THE SAUCE:

15 sprigs fresh Italian parsley, leaves only

2 medium-size cloves garlic, peeled

2 ounces pancetta or prosciutto, in one
  piece

¼ cup extra virgin olive oil

1 pound ripe tomatoes or drained canned
  tomatoes, preferably imported Italian

Salt and freshly ground black pepper

2 cups completely defatted chicken or meat
  broth, preferably homemade

TO SERVE:

Fresh Italian parsley leaves

Squeeze the lemon halves into a crockery or glass bowl of cold water, add the artichokes, and soak for half an hour.

Bring a large pot of cold water to a boil over medium heat. Clean the artichokes (see technique on page 4), removing the tough leaves and chokes, cut them into quarters, and place them back in the acidulated water until needed. When the water reaches a boil, add coarse salt to taste, then drain the artichokes, add them to the pot, and boil for 5 minutes. Transfer the artichokes to a crockery or glass bowl, place a paper or kitchen towel dampened in cold water on top, and let rest until needed.

Prepare the sauce. Finely chop the parsley and garlic together on a cutting board; cut the pancetta or prosciutto into tiny pieces. Place a nonreactive medium-size casserole with the olive oil over medium heat; when the oil is warm, add the garlic mixture along with the pancetta or prosciutto and sauté for 5 minutes, mixing every so often with a wooden spoon. If using fresh tomatoes, cut them into small pieces. Whether using fresh or canned tomatoes, pass them through a food mill fitted with the disk with the smallest holes into a crockery or glass bowl. Add the strained tomatoes to the casserole, season with salt and pepper, and cook for another 15 minutes. Add the artichokes, pour in ¾ cup of the broth, cover the casserole, and cook for 15 minutes more, adding broth as needed and mixing every so often with a wooden spoon. By that time the artichokes should be cooked and quite soft and coated with a rather thick sauce. Serve hot with the parsley leaves.

MELANZANE AL ROSMARINO
Rosemary Eggplant

Makes 10 to 12 servings

Eggplant, though a signature vegetable of Sicily, is popular all over Italy, grilled, sautéed, or, most often, fried. For best results for most dishes, the cut eggplant should be salted and placed under a light weight for a short time to remove some of its bitter liquid. Then it is cooked as you wish. Sautéed for this dish, the eggplant is intensely flavored with rosemary. The soft cubes of eggplant are placed on toasted bread slices, called *crostoni* (they are larger than *crostini*), and may be eaten as a vegetable course or as an appetizer.

3 medium-size eggplant (about 2 pounds), peeled and cut into ½-inch cubes

Coarse-grained salt

3 tablespoons rosemary leaves, fresh or preserved in salt (page 2)

4 large cloves garlic, peeled

Salt and freshly ground black pepper

¾ cup extra virgin olive oil

20 sprigs fresh Italian parsley, leaves only

TO SERVE:

10 to 12 slices crusty Italian country bread, about 1 inch thick, lightly toasted

Place the eggplant cubes on a serving platter, sprinkle about 2 tablespoons of coarse salt over them, then place a second platter over the eggplant cubes as a weight, but do not crush them. Let rest at room temperature for at least 1 hour.

Meanwhile, finely chop the rosemary and garlic together on a cutting board. Transfer the garlic mixture to a small bowl, season with salt and pepper, and mix very well.

Rinse the eggplant cubes many times under cold running water, then pat dry with paper towels. Heat the olive oil in a large heavy skillet over medium heat. When the oil is moderately hot, about 300 degrees, add the eggplant cubes, preferably in a single layer, and cook, covered, for 3 to 4 minutes. By that time the lower part of the eggplant should have a thin golden crust. Turn the eggplant cubes over, cover the skillet, and cook for 3 to 4 minutes more. Sprinkle the garlic mixture over the eggplant and a little salt and pepper and mix very well with a wooden spoon. Some cubes may fall apart; this is all right. Keep cooking until all the cubes are soft. With a skimmer, transfer the eggplant to a crockery or glass bowl. Add the parsley leaves to the eggplant and mix again. Immediately place the eggplant mixture over the slices of bread and serve. This dish may be served as an appetizer or a vegetable, but should always be warm.

PARMIGIANA DI ZUCCHINE
Parmigiana of Zucchini

Makes 8 to 10 servings

Recipes *"alla Parmigiana"* originally meant made in the homey style of a housewife from Parma. Because this usually meant that Parmigiano cheese was in the recipe, the meaning spread to dishes that were based on that cheese and even some other cheeses, sometimes in combination. This *"Parmigiana"* of zucchini is not from Parma at all, but rather from Sicily, where they gave the name to a vegetable dish utilizing three different cheeses—Parmigiano, of course, Groviera, and mozzarella. The three are coarsely grated and alternated in layers with the thinly sliced zucchini and tomato sauce.

Those Italian dishes called *gratinati,* which use cheese in the recipe, are usually prepared in a more French style, with a cheese layer on top, and the word itself is probably a translation of *gratinée.* A dish like this *Parmigiana* is a more authentically Italian one, which avoids allowing the cheese on top to become brown in the French manner, because the Italians feel it makes the cheese bitter.

For me, this is one of the most flavorful treatments of zucchini and one of my own favorites.

FOR THE TOMATO SAUCE:

2 pounds very ripe tomatoes or drained
    canned tomatoes, preferably imported
    Italian

3 tablespoons extra virgin olive oil

6 fresh basil leaves

Salt and freshly ground black pepper

FOR THE ZUCCHINI:

2 pounds thin zucchini, but not the
    Japanese type

Coarse-grained salt

4 ounces mozzarella cheese

4 ounces Groviera cheese or imported Swiss
    cheese

6 tablespoons freshly grated Parmigiano
    cheese

Salt and freshly ground black pepper

15 fresh basil leaves

Several pats of sweet butter

If using fresh tomatoes, cut them into large pieces. Place the tomatoes in a medium-size nonreactive casserole, add the olive oil and basil, and set over medium heat for 20 minutes, stirring every so often with a wooden spoon.

Preheat the oven to 375 degrees. Meanwhile, trim the ends off the zucchini and cut them lengthwise into about ¼-inch-thick slices. Place the cut zucchini in a bowl of cold water with a little coarse salt added and let them soak for half an hour.

Bring a large nonreactive casserole of cold water to a boil over medium heat, add coarse salt to taste, then drain one-fourth of the zucchini and boil for 2 minutes. Transfer to lightly oiled jelly-roll pans in a single layer and bake for 5 minutes to remove excess moisture. Repeat the same procedure with the rest of the zucchini.

Pass the cooked-down tomatoes through a food mill fitted with the disk with the smallest holes back into the casserole and set it over medium heat. Season with salt and pepper and cook for another 15 minutes, stirring every so often.

Coarsely grate the mozzarella and Groviera and mix together, along with the Parmigiano. Pour ¼ cup of the tomato sauce over the bottom of a 13½ × 8¾-inch glass baking dish, then arrange one-third of the zucchini slices in a layer over the tomato sauce. Sprinkle a little salt and pepper over them, then add four or five basil leaves and two pats of butter. Make a layer using one-third of the mixed cheeses, then spread 1 cup of the tomato sauce over that. Repeat the layers in the same order and quantities, except for the top layer of tomato sauce, which will use all the remaining tomatoes (more than 1 cup); the top layer of sauce should completely cover all the layers below. Bake in the preheated oven for 50 minutes; the zucchini should be very soft and juicy. Remove from the oven and cool for at least 10 minutes before serving.

EMILIA-ROMAGNA

SFORMATINI DI ZUCCHINE
Zucchini Timbales

Makes 14 timbales

Sformatini are small molds or timbales and are an important part of the Italian vegetable repertory, especially when an elaborate vegetable course is needed. They can be made as one large mold, called a *sformato*, or in smaller individual ones as is done in this recipe. The vegetables usually are precooked (for an exception, see *Patate in Forma*, page 160), pureed, and combined with *balsamella* (bechamel) made from butter, flour, and milk, and occasionally eggs, as is the case here. This delicately flavored mold is served with a rich sauce meat, a little of which is placed on top. Though the butter, cream, and cheese are particularly typical of the Emilia region, these *sformatini* are made all over Italy.

continued

FOR THE ZUCCHINI MIXTURE:

6 medium-size zucchini (about 1½ pounds),
    ends removed

Coarse-grained salt

1 very small red onion, cleaned

1 medium-size carrot, scraped

1 stalk celery

10 sprigs fresh Italian parsley, leaves only

½ cup extra virgin olive oil

Fine salt and freshly ground black pepper

About 1 cup completely defatted chicken
    broth, preferably homemade

FOR THE *BALSAMELLA* (BECHAMEL):

6 tablespoons (3 ounces) sweet butter

¼ cup unbleached all-purpose flour

1½ cups whole milk

Salt and freshly ground black pepper

4 extra-large eggs

FOR THE MOLDS:

About 2 tablespoons (1 ounce) sweet butter

1 lemon (optional), cut in half

TO FINISH THE TIMBALE MIXTURE:

2 tablespoons heavy cream

4 ounces Parmigiano cheese, freshly grated

FOR THE SAUCE:

3 sweet Italian sausages without fennel seeds
    (about 12 ounces) or 12 ounces
    ground pork

2 cups completely defatted chicken broth,
    preferably homemade

2 tablespoons tomato paste, preferably
    imported Italian

15 large sprigs fresh Italian parsley, leaves only

1 large clove garlic, peeled

Salt and freshly ground black pepper

TO SERVE:

Fresh Italian parsley leaves

Cut the zucchini into 1-inch cubes and soak them in a bowl of cold water with a little coarse salt for half an hour.

Finely chop the onion, carrot, celery, and parsley together on a cutting board. Place a medium-size casserole with the olive oil over medium heat; when the oil is warm, add the onion mixture and sauté for 5 minutes, stirring constantly with a wooden spoon.

Drain the zucchini, rinse them under cold running water, sprinkle with a little fine salt and pepper, and add them to the casserole. Sauté for 10 minutes, mixing with a wooden spoon. Add ½ cup of the broth, reduce the heat to medium-low, and simmer, adding more broth if needed, until the zucchini are soft and all the juices have been absorbed. Transfer the contents of the casserole to a crockery or glass bowl and let rest until cool, about half an hour.

Meanwhile, prepare the *balsamella* with the ingredients and quantities listed above according to the instructions on page 4 and transfer it to a crockery or glass bowl. Immediately add the eggs one at a time, mixing very well with a wooden spoon. Press on top of the *balsamella* a sheet of buttered waxed paper to prevent a skin from forming and let the *balsamella* cool completely.

Lightly butter 14 glass custard cups, preheat the oven to 375 degrees, and prepare a water bath (*bagno Maria*) by placing a kitchen towel or paper towels on the bottom of a roasting pan. If using a metal roasting pan, place a lemon cut in half in the water so the pan does not discolor.

In a food processor or blender process the zucchini mixture until smooth. Transfer to a large bowl, add the cooled egg-enriched *balsamella,* then add the cream and Parmigiano. Mix very well with a wooden spoon and taste for salt and pepper. Pour ½ cup of the mixture into each prepared custard cup and place the cups in the roasting pan. Add lukewarm water to the pan to come up to the height of the zucchini mixture in the cups. Bake until the tops of the timbales are lightly golden and quite firm, about 45 minutes. Remove the cups from the water and let rest for at least 5 minutes before unmolding them onto individual plates.

As the timbales are baking, prepare the sauce. Remove the casings from the sausages and place them, cut into large pieces, in a nonreactive medium-size saucepan. Add the broth and place the pan over medium heat. Cook for 15 minutes, breaking the sausages into small, even pieces. Add the tomato paste and cook for 10 minutes more. Finely chop the parsley and garlic together on a cutting board, add to the pan, mix very well, and season with salt and pepper. Cook for 5 minutes more. Transfer the contents of the pan to a blender or food processor and process to get a rather smooth sauce. Return the sauce to the pan and reduce it for about 10 minutes over medium heat.

When the zucchini timbales are unmolded and ready to be served, pour some of the sauce on one side of each plate, sprinkle the parsley leaves over, and serve.

VARIATION: The *sformatini* may also be eaten with a very light tomato sauce prepared with the following ingredients:

1½ pounds very ripe tomatoes or drained canned tomatoes, preferably imported Italian	2 tablespoons extra virgin olive oil
	6 fresh basil leaves
	Salt and freshly ground black pepper
1 small clove garlic, peeled	

If fresh tomatoes are used, cut them into small pieces. Place the tomatoes in a small nonreactive saucepan along with the garlic, olive oil, and basil. Set the pan over medium heat and let cook for about 30 minutes, stirring every so often with a wooden spoon. Pass the contents of the pan through a food mill fitted with the disk with the smallest holes into a clean pan. Season with salt and pepper, then reduce over low heat until a rather thick sauce forms.

CAVOLFIORE ALLA CALABRESE
Stewed Cauliflower Calabrian Style

Makes 4 to 6 servings

In this hot dish, the whole cauliflower is briefly parboiled, then the detached florets are sautéed in olive oil and garlic and the other sauce ingredients added. As in the cold *Insalata di Cavolfiore* on page 146, the cauliflower sauce is made with savory ingredients. Italians prefer cauliflower and broccoli completely cooked, but not overcooked.

1 large head cauliflower, large green leaves removed

Coarse-grained salt

⅓ cup extra virgin olive oil

2 medium-size cloves garlic, peeled and finely chopped

1 tablespoon tomato paste, preferably imorted Italian

½ cup lukewarm water

2 tablespoons capers in wine vinegar, drained

2 whole anchovies preserved in salt (see Note on page 10) or 4 anchovy fillets packed in oil, drained

5 sprigs fresh Italian parsley, leaves only

Salt and freshly ground black pepper

TO SERVE:

Abundant fresh basil leaves

Soak the cauliflower in a bowl of cold water for half an hour. Bring a large pot of cold water to a boil, add coarse salt to taste, then the cauliflower, and cook for 2 minutes. Transfer the cauliflower to a cutting board and carefully detach all the florets, discarding the rest.

Heat the olive oil in a nonreactive medium-size casserole, preferably made of terra-cotta or enamel, over medium heat. Add the garlic, sauté for a few seconds, then arrange all the cauliflower florets in a single layer in the casserole. Reduce the heat to medium-low and cook for 5 minutes, turning the cauliflower once.

Dissolve the tomato paste in the lukewarm water. Finely chop the capers, anchovies, and parsley together on a cutting board. Combine the caper mixture with the dissolved tomato paste, mix very well, and add to the cauliflower. Season with salt and pepper and cook until almost all the liquid is absorbed and the cauliflower is completely cooked but not mushy. Transfer the contents of the casserole to a large serving platter and serve with the basil leaves.

CAVOLO ALL'ALLORO
Stewed Savoy Cabbage with Bay Leaves

Makes 6 to 8 servings

The method for this flavorful Savoy cabbage dish is to cook it virtually without water, only the little that clings to the soaked thin slices. Stewed cabbage is unique to Friuli among Italian regions. The method described in this recipe is worth noting because the region does have many cabbage dishes.

1 Savoy cabbage (about 2½ pounds)	8 bay leaves
1 large red onion, cleaned and thinly sliced	¼ cup extra virgin olive oil
2 large cloves garlic, peeled and cut into slivers	2 cups completely defatted chicken or meat broth, preferably homemade
3 ounces pancetta or prosciutto, ground	Salt and freshly ground black pepper

Clean the cabbage, removing the tough outer leaves and the core. Thinly slice the cabbage and place it in a bowl of cold water for half an hour.

Make a layer of the sliced onion on the bottom of a casserole. Sprinkle the garlic on top, then the ground pancetta or prosciutto. Drain the cabbage, leaving a little water on it, and add it to the casserole. Arrange the bay leaves over that and drizzle the olive oil all around. Cover the casserole, set it over medium heat, and let cook for 15 minutes without uncovering or mixing. Then open the casserole, add the broth, and season with salt and pepper. Cover again and cook for 20 minutes more, shaking the casserole several times to prevent sticking. Remove the lid, mix very well, and raise the heat high to evaporate almost all the broth, 3 to 4 minutes. Discard the bay leaves and serve hot.

POMODORI AL FORNO ALLA SARDA
Baked Tomatoes Sardinian Style

Makes 4 servings

Tomato halves are baked with garlicked bread crumbs and saffron, a Sardinian touch. Olive oil with chopped garlic and parsley form a sauce, and a basil leaf is placed over each tomato half.

4 large ripe tomatoes

Coarse-grained salt

¼ cup extra virgin olive oil

3 large cloves garlic, peeled and finely chopped

½ cup very fine unseasoned bread crumbs, preferably homemade, lightly toasted

Salt and freshly ground black pepper

Large pinch of ground saffron

TO SERVE:

1 medium-size clove garlic, peeled

15 sprigs fresh Italian parsley, leaves only

Salt and freshly ground black pepper

¼ cup extra virgin olive oil

8 large fresh basil leaves

Carefully wash the tomatoes and cut them in half. Do not seed them. Sprinkle a little coarse salt over the cut sides and let them stand upside down on paper towels for 15 minutes to drain. Stand them right side up again, pour the olive oil over, and let rest for 5 minutes.

Preheat the oven to 375 degrees and oil a glass baking pan. Mix the chopped garlic with the bread crumbs and season with salt and pepper. Add the saffron and mix again. Coat the cut side of the tomatoes with this mixture and arrange them in a single layer in the pan. Bake until the tomatoes are soft, about 45 minutes. To serve, finely chop the garlic and parsley together on a cutting board, transfer to a small crockery or glass bowl, and season with salt and pepper. Add the olive oil and mix very well. Serve the tomatoes with the olive-oil mixture drizzled all over and a basil leaf on each tomato half.

SFORMATO O TORTA DI BIETOLE

Swiss Chard Torte

Makes 6 to 8 servings

From the repertory of the ancient Roman Jewish *cucina*, this *torta* of Swiss chard has become a favorite in Rome. Mixed with ricotta, Parmigiano, and eggs and flavored with cinnamon and nutmeg, it makes a substantial vegetable course by itself. The tomatoes were obviously added in recent centuries and the Parmigiano probably precluded any ingredient to make it "sweet and sour," as some traditional Italian Jewish dishes are. Parmigiano and other types of Grana cheese go back to the ancient Etruscans and were originally made with wild artichoke rennet. This vegetarian rennet is still used to make kosher Parmigiano for modern Italian Jews.

This *torta* has become a useful dish on nonmeat days for the Roman population at large.

1½ pounds Swiss chard (yields 1 pound cleaned, with large stems removed)

Coarse-grained salt

1 pound ripe tomatoes or drained canned tomatoes, preferably imported Italian

½ cup plus 1 tablespoon extra virgin olive oil

Salt and freshly ground black pepper

7½ ounces whole-milk ricotta

4 extra-large eggs

½ cup freshly grated Parmigiano cheese

Pinch of freshly grated nutmeg

Pinch of ground cinnamon

Cut the Swiss chard into 2-inch lengths and soak in a bowl of cold water for half an hour. Bring a large pot of cold water to a boil over medium heat, add coarse salt to taste, then drain the chard, add it to the boiling water, and let cook for 4 minutes.

Meanwhile, if using fresh tomatoes, cut them into small pieces. Whether using fresh or canned tomatoes, pass them through a food mill fitted with the disk with the smallest holes into a small crockery or glass bowl. Heat the ½ cup olive oil in a large nonreactive skillet over medium heat; when the oil is warm, add the tomatoes, season with salt and pepper, and let simmer for 15 minutes.

Drain the chard, cool it under cold running water, and squeeze it very well. Coarsely chop the chard and add it to the tomato sauce. Mix well and cook for 15 minutes more, stirring every so often with a wooden spoon. By that time almost no liquid should be left in the skillet. Transfer to a large crockery or glass bowl and let cool for about half an hour.

continued

Drain the ricotta very well and mix it with the eggs and 6 tablespoons of the Parmigiano in a large crockery or glass bowl. Season with salt, pepper, nutmeg, and cinnamon, cover the bowl with plastic wrap, and refrigerate until needed.

Preheat the oven to 375 degrees. With the remaining tablespoon oil, heavily oil a 10-inch pie plate. When the chard is cold, add it to the ricotta mixture, stir all the ingredients together, then transfer it all to the oiled plate. Sprinkle the remaining Parmigiano over and bake until the *torta* pulls away from the sides of the plate, about 40 minutes. Remove from the oven, and let rest on a wire rack for at least 10 minutes before unmolding it onto a round serving platter. Serve it sliced like a pie.

SICILY

PEPERONI ARROTALATI
Stuffed Rolled-Up Peppers

Makes 6 servings

On skinned peppers, opened and flattened, is placed an elaborate stuffing made with savory capers, olives, bread crumbs, parsley, oregano, and tomatoes combined with sweet raisins and *pignoli*. The stuffed flattened peppers are rolled up into *involtini*, baked, and served hot.

In Italy, yellow, orange, and red bell peppers are preferred to green ones. Red peppers should not be confused with pimientos.

6 large red or yellow bell peppers

6 tablespoons very fine unseasoned bread
    crumbs, preferably homemade, lightly
    toasted

1 cup completely defatted chicken or meat
    broth, preferably homemade

15 sprigs fresh Italian parsley, leaves only

2 tablespoons capers in wine vinegar, drained

4 ounces green olives in brine, drained and
    pitted

½ pound ripe tomatoes, blanched for
    1 minute, peeled, and seeded, or
    canned tomatoes, preferably imported
    Italian, drained and seeded

2 tablespoons raisins

2 tablespoons pine nuts (*pignoli*)

Salt and freshly ground black pepper

Large pinch of dried oregano

¼ cup extra virgin olive oil

TO SERVE:

Fresh Italian parsley leaves

Remove the skins from the peppers (page 176), then put them in a bowl of cold water and remove the stems and pulp with all the seeds. Cut open the peppers on only one side, so each remains in one flattened piece. Let the skinned cleaned peppers rest on paper towels until needed.

Preheat the oven to 375 degrees. Prepare the stuffing. Soak the bread crumbs in the broth for 10 minutes. Meanwhile, finely chop the parsley, capers, and olives together on a cutting board. Drain the bread crumbs and place them and the olive mixture in a small crockery or glass bowl. Add the tomatoes, raisins, and pine nuts, and season with salt, pepper, and oregano. Mix very well with a wooden spoon, breaking the tomatoes up into small pieces. Spread the stuffing over the prepared peppers and roll them up like *involtini*.

Oil a baking dish with 2 tablespoons of the olive oil. Place the stuffed peppers in the baking dish with the top facing down, so they remain closed while baking. Pour the remaining oil over and bake until soft to the touch, about 35 minutes. Serve hot with the parsley leaves sprinkled over with some of the juices of the peppers.

NOTE: The peppers may be served at room temperature after a few hours; in that case, cover the baking pan to prevent them from drying out too much. You may also serve the peppers at room temperature as an appetizer, drizzling over each pepper ½ tablespoon olive oil mixed with 1 teaspoon wine vinegar.

PEPERONI IN CASSERUOLA
Sweet Peppers Baked with Grated Cheese

Makes 6 to 8 servings

Here aromatic vegetables and tomatoes are sautéed, then peeled peppers lightly precooked. Peppers can be skinned using two different methods, depending on the dish. If they are to be eaten alone or combined with eggplant or with different versions of the eggplant-based caponata, it is preferred to roast them on charcoals, which gives them a smoky flavor. In dishes with tomatoes, as this one, it is preferred to roast them in the oven to avoid having a smoky flavor which does not combine well with tomatoes.

6 large bell peppers (preferably red and
    yellow)

1 large red onion, cleaned

2 large carrots, scraped

3 stalks celery

10 sprigs fresh Italian parsley, leaves only

½ cup extra virgin olive oil

1 pound ripe tomatoes, blanched for
    1 minute, peeled, and seeded, or
    canned tomatoes, preferably imported
    Italian, drained and seeded

Salt and freshly ground black pepper

Large pinch of dried oregano

½ cup very fine unseasoned bread crumbs,
    preferably homemade, lightly toasted

3 extra-large eggs

¾ cup freshly grated Parmigiano cheese

TO SERVE:

¼ cup freshly grated Parmigiano cheese

To remove the skins from the peppers, preheat the oven to 400 degrees. Place the peppers on the middle shelf of the oven, put a roasting pan full of cold water on the bottom shelf, then bake until their skins start detaching, about 35 minutes. Remove the peppers from the oven, put them in a plastic bag for 15 minutes to allow the skins to detach, then clean them under cold running water, removing the stems and the pulp and seeds inside. Cut the peppers into strips about 1 inch wide. Let the peppers rest until needed.

    Meanwhile, coarsely chop the onion, carrots, celery, and parsley together on a cutting board. Heat the olive oil over medium heat in a large nonreactive skillet. When the oil is warm, add the onion mixture and sauté for 15 minutes, stirring every so often with a wooden spoon. If fresh tomatoes are used, quarter them. Add the tomatoes to the skillet, season with salt, pepper, and oregano, and sauté over high heat, stirring, for 5 minutes, then add the peppers and cook for another 2 minutes. Remove from the heat and transfer the contents of the skillet to a crockery or glass bowl to cool for at least half an hour.

Reduce the oven heat to 375 degrees. Lightly oil a 13½ × 8¾-inch baking dish, then coat it evenly with the bread crumbs. Mix the eggs and Parmigiano together in a small bowl. Transfer the pepper mixture from the bowl to the dish, then pour the egg mixture over and bake until the eggs are cooked completely, about 20 minutes. Remove from the oven, sprinkle the grated Parmigiano over, and serve hot.

❖

PATATE IN TEGLIA ALLA PADOVANA
Potato Casserole Padua Style

Makes 6 servings

The Veneto region takes particular care in sautéing aromatic herbs as the first step in preparing a dish; they consider this to be the "secret" of the flavor of their cuisine. To indicate an incompetent cook, the Veneti say, "He/she does not know how to sauté." Traditionally, brides-to-be had to pass the mothers-in-law's tests of sautéing and of making *bigoli,* the traditional Veneto pasta (see page 86).

2 pounds all-purpose potatoes, peeled and cut into 1½-inch cubes

8 cups cold water

Coarse-grained salt

1 large red onion, cleaned

3 ounces pancetta or prosciutto, in one piece

1 tablespoon (½ ounce) sweet butter

¼ cup extra virgin olive oil

About 1 cup completely defatted chicken or meat broth, preferably homemade, as needed

Salt and freshly ground black pepper

1 heaping tablespoon rosemary leaves, fresh or preserved in salt (page 2), finely chopped

Fresh Italian parsley leaves

Place the potatoes in a bowl of cold water. Heat the 8 cups cold water in a medium-size saucepan over medium heat; when the water reaches a boil, add coarse salt to taste, then drain the potatoes and add them to the saucepan and let boil for 5 minutes. Drain and set aside.

Meanwhile, coarsely chop the onion and cut the pancetta or prosciutto into very small pieces or grind it with a meat grinder. Set a medium-size skillet with the butter and olive oil over medium heat; when the butter is melted, add the onion and pancetta or prosciutto and sauté for 2 minutes. Add the potatoes and mix very well. Cook the potatoes, stirring almost constantly with a wooden spoon, until they are cooked but still have a little bite. Add a little broth if needed for extra cooking. The cooking time should be about 15 minutes. Halfway through, season with salt and pepper and add the chopped rosemary. Transfer to a large serving platter, sprinkle the parsley leaves over, and serve hot.

PATATE SABBIOSE
"Sandy" Potatoes

Makes 6 servings

Sprinkling dishes with grated cheese has been done only in recent centuries. Previously the sprinkling was with bread crumbs, for both taste and a "sandy" texture. Sometimes the crumbs were combined with chopped aromatic herbs, as in this dish, which is probably many centuries old.

1½ pounds all-purpose potatoes

1 tablespoon rosemary leaves, fresh or
    preserved in salt (page 2)

4 sage leaves, fresh or preserved in salt
    (page 2)

Large pinch of dried oregano

6 tablespoons extra virgin olive oil

Salt and freshly ground black pepper

Coarse-grained salt

2 tablespoons (1 ounce) sweet butter

¼ cup very fine unseasoned bread crumbs,
    preferably homemade, lightly toasted

TO SERVE:

Sprigs fresh rosemary and sage

Peel the potatoes and cut them into ½-inch-thick slices. Let them rest in a bowl of cold water until needed. Finely chop the rosemary, sage, and oregano together on a cutting board and transfer to a small crockery or glass bowl. Add the olive oil and season with salt and pepper. Mix very well.

Bring a medium-size casserole with cold water to a boil, add coarse salt to taste, then drain the potatoes and add them to the casserole to simmer for about 6 minutes. At that point the potatoes should be half cooked; transfer them to a serving platter lined with paper towels to remove excess water. Let cool, covered with wet paper towels, for half an hour.

Melt the butter in a large skillet over medium heat, add the potatoes, then pour the olive oil mixture over. Lightly sauté the potatoes until completely cooked and rather crisp, about 5 minutes per side. Sprinkle over the bread crumbs, mix very well, and sauté for 1 minute more. Transfer to a serving platter and serve warm with the rosemary and sage sprigs.

FRITTELLE DI PATATE
Crab-Shaped Potato Fritters

Makes 6 servings

To make *Frittelle di Patate,* we shred raw potatoes, mix them with eggs and cheese, and fry them in vegetable oil. In frying, the shredded potatoes acquire a shape that resembles that of a crab. The crisp fritters, their oil drained off, sprinkled with salt and lemon juice, are light and delicious.

1 pound boiling potatoes (don't use new
    potatoes)

3 extra-large eggs

3 tablespoons freshly grated Pecorino
    Romano cheese

Salt and freshly ground black pepper

1 quart vegetable oil (½ sunflower oil and
    ½ corn oil)

TO SERVE:

Salt

1 lemon, cut into wedges

Peel the potatoes and put them in a bowl of cold water to remove some of the starch and to keep them from discoloring. Mix the eggs with the cheese in a medium-size crockery or glass bowl and season with salt and pepper. Drain the potatoes and dry them with paper towels. Coarsely shred the potatoes with a hand grater into the bowl containing the cheese mixture. Mix everything together very well, using a wooden spoon.

Meanwhile, heat the vegetable oil in a large, heavy, deep-sided skillet over medium heat. When the oil is hot, about 375 degrees, take 1 heaping tablespoon of the potato mixture, trying not to take a lot of the separated liquid (the potatoes will shed a lot of water), and gently drop it in the hot oil. After adding each tablespoon, stir the potato mixture to keep too much liquid from separating. Use a strainer-skimmer to turn the *frittelle* and when they are golden on both sides, about 30 seconds per side, transfer them to a serving dish lined with paper towels to absorb excess oil. When all the fritters are on the dish, remove the paper towels, sprinkle with a little salt, and serve accompanied by the lemon wedges.

FAGIOLINI ALLA SALSA VERDE CON OLIVE

String Beans with Green Sauce

Makes 6 to 8 servings

What we call string beans are eaten young, thin, and tender in Italy; there is almost never the string along the side found in older string beans. After they are boiled, they are often simply dressed with olive oil or sautéed with chopped garlic. But they are also prepared with many regional dressings.

The green herb sauce used in this Ligurian recipe is made from parsley rather than the more famous basil green sauce known as pesto. But this parsley version is different from the famous Tuscan *salsa verde* in its savory ingredients, here capers in wine vinegar and black olives. It shares with that version uncooked garlic and anchovies. This *salsa verde* still retains a touch of its Ligurian basil in the fresh whole leaves added at the end. Green pesto sauces can also be made with mint and other fresh herbs.

2 pounds string beans, preferably the very
    thin ones, ends trimmed
Coarse-grained salt

FOR THE SAUCE:

2 medium-size cloves garlic, peeled

6 large black Greek olives, pitted

1 tablespoon capers in wine vinegar, drained

2 whole anchovies preserved in salt
    (see Note on page 10) or 4 anchovy
    fillets packed in oil, drained

15 sprigs fresh Italian parsley, leaves only

⅓ cup extra virgin olive oil

Salt and freshly ground black pepper

TO SERVE:

Fresh basil leaves

Set a pot of cold water over medium heat; when the water reaches a boil, add the beans and coarse salt to taste. Cook until the beans are completely cooked but not mushy. The cooking time depends on the variety and size of the beans you use. For the very thin ones, 5 to 6 minutes is enough.

Meanwhile, finely chop the garlic, olives, capers, anchovies, and parsley together on a cutting board or in a blender or a food processor. Transfer the garlic mixture to a small crockery or glass bowl, add the olive oil, and season with salt and pepper. Drain the beans, place them in a crockery or glass bowl, and cover with a wet paper or kitchen towel until cool, about half an hour. When ready, dress the beans with the prepared sauce, then transfer everything to a serving platter and serve with the basil leaves scattered over.

FAGIOLINI IN SALSA DI CAPPERI
String Beans in Caper-Walnut Sauce
Makes 6 servings

Here the boiled string beans are dressed with oil, salt, and pepper and allowed to cool. Then a caper sauce is prepared separately with ground parsley, scallions, and capers, as well as ground walnuts, which are a survival of so many Renaissance green sauces. Ground nuts were then more commonly added for thickening than flour. The chopped ingredients are sautéed with butter and oil, adding wine vinegar, bay leaves, and white wine.

The tomatoes are used as a receptacle for the small string beans and the thick sauce is poured over before serving. Again basil leaves are placed on top of each portion, consisting of one stuffed tomato.

¾ pound string beans, preferably the very
   thin ones, ends trimmed
Coarse-grained salt
3 tablespoons extra virgin olive oil
Salt and freshly ground black pepper

FOR THE SAUCE:
Generous ¼ cup capers in wine vinegar,
   drained
2 ounces shelled walnuts
20 sprigs fresh Italian parsley, leaves only
10 scallions, white part only

3 tablespoons (1½ ounces) sweet butter
1 tablespoon extra virgin olive oil
¼ cup white wine vinegar
2 bay leaves
Salt and freshly ground black pepper
½ cup dry white wine

FOR THE TOMATO CUPS:
6 large ripe tomatoes
Coarse-grained salt

TO SERVE:
Fresh basil leaves

Soak the beans in a bowl of cold water for half an hour. Bring a large saucepan of cold water to a boil over medium heat, add coarse salt to taste, then drain the beans, add to the pan and cook until completely cooked but not mushy, 5 to 6 minutes. Drain the beans, cut them into thirds, transfer to a crockery or glass bowl, then add the olive oil and season with salt and pepper. Mix very well and let cool, covered with a wet paper or cotton kitchen towel for about 1 hour.

Prepare the sauce. Place the capers, walnuts, parsley, and scallions in a food processor or blender and process until almost a paste is formed. Melt the butter along with the olive oil in a medium-size saucepan over low heat, add the caper mixture, and sauté for 2 minutes, stirring constantly with a wooden spoon. Raise the heat to medium, add the vinegar and bay leaves, and season with salt and pepper. When the vinegar has evaporated, add the wine and cook for 5 minutes more. By that time a rather thick sauce should have formed. Discard the bay leaves.

Cut off the tops of the tomatoes and use a melon baller to remove the seeds and pulp from inside. Rinse under cold running water, sprinkle a little coarse salt inside, and let rest upside down on paper towels for 10 minutes. When ready, stuff each tomato with the string beans, pour over some of the sauce, and serve with the basil leaves.

PIEDMONT

FAGIOLI SERPENTI ALLA PIEMONTESE
Long Beans Piedmont Style
Makes 6 servings

Fagioli serpenti are long beans, which are most commonly found in Asian markets. They are much used in Italy. First the ground pancetta, garlic, parsley, and basil are sautéed, then the beans placed over them and covered with tomato sauce and the full-bodied Barolo red wine native to Piedmont. The long beans require a long cooking time in the covered casserole.

This is the classic way of cooking string beans in order to bring out the taste of the wine. Some add a little oil or butter to the pancetta. This dish is used mainly to accompany boiled meats.

2 pounds long beans, ends trimmed and cut
  into thirds

FOR THE COOKING SAUCE:
3 ounces pancetta, coarsely ground or cut
  into small pieces
2 cloves garlic, peeled
15 sprigs fresh Italian parsley, leaves only

10 fresh basil leaves
1 pound ripe tomatoes or drained canned
  tomatoes, preferably imported Italian
1 cup Barolo wine
Salt and freshly ground black pepper
About 2 cups completely defatted chicken
  or meat broth, preferably homemade

Soak the beans in a bowl of cold water for half an hour. Arrange the ground pancetta over the bottom of a large nonreactive casserole. Finely chop the garlic, parsley, and basil together on a cutting board. If fresh tomatoes are used, cut them into large pieces. Whether using fresh or canned tomatoes, pass them through a food mill fitted with the disk with the smallest holes into a crockery or glass bowl. Drain the beans and put them in the casserole on top of the pancetta. Sprinkle all the garlic mixture over the beans, then pour the strained tomatoes and wine over. Season with salt and pepper. Do not mix or stir. Cover the casserole and place it over medium heat. Shake the casserole every so often to make sure the beans do not stick to the bottom, adding broth as needed. After 30 minutes the beans should be almost cooked. Mix very well and cook, uncovered, for 2 to 3 minutes more. Transfer to a warm serving platter and serve warm.

FAGIOLI AL FIASCO ALL'ALLORO
Beans with Bay Leaves
Makes 6 to 8 servings

Cannellini, white kidney beans, are the favorite beans of Tuscany. This special method of placing beans in a wine flask with just the right amount of liquid and seasonings, and setting the flask in a pot of water to cook, is done in order to retain the full flavor of the seasoned beans. The secret of keeping the glass flask from cracking in the boiling water is to have the water inside and outside the flask always remain at the same temperature, which means beginning with both of them cold and then being sure that any water added later is simmering like the water in the pot and inside the flask. Non-Tuscans are usually surprised that the flask does not crack, but in many years of cooking beans this way, I have never had one crack. And, of course, the presentation is beautiful. The beans emerge with a rich flavor that it is difficult to duplicate with other methods of cooking.

1½ cups dried cannellini (white kidney) beans, picked over

2 ounces prosciutto, preferably Tuscan type, or pancetta, in one piece

2 sage leaves, fresh or preserved in salt (page 2)

1 tablespoon rosemary leaves, fresh or preserved in salt (page 2)

1 medium-size clove garlic, peeled

3 bay leaves

10 black peppercorns

2 tablespoons extra virgin olive oil

Fine salt

TO SERVE:

Salt and freshly ground black pepper

Extra virgin olive oil for each serving

Soak the beans in a bowl of cold water overnight. The next morning drain the beans and transfer them to an old-fashioned wine flask, with the straw removed, or to another flask. In a meat grinder, grind together the prosciutto or pancetta, sage, rosemary, and garlic. Add the mixture to the flask along with the bay leaves and peppercorns. Pour the olive oil into the flask and enough cold water to cover everything. Cover the mouth of the flask with absorbent cotton and place it in a stockpot. Pour enough cold water into the stockpot to reach several inches above the level of the water inside the flask and set it over medium heat. Let the water simmer for about 2 hours. Keep a kettle or pot of simmering water next to the stockpot, as you may need to add some to the stockpot later. After 2 hours the beans should be perfectly cooked and the taste and the texture will be much superior to those boiled in water. The flask will not break unless a change of temperature occurs in the pot, which can happen if, when the water evaporates either in the pot or inside the flask, you are not careful to add simmering or strongly boiling water rather than cold. Transfer the beans to a bowl, discard the bay leaves, and season with fine salt. In Tuscany they have recently developed a special *fiasco per fagioli*, because removing the beans from a wine flask takes patience. Drain the excess liquid from the beans and transfer them to a serving platter. Season with salt, pepper, and olive oil and serve. These are very good at room temperature as well.

❖

CANNELLINI E BIETOLA
Cannellini and Swiss Chard Casserole

Makes 6 servings

Cannellini beans and Swiss chard are both Tuscan favorites. This dish has a special method of cooking, in which the soaked beans are placed between layers of chard on bottom and top, water is poured into the casserole, and everything is topped with chopped garlic and onion and tomato slices. The casserole is covered and nothing is stirred while cooking, only mixed together in the last five minutes.

1 cup dried cannellini (white kidney) beans, picked over

3 pounds Swiss chard, cleaned and stalks and leaves cut into ½-inch-thick slices

3 very large cloves garlic, peeled and finely chopped

1 very large red onion, cleaned and thinly sliced

2 large ripe tomatoes, thinly sliced

4 cups lukewarm water

¼ cup extra virgin olive oil

Freshly ground black pepper

Coarse-grained salt

TO SERVE:

1 tablespoon extra virgin olive oil for each serving

Freshly ground black pepper

Soak the beans in a bowl of cold water overnight. The next morning drain the beans and soak the chard in a bowl of cold water for half an hour. When ready, drain the chard and arrange half of it over the bottom of a heavy nonreactive casserole. Place the beans over the bed of chard, making sure that the beans do not reach to the sides of the casserole. On top of the beans arrange the remaining chard to completely cover them. Sprinkle the chopped garlic all over, then make a layer of the sliced onion, then one of the tomatoes. Pour the water over, drizzle the olive oil on, and season with pepper.

Cover the casserole and set over medium heat. Bring to a boil, then reduce the heat to medium-low and simmer for 50 minutes, without mixing or stirring, adding a little more water if needed. By that time the beans should be almost cooked. Season with coarse salt and cook for 5 minutes more. Gently mix the beans and chard together and taste for salt and pepper. Use a slotted spoon to serve the mixed beans and chard. To serve, add the olive oil and some black pepper to each serving.

FAGIOLI IN SAOR ALLA VENEZIANA

Beans in Venetian Vinegar Sauce

Makes 6 servings

The speckled red-and-white borlotti beans, sometimes called Roman beans, are the favorite of the Veneto. In the sweet-and-sour *Fagioli in Saor,* the beans are dressed with a favorite Venetian sauce that is even more famously used with such fried fish as sardines or sole. Some butter and onions provide the sweetness, while the bay leaves and vinegar supply the savory bite. The beans are served warm with chopped parsley and garlic over the top.

1 cup dried borlotti (Roman) or cannellini
    (white kidney) beans, picked over

3 quarts cold water

1 large clove garlic, peeled

2 tablespoons extra virgin olive oil

Coarse-grained salt

FOR THE SAUCE:

2 tablespoons (1 ounce) sweet butter

2 tablespoons extra virgin olive oil

1 large red onion (such as the Tropea),
    cleaned and thinly sliced

6 bay leaves

¼ cup red wine vinegar

1 cup cold water

Salt and freshly ground black pepper

TO SERVE:

15 sprigs fresh Italian parsley, leaves only

1 medium-size clove garlic, peeled

Soak the beans in a bowl of cold water overnight. The next morning drain the beans and place them in a medium-size casserole with the 3 quarts cold water, the garlic, and olive oil. Set the casserole over medium heat and simmer for 45 minutes. By that time the beans should be almost cooked, but still a little firm. Add coarse salt to taste and simmer for another 5 minutes.

Meanwhile, prepare the sauce. Place a medium-size skillet with the butter and olive oil over medium heat; when the butter is melted, add the onion and lightly sauté for 5 minutes. Add the bay leaves and cook for another 5 minutes. Add the vinegar and let evaporate for 5 minutes. Pour in ½ cup of the water, season with salt and pepper, and cook for 5 minutes more. Drain the beans and add them to the skillet. Simmer slowly, mixing every so often with a wooden spoon, until the beans are completely cooked, adding more water if needed. The sauce should be rather thick.

Meanwhile, finely chop the parsley and garlic together on a cutting board. Transfer the beans with some of their sauce to a serving platter, sprinkle the garlic mixture over, and serve warm.

FAGIOLI IN SALSA ALLA PADOVANA
Roman Beans in Savory Sauce Padua Style
Makes 8 servings

The savory sauce for *Fagioli in Salsa alla Padovana* repeats the onion, garlic, and wine vinegar found in *Fagioli in Saor*, but olive oil is used without butter, and the anchovies, pancetta, rosemary, and sage make the sauce fully savory, without any sweetness. Padua, though close to Venice, has its own culinary traditions and even the recipes it shares somewhat with Venice have their own distinctive touches.

2 cups dried borlotti (Roman) beans,
    picked over
2 tablespoons extra virgin olive oil
Coarse-grained salt

FOR THE SAUCE:
1 medium-size red onion (such as the
    Tropea), cleaned
2 medium-size cloves garlic, peeled
4 whole anchovies preserved in salt
    (see Note on page 10) or 8 anchovy
    fillets packed in oil, drained

3 ounces pancetta or prosciutto, ground
¼ cup extra virgin olive oil
Salt and freshly ground black pepper
10 sprigs fresh Italian parsley, leaves only
1 stalk celery
1 tablespoon rosemary leaves, fresh or
    preserved in salt (page 2)
6 sage leaves, fresh or preserved in salt
    (page 2)
½ cup red wine vinegar
½ cup cold water

Soak the beans in a bowl of cold water overnight. The next morning place a medium-size stockpot of cold water over medium heat; when the water reaches a boil, drain the beans and add them to the pot along with the olive oil. Cook for about 40 minutes or less, depending on how old they are. They are ready when they are soft but still retain their shape. Season with coarse salt, simmer for another 2 minutes, then drain and arrange the beans on a serving platter. Cover the beans with dampened paper towels to keep the skins from splitting. (The beans may be cooked up to 1 day in advance.)

Meanwhile, prepare the sauce. Finely chop the onion, garlic, and anchovies together on a cutting board and mix them together with the ground pancetta or prosciutto. Place a medium-size saucepan with the olive oil over medium heat; when the oil is warm, add the meat mixture and lightly sauté for 15 minutes, lowering the heat if too high. Season with salt and pepper. Meanwhile, finely chop the parsley, celery, rosemary, and sage together on a cutting board and add these to the saucepan. Mix very well, raise the heat to medium if it was lowered, and cook for 2 minutes, stirring. Add the vinegar and, after a minute, the water. Taste for salt and pepper and cook for 10 minutes more. Remove the paper towels from the beans and pour the sauce over them. You may serve immediately or at room temperature after a few hours.

FAGIOLI ALLA TREVISANA
Beans Treviso Style

Makes 6 servings

Fagioli alla Trevisana are made with either cannellini or borlotti beans and the sauce is simpler than for the other two *fagioli* dishes, omitting the onions and several of the herbs, but adding basil. Most interesting is that these three treatments of beans, each with its completely integrated sauce, produce quite different taste results.

FOR THE BEANS:

1 cup dried cannellini (white kidney) or
    borlotti (Roman) beans, picked over
1 tablespoon extra virgin olive oil
Coarse-grained salt

FOR THE SAUCE:

3 whole anchovies preserved in salt
    (see Note on page 10) or 6 anchovy
    fillets packed in oil, drained

15 sprigs fresh Italian parsley, leaves only
1 large clove garlic, peeled
¼ cup extra virgin olive oil
Salt and freshly ground black pepper

TO SERVE:

Fresh basil leaves

Soak the beans in a bowl of cold water overnight. The next morning drain the beans and add them to a medium-size saucepan of cold water. Set the pan over medium heat, add the olive oil, and simmer for about 45 minutes. By that time the beans should be almost cooked and rather soft. Season with coarse salt and simmer another 5 minutes. Drain the beans, put them in a crockery or glass bowl covered with dampened paper or kitchen towels (to keep the skins from splitting), and let cool completely, about half an hour.

When ready, finely chop the anchovies, parsley, and garlic together on a cutting board. Transfer to a small bowl, add the olive oil, season with salt and pepper, and mix very well. Pour the sauce over the beans, mix very well, then transfer everything to a serving platter and serve with a lot of basil leaves.

LENTICCHIE IN UMIDO
Lentils in Sauce

Makes 6 to 8 servings

Lentils are among the three beans or legumes that are native to the Eastern Hemisphere, the other two being chick peas and fava beans. All others used in gastronomy came from the New World. Purees of lentils and lentil sauces are used with pasta and whole lentils in various sauces are employed as a vegetable course or accompaniment, in soups, or, again, combined with pastas. Of the lentil's many symbolisms, the one that remains most traditional is the eating of a lentil dish at the New Year's dinner to bring luck, wealth, and fecundity, and this one is a particular holiday favorite.

2 cups dried lentils, picked over

2 tablespoons extra virgin olive oil

2 large cloves garlic, peeled

2 stalks celery, cut into thirds

1 medium-size red onion, cleaned

Coarse-grained salt

FOR THE SAUCE:

¼ cup extra virgin olive oil

4 cloves garlic, peeled and cut into thin slivers

4 heaping tablespoons tomato paste, preferably imported Italian

Salt and freshly ground black pepper

Hot red pepper flakes

1 large sprig fresh rosemary or 1 tablespoon fresh rosemary leaves, plus more sprigs for serving

About 1 cup completely defatted chicken or meat broth, preferably homemade

Soak the lentils in a bowl of cold water for several hours. When ready, bring a medium-size stockpot of cold water to a boil over medium heat. When the water reaches a boil, drain the lentils and add them to stockpot, along with the olive oil, garlic cloves, celery, and onion and simmer for about 35 minutes (see Note). By that time the lentils should be cooked but still a little firm. Add coarse salt to taste and simmer for 2 or 3 minutes more. Drain the lentils, transfer them to a crockery or glass bowl, and discard the garlic, celery, and onion. Place wet paper towels on top to prevent the lentils from drying and breaking and let rest until needed.

To make the sauce, place a nonreactive skillet with the olive oil over medium heat; when the oil is warm, add the garlic slivers and lightly sauté for a few seconds. Add the tomato paste, stir, and immediately add the drained lentils. Season with salt, black pepper, and hot pepper flakes and place the rosemary sprig, or the rosemary leaves wrapped in a small piece of cheesecloth, in the skillet. Sauté for 1 minute, mixing constantly, then start adding the broth ¼ cup at a time. Gently mix the lentils, being sure the tomato paste is completely dissolved and the lentils have acquired a coating. The lentils are ready when they are completely cooked and a medium-thick sauce has formed. Transfer to a serving platter, discard the rosemary, replace with fresh rosemary sprigs, and serve.

NOTE: In the past we soaked the lentils overnight and cooked them for 2 hours. Some packages still give those instructions, but the methods of drying lentils must have improved in recent years, as both soaking and cooking times have become much shorter.

LIGURIA

"POLPETTONE" ALLA GENOVESE
Genoese Vegetable Loaf

Makes 8 servings

Though called a *polpettone* or loaf, this is really closer to a soufflé-like *budino*, which is, however, like most Italian soufflés, unmolded. It is prepared with a variety of vegetables in Liguria, including a popular version with artichokes. The crustless white bread is broken up but not pureed, because it is used in place of the original sweetbreads and is left with a texture that recalls that delicacy.

1 pound all-purpose potatoes

1 pound string beans, the thinnest you
    can find

Coarse-grained salt

1 large or 2 medium-size red onions,
    cleaned

3 tablespoons (1½ ounces) sweet butter

2 tablespoons extra virgin olive oil

1½ cups vegetable or completely defatted
    chicken broth, preferably homemade

15 sprigs fresh Italian parsley, leaves only

30 small fresh marjoram leaves or
    1 teaspoon dried

Salt and freshly ground black pepper

About ⅓ cup very fine unseasoned bread
    crumbs, preferably homemade, lightly
    toasted

2 ounces crustless white bread

1 cup milk

4 extra-large eggs

½ cup freshly grated Parmigiano cheese

Large pinch of freshly grated nutmeg

2 tablespoons (1 ounce) sweet butter, cut
    into small pieces

continued

In a medium-size pot, boil the potatoes, with the skins on, in salted water, until very soft, about 35 minutes, depending on their size.

Meanwhile, remove the ends from the string beans, then soak the beans in a bowl of cold water for half an hour. Bring a medium-size pot of cold water to a boil, add coarse salt to taste, drain the beans, and add them to the boiling water. Cook until quite soft, about 15 minutes or more, depending on their size. The string beans should still retain their shape. Transfer the beans to a crockery or glass bowl, cover them with a dampened cotton kitchen towel or paper towels, and let rest until needed.

When the potatoes are ready, drain, transfer to a cutting board, and, immediately, while still very hot, peel and rice them, using a potato ricer with the smallest holes, into a crockery or glass bowl. Let rest until needed.

Finely chop the onion on a cutting board. Place a large skillet with the butter and olive oil over medium heat; when the butter is barely melted, add the onion, reduce the heat to medium-low, and cook for 15 minutes, stirring occasionally. Add the broth, raise the heat to medium, and cook until the onion is almost a paste, about another 10 minutes.

Meanwhile, finely chop the parsley and marjoram together on a cutting board and cut the string beans into very small pieces. Add the herb mixture to the skillet, then the cut-up beans and riced potatoes. Season with salt and pepper. Cook for 5 minutes, constantly stirring with a wooden spoon to prevent the potatoes from sticking to the bottom. Transfer the contents of the skillet to a crockery or glass bowl and let rest until cool, about 1 hour.

Preheat the oven to 375 degrees. Lightly butter an 8½-inch soufflé dish and coat it evenly with the bread crumbs.

Place the bread in a small bowl with the milk for a few minutes, then add the eggs and Parmigiano to the bowl. Mix very well, then season with salt, pepper, and nutmeg. Add this bread mixture to the potato mixture and combine the ingredients very well. Empty the combined ingredients into the prepared soufflé dish. Distribute the butter pieces over the top and bake until golden on top, about 1 hour. Remove from the oven and let rest for at least 15 minutes before unmolding onto a large plate. Place a serving dish over the top and flip again so the golden part is on top. Serve, slicing the *polpettone* like a cake.

VARIATION: You can bake the *polpettone* in twelve well-buttered custard cups coated with bread crumbs. The baking time will be about 45 minutes.

MAIN COURSES

In Italy, after the first course, the plate is changed and the second course is served alone on its own plate. There are almost never vegetables on the same plate, with rare exceptions when one vegetable is always associated with a particular meat treatment, in effect making it part of the dish. An example is Sausages with Cannellini Beans, and indeed the beans are sautéed in the juices of the sausage. Another is slices of the large boiled sausage called *cotechino* accompanied by potato purée, almost a requirement for the dish. As will be seen, the vegetable is usually presented as a separate course, after the main one, on its own plate.

Because the main course is preceded by one or two others and followed by a vegetable, the portions of meat, fish, or fowl are much smaller than in most other cuisines, in which the main course forms the bulk of the meal and is preceded by only a small appetizer or soup. For example, when steak is served in Italy, one large steak is sliced and serves four to six people, each getting one or two slices. For this reason, much less meat is traditionally eaten in this vegetable- and grain-oriented country. Hence the popularity of such "Mediterranean cooking" to the health-food-oriented.

Italy is surrounded by seas, so it has fish in great variety and abundance. It retains its wooded areas, so that there is much game and still many rabbits and "free-range" chickens. Small chickens, capons, and mature hens each have their own recipes. Sheep raising is important and traditional in many areas, and lamb, which is always served very young, older sheep, which includes what is called lamb in many other countries, and mutton again each have their own repertory of dishes. Pork is outstanding and used both fresh and preserved. And the beef repertory includes the remarkable steaks of Tuscany.

Every region cooks these different meats in its own special ways, so, as you can imagine, this is just a small selection of main dishes one can find in Italian cooking.

FISH AND SHELLFISH

❖

ZUPPA DI PESCE ALLA VENETA
Venetian-Style Fish "Zuppa"

Makes 6 servings

Each port of Italy has its own fish soup. One can venture even further and say that most every Mediterranean port, no matter what the country, has its own fish soup. So bouillabaise from Marseille is hardly unique; indeed, it shares its famous selection of fish, even the combination, with other great ports nearby, such as Genoa. It is speculated that such fish soups are particularly characteristic of port cities founded by the ancient Greeks, as Marseille, Pisa, Siracusa, and Barcelona were.

One would certainly expect the Queen of the Adriatic to have its own *zuppa di pesce*, and it does. While most Italian ports prefer to cook the small fish whole and the large fish in pieces with the bones, Venice, almost alone, prefers to use fillets. Going through the great Rialto fish market, one notices that at least one fish is always sold filleted, and that is John Dory, also called St. Peter fish on the Adriatic, where it so often is found. One can speculate that the reason for this is the unappetizing look of the whole fish—scrawny, wrinkled, and ugly. One almost never sees fillets of fresh fish sold in other Italian markets.

In addition to the John Dory, the Venetians use other fish plentiful in their own waters, and we have included *branzino*, a type of bass, and dorade. Here, as in most fish soups, a combination of fish is employed. Aside from the filleting, also unusual to the Venetian version is the absence of shellfish and squid.

continued

FOR THE BROTH:

4 quarts cold water

2 medium-size carrots, scraped and cut into
  large pieces

1 large yellow onion, cleaned and thinly sliced

2 stalks celery, cut into large pieces

5 sprigs fresh Italian parsley, leaves only

1 cup dry white wine

½ pound fish heads (you can get these from
  your fishmonger)

Coarse-grained salt

FOR THE FISH:

1 lemon, cut in half

Coarse-grained salt

1 pound sea bass fillets or slices with bones
  (*branzino* in Italian), cut into 4-ounce
  pieces

1 pound John Dory fillets or slices with
  bones (*San Pietro* in Italian), cut into
  4-ounce pieces

1 pound dorade fillets or slices with bones
  (*orata* in Italian), cut into 4-ounce pieces

FOR THE SAUCE:

3 large cloves garlic, peeled

30 sprigs fresh Italian parsley, leaves only

Hot red pepper flakes

½ cup extra virgin olive oil

1 cup dry white wine

Salt and freshly ground black pepper

2 pounds ripe tomatoes or drained canned
  tomatoes, preferably imported Italian

TO SERVE:

Fresh Italian parsley leaves

Bring the cold water to a boil in a casserole over medium heat. Add the carrots, onion, celery, parsley, wine, fish heads, and coarse salt to taste and simmer for about 25 minutes, skimming any foam off the surface. Strain the broth, discarding all the vegetables and fish heads, and save the broth. Meanwhile, squeeze the lemon halves, put the fish fillets in a large crockery or glass bowl of cold water, add a little coarse salt and the lemon juice, and soak the fish for half an hour. Drain the fish and pat dry with paper towels.

Bring the fish broth back to a simmer, add the fish, and parboil for just a few minutes to half-cook the fish. Carefully lift out the fish and place on a serving platter. If using fish with bones, at this point you can fillet it or not, depending on how you like it. For the sauce, finely chop the garlic, 15 sprigs of the parsley, and the hot pepper flakes together on a cutting board. Heat the olive oil in a large nonreactive skillet over medium heat; when the oil is warm, add the chopped mixture and lightly sauté for 5 minutes. Pour in the wine and let it evaporate for 5 minutes. Season with salt and pepper. If fresh tomatoes are used, cut them into small pieces. Whether using fresh or canned tomatoes, pass them through a food mill fitted with the disk with the smallest holes into a crockery or glass bowl. Add the tomatoes to the skillet and reduce until the sauce is rather thick, about another 10 minutes. Finely chop the remaining parsley.

If using fish fillets, cut the parboiled fillets into 2-inch pieces. Add the fish to the skillet. Sprinkle the chopped parsley over the top and simmer until the fish is completely cooked but still retains its shape, 1 or 2 minutes. Serve the fish and sauce over some slices of grilled polenta with a few parsley leaves sprinkled over each serving.

ORATA AL LIMONE ALLA VENETA
Dorade with Lemon Venetian Style

Makes 4 to 6 servings

In recent years, types of fish that have always been popular in Mediterranean cookery, but that were considered junk fish to be thrown back or used as bait by Atlantic fishermen, have been increasingly accepted outside the Mediterranean area. These fish include John Dory, dorade, and monkfish. In some parts of Italy, dorade is considered the finest of all fish for baking and grilling and for other delicate dishes.

This Venetian preparation uses a cold uncooked herb sauce over the dorade, which is first lightly marinated in lemon juice, then baked in tomatoes and white wine. It is finished with black olives and parsley.

2 large lemons, cut in half

Coarse-grained salt

2 dorades (*orate* in Italian), about 2 pounds
    total, scales removed and fish completely
    cleaned but with head and tail left on

Freshly ground black pepper

FOR THE HERB SAUCE:

Large pinch of dried oregano or 1 teaspoon
    fresh oregano leaves

2 large cloves garlic, peeled

3 tablespoons capers in wine vinegar,
    drained

15 sprigs fresh Italian parsley, leaves only

2 fresh basil leaves

2 whole anchovies preserved in salt
    (see Note on page 10) or 4 anchovy
    fillets packed in oil (optional), drained

½ cup extra virgin olive oil

Salt and freshly ground black pepper

FOR THE TOMATO SAUCE:

1 pound ripe tomatoes or drained canned
    tomatoes, preferably imported Italian

3 tablespoons extra virgin olive oil

Salt and freshly ground black pepper

TO BAKE:

1 cup dry white wine

TO SERVE:

Black olives

Sprigs fresh Italian parsley

continued

Squeeze one of the lemon halves into a large crockery or glass bowl of cold water, add a little coarse salt, and soak the fish in it for half an hour. Drain the dorades, rinse, and dry them with paper towels. Place the fish on a platter, squeeze the remaining lemon halves over them, season with salt and pepper, and let rest for 1 hour in a cool place or in the refrigerator.

Meanwhile, prepare the sauce. Finely chop the oregano, garlic, capers, parsley, basil, and anchovies, if used, together on a cutting board. Transfer to a small crockery or glass bowl, add the oil, season with salt and pepper, and mix very well. Refrigerate the sauce, covered, until needed.

If fresh tomatoes are used, cut them into pieces. Whether fresh or canned, pass the tomatoes through a food mill fitted with the disk with the smallest holes into a crockery or glass bowl. Add the olive oil, season with salt and pepper, and mix very well.

Preheat the oven to 375 degrees and lightly oil a large crockery or glass baking dish. Transfer the fish to the dish, pour the tomato mixture over, and bake for about 20 minutes; the fish should be completely cooked but still very juicy. If during the baking the tomato sauce dries too much, add a little wine.

Transfer the fish and all of the solid part of the sauce to a serving platter. Arrange the refrigerated herb sauce all over the fish in its tomato sauce and serve with the fish still hot, accompanied by the black olives and sprigs of Italian parsley.

CAMPANIA

PESCATRICE IN SCABECIO
Monkfish in a Savory Sauce

Makes 4 servings

Monkfish, *coda di rospo* in Italian and *lotte* in French, is a great favorite in the Mediterranean and has recently come into its own in other climes. In America it is most often sold boned as a large fillet or as boneless slices. It has a firm texture that some like to compare to lobster meat. In Italy it most often is eaten in slices with the bone.

This preparation from the Naples area simmers the fish with vinegar, onion, and bay leaf, removes it from the heat, and allows it to rest for an hour. Then the scallions, garlic, and sage are simmered separately in vinegar and a little cold water. A bed is prepared of arugula and tomato slices, and the fish is drained and laid on top. This *in scabecio* type of savory vinegar-flavored dish is much used in the Naples area.

1 lemon, cut in half

Coarse-grained salt

12 slices monkfish (from the tail, with the bone), about 2 inches thick

2 quarts plus ½ cup cold water

½ cup red wine vinegar

1 large red onion, cleaned and quartered

6 bay leaves

25 large scallions, white part only

6 tablespoons extra virgin olive oil

3 large cloves garlic, peeled and cut into slivers

8 large sage leaves, fresh or preserved in salt (page 2)

Salt and freshly ground black pepper

TO SERVE:

1 large bunch arugula

1 large ripe but not overripe tomato (about 1 pound)

Fresh basil leaves

Squeeze the lemon halves into a crockery or glass bowl of cold water, add a little coarse salt, and soak the fish in it for half an hour. Place a medium-size nonreactive casserole with 2 quarts of the cold water, 3 tablespoons of the vinegar, the onion, and two of the bay leaves over medium heat; when the water reaches a boil, add coarse salt to taste and simmer for 30 minutes.

Drain the fish and rinse under cold running water, then add the fish to the casserole and simmer for 3 minutes, or less if the fish pieces are narrow ones from the end of the tail. Remove the casserole from the heat, cover, and let rest for 1 hour or even longer if desired at room temperature.

When ready, coarsely chop the scallion whites and place the olive oil in a medium-size saucepan over medium heat. When the oil is warm, add the scallion whites, the garlic over the scallions, then the sage leaves. Do not mix. Season with salt and pepper. Finally, on top of all these ingredients, place the remaining four bay leaves and pour the remaining 5 tablespoons of vinegar mixed with the remaining ½ cup cold water. Simmer for 15 minutes, mix, and cook 1 minute more. By that time the scallions should be very soft; otherwise, add more water and cook, still without mixing, until very soft but not dry. Meanwhile, transfer the fish to a platter lined with paper towels to remove excess liquid. Remove the large stems from the arugula and arrange them on a serving platter. Cut the tomato into 6 slices and place them over the arugula. When the sauce is ready, remove and discard the bay leaves and sage leaves, then transfer the fish onto the tomato slices and cover with the contents of the saucepan. Serve with the basil leaves.

"SARTÙ" DI SOGLIOLE
Rice Timbale Stuffed with Sole
Makes 6 to 8 servings

Rice molds form an important area of Italian cooking; they may be savory or sweet. With a meat stuffing, they are often called *bombe*; as desserts, they may be stuffed with fruit.

The *sartù* exists in Naples and in Tuscany. In Naples it is a layering of rice alternating with many other ingredients, whereas in Tuscany, the bottom and top layers are flavored rice, while the stuffing is of fish, specifically sole. It is a type of timbale with the rice acting as a crust and the whole wrapped in lettuce leaves. The fish is first put in a savory marinade and then placed uncooked between the flavored rice layers. After baking, the timbale is sliced and served with a caper sauce.

1 lemon, cut in half

Coarse-grained salt

1 pound sole fillets or fillets of another
    flatfish such as flounder

FOR THE MARINADE:

2 tablespoons capers in wine vinegar, drained

2 medium-size cloves garlic, peeled

4 anchovy fillets packed in oil, drained

5 large sprigs fresh Italian parsley, leaves only

Salt and freshly ground black pepper

3 tablespoons extra virgin olive oil

FOR THE RICE:

Coarse-grained salt

1 pound raw short-grain rice, preferably
    Italian Arborio

Juice of 1 lemon

10 sprigs fresh Italian parsley, leaves only

2 cloves garlic, peeled

2 tablespoons extra virgin olive oil

Salt and freshly ground black pepper

¼ cup capers in wine vinegar, drained

2 extra-large eggs

TO LINE THE PAN:

2 heads Boston lettuce

Coarse-grained salt

2 tablespoons extra virgin olive oil

FOR THE CAPER SAUCE:

¼ cup capers in wine vinegar, drained

¼ cup extra virgin olive oil

2 tablespoons (1 ounce) sweet butter, at
    room temperature

1 tablespoon unbleached all-purpose flour

1 large clove garlic, peeled and finely
    chopped

1 cup completely defatted light chicken
    broth, preferably homemade

Salt and freshly ground black pepper

1 tablespoon red wine vinegar

Squeeze the lemon halves into a large crockery or glass bowl of cold water, add a little coarse salt, and soak the fillets in the bowl for half an hour.

Meanwhile, prepare the marinade. Finely chop the capers, garlic, anchovies, and parsley together on a cutting board. Transfer the caper mixture to a medium-size bowl, season with salt and pepper, add the olive oil, and mix very well. Drain the fish and rinse under cold running water. Cut the fillets into 2-inch-wide strips. Place the fish in the bowl with the marinade, mix very well, cover the bowl with plastic wrap, and refrigerate until needed.

Bring a large pot of cold water to a boil over medium heat, add salt to taste, then the rice, and cook for about 16 minutes. Drain the rice, put it into a crockery or glass bowl, add the lemon juice, and mix very well. Let the rice, covered, cool completely. Next, coarsely chop the parsley and finely chop the garlic. Mix the parsley and garlic with the olive oil and season with salt and pepper. When the rice is cold, add this mixture to it along with the whole capers and eggs. Mix very well.

Blanch the green outer leaves of the lettuce in boiling salted water for 20 seconds, transfer to a bowl of cold water, then open them onto kitchen towels dampened with cold water. Preheat the oven to 375 degrees and lightly oil a 10-inch springform pan. Line the pan, bottom and sides, with the blanched lettuce leaves. Make a layer of rice, using two-thirds of the mixture, on the bottom of the pan. Arrange the fish with its marinade over the rice, then make another layer with the remaining rice. On top of that make a layer of blanched lettuce leaves, then take the lettuce edges hanging from the sides and fold them over the top. Brush the lettuce with the oil, cover the mold with a sheet of aluminum foil, and bake for 1 hour.

Meanwhile, prepare the caper sauce. Finely chop the capers and place them in a small saucepan with the olive oil. Use a fork to mash together the butter, flour, and garlic. Heat the broth in another small saucepan and set the saucepan containing the capers over low heat. Sauté capers, stirring, for 1 minute. Dissolve the butter mixture in the warmed broth and immediately pour it in with the capers. Mix very well, season with salt and pepper, and simmer for 15 minutes.

Remove the rice mold from the oven and let it rest for 10 minutes before releasing the sides of the springform and transfering the mold to a round serving platter. When the sauce is reduced by half, add the vinegar and let it evaporate for 1 minute. Serve the rice mold, slicing it like a pie, with some of the caper sauce on the side.

TONNO ALL'AGRO
Fresh Tuna in Savory Wine Lemon Sauce
Makes 6 servings

Fresh tuna or swordfish, cut thin and sometimes pounded even thinner, is enjoyed in Southern Italy stuffed and rolled up into an *involtino*. The famous Sicilian *involtini* are of swordfish, with a typical Sicilian stuffing containing raisins and *pignoli*; they are broiled on skewers over a wood fire and served simply, without a sauce.

These more complex *involtini* of tuna from Sardegna are marinated a bit with wine vinegar, then sautéed in a savory sauce containing anchovies, white wine, thyme, and bay leaf. The sauce is reduced and the sauced fish served with lemon juice drizzled over and diced tomatoes and more fresh thyme.

2 pounds fresh tuna, in one piece

6 cups cold water

½ cup red wine vinegar

2 small red onions, cleaned

2 medium-size carrots, scraped

2 medium-size stalks celery

3 whole anchovies preserved in salt (see
    Note on page 10), or 6 anchovy fillets
    packed in oil (optional), drained

Fresh thyme leaves or dried thyme
    to taste

Freshly ground black pepper

Salt

½ cup extra virgin olive oil

2 tablespoons (1 ounce) sweet butter

6 bay leaves

About ½ cup unbleached all-purpose flour

1 cup dry white wine

Juice of 1 medium-size lemon

TO SERVE:

1 large ripe tomato, seeded and diced

Fresh thyme leaves

Clean the tuna, removing the skin, and cut it into 6 slices. Combine the water and vinegar in a large crockery or glass bowl, add the tuna, and let soak for half an hour. Finely chop the onions, carrots, and celery together on a cutting board and set aside.

When ready, drain the tuna and dry the slices with paper towels. Lightly pound the slices, placing them between two sheets of wet waxed paper. If using anchovies, place on top of each tuna slice an anchovy fillet cut into four pieces. Season each with a few leaves of fresh thyme or a pinch of dried thyme and a little black pepper. If you do not use anchovies, season with salt and pepper and be more plentiful with the thyme. Roll up each slice and tie like an *involtino* with kitchen string (to tie like a salami, see page 5).

Place a medium-size skillet with the olive oil and butter over medium heat; when the butter is melted, add the chopped onion mixture and the bay leaves. Sauté until the onions are translucent. Lightly flour the *involtini* and add them to the skillet. Cook for 4 minutes, turning the fish several times. Season with salt and pepper. Transfer the fish, not yet completely cooked, to a serving dish and let rest, covered, until needed. Add the wine to the skillet and reduce it by half, about 5 minutes. Place the tuna back in the skillet, turn the slices several times to be sure they are completely coated with the sauce, cover the skillet, and simmer until the *involtini* are completely cooked but still very juicy, 3 to 4 minutes.

Drizzle the lemon juice all over, discard the bay leaves, and transfer the *involtini* to a large serving platter. Spoon the sauce over the fish and sprinkle the diced tomatoes and thyme leaves over. Serve hot.

GAMBERI ALLE ERBE
Shrimp in Herbed Horseradish Sauce

Makes 4 servings

Seafood dishes from Friuli proper rather than Trieste are sometimes made with mountain ingredients; in this case the sauce contains the seeds of mountain fennel, that is, caraway seeds, and the root called *rafano,* the type of horseradish that exists in Italy. Both of these give a distinctive flavor to the shrimp not found in other regions of Italy.

1 large lemon, cut in half

Large pinch of coarse-grained salt

1½ pounds medium-size shrimp, shelled
    and deveined

FOR THE SAUCE:

2 medium-size stalks celery

1 medium-size red onion, cleaned

2 cloves garlic, peeled

20 sprigs fresh Italian parsley, leaves only

1 teaspoon dried marjoram

4 ounces pancetta, in one piece

¼ cup extra virgin olive oil

2 tablespoons (1 ounce) sweet butter

1 tablespoon caraway seeds

2 tablespoons tomato paste, preferably
    imported Italian

1½ cups lukewarm completely defatted
    chicken or meat broth, preferably
    homemade

Salt and freshly ground black pepper

TO COOK THE SHRIMP:

1 tablespoon extra virgin olive oil

1 tablespoon (½ ounce) sweet butter

Salt and freshly ground black pepper

1½ tablespoons peeled and freshly grated
    horseradish

TO SERVE:

15 sprigs fresh Italian parsley, leaves only

Squeeze the lemon halves into a large crockery or glass bowl of cold water, add the coarse salt, and soak the shrimp in it for an hour.

Meanwhile, prepare the sauce. Finely chop the celery, onion, garlic, parsley, and marjoram together on a cutting board. Cut the pancetta into tiny pieces. Place a medium-size casserole with the olive oil and butter over medium heat; when the butter is melted, add the celery mixture and sauté for 5 minutes, stirring every so often with a wooden spoon. Add the pancetta and cook for another 5 minutes, stirring several times.

Meanwhile, use a mortar and pestle to finely grind the caraway seeds. This will take you several minutes, because caraway seeds are quite hard. In a small bowl, dissolve the tomato paste in the broth. Add ½ cup of the tomato broth to the casserole and keep adding broth, waiting each time until it is reduced by half, until it is used up. Season with salt, pepper, and a large pinch of ground caraway seeds.

When the sauce has some body, drain the shrimp and rinse them under cold running water. Place a large skillet with the tablespoons of olive oil and butter over medium heat; when the butter is melted, add the shrimp, season with salt and pepper, and sauté for 1 minute. Pour the prepared sauce over the shrimp, sprinkle the horseradish over that, and cook for 2 to 3 minutes more. Coarsely chop the parsley leaves and serve the shrimp with some of the sauce and some of the chopped parsley.

NOTE: If the horseradish is grated in advance, let it soak in a small bowl of cold water with ¼ cup dry white wine added so it retains its full flavor.

The ingredient list calls for 1 tablespoon caraway seeds but the recipe requires only a pinch of the ground seeds. The reason for the discrepancy is that trying to grind less than 1 tablespoon of caraway seeds at a time is next to impossible.

SICILY

SPIEDINO DI GAMBERI AL MARSALA
Shrimp Wrapped in Pancetta Cooked on Skewers

Makes 6 servings

In Italy, bushes of *alloro*, bay leaf, are so common that they are used to enclose many gardens. A non-Italian friend of mine living in Florence once invited me to a fish lunch and complained that the herb markets had no bay leaves. I suggested that he step outside and pull them off the copious bushes that surrounded the local park, as any Florentine would have done. So it is very easy to find bay leaf branches to use as skewers in Italy. If you cannot find them, use rosemary twigs that are thick enough to use for that purpose.

Several cuisines have shrimp-wrapped-in-bacon dishes, but this Italian version uses the unsmoked type of bacon, which is, of course, the pancetta that is so common in Italian cooking. After cooking the shrimp quickly, the pan is deglazed with the Marsala or brandy and a little broth is added in order to make a delicious sauce.

continued

1 lemon, cut in half

Coarse-grained salt

18 large or jumbo shrimp, shelled and
deveined

18 thin slices pancetta

6 skewers made from branches of the bay
leaf bush with some of the leaves left on
top, or rosemary twigs, or wooden
skewers soaked in water for half an hour

¼ cup (2 ounces) sweet butter

Freshly ground black pepper

1 tablespoon unbleached all-purpose flour

½ cup dry Marsala or brandy

½ cup vegetable or completely defatted
chicken broth, preferably homemade

TO SERVE:

Bay leaf branches or sprigs fresh rosemary

Squeeze the lemon halves into a large crockery or glass bowl of cold water. Add a little salt and soak the shrimp in it for half an hour. Drain the shrimp, rinse, and pat them dry with paper towels. Wrap each shrimp with a slice of pancetta. Thread the shrimp onto the skewers, three per skewer.

Heat the butter in a medium-size skillet over medium heat; when the butter is melted, add the skewers, lightly season with salt and pepper, and sauté until the shrimp are completely cooked, about 3 minutes per side.

Transfer the skewers to a serving platter. Raise the heat under the skillet to medium-high, add the flour, and mix very well with a wooden spoon. After a few seconds, add the Marsala or brandy, mix well again, and cook for 1 minute. Add the broth, taste for salt and pepper, and cook until the sauce is reduced by half. Pour the sauce over the shrimp on the serving platter and serve hot with the bay leaf branches or sprigs of rosemary on the side.

"GAMBARI" ALLA TREVIGIANA
Shrimp, Radicchio, and Beans Treviso Style

Makes 4 servings

The three main ingredients, marjoram, Treviso radicchio, and borlotti beans, all so typical of the Veneto, are combined into a very attractive and delicious dish. Marjoram is the distinguishing herb; many are not aware that marjoram—and thyme—are just as Italian as basil and sage and is used in many dishes, particularly in the northern and central regions.

The long-stemmed Treviso radicchio comes from a town in the Veneto and is sometimes cooked before being used in this dish. Cooking changes the color to a less attractive brownish tone rather than red. And since we have the option of the more attractive uncooked salad, I suggest that. Radicchio, however, is also delicious cooked, whether grilled or sautéed, and the Treviso type is more delicate and less bitter.

1 cup dried borlotti (Roman) beans,
    picked over

6 cups cold water

1 large clove garlic, peeled

1 tablespoon extra virgin olive oil

Coarse-grained salt

1 small head red radicchio, preferably the
    Trevigiano type, thinly sliced

FOR THE SHRIMP:

1 lemon, cut in half

Coarse-grained salt

1½ pounds medium-size shrimp, shelled
    and deveined

3 skewers made from rosemary branches
    or wooden skewers soaked in water for
    half an hour

FOR THE SAUCE:

3 large cloves garlic, peeled

1 heaping tablespoon fresh marjoram leaves

15 sprigs fresh Italian parsley, leaves only

⅓ cup extra virgin olive oil

3 bay leaves

Salt and freshly ground black pepper

TO COOK THE SHRIMP:

About ½ cup unbleached all-purpose flour

Salt and freshly ground black pepper

⅓ cup dry white wine

TO SERVE:

Sprigs fresh marjoram

3 bay leaves

continued

Soak the beans in a bowl of cold water overnight. The next morning bring a small pot with the 6 cups water to a boil. Drain the beans, add them to the water along with the garlic and olive oil, reduce the heat to medium, and simmer for 45 minutes. By that time the beans should be almost cooked. Season with salt and cook another 5 minutes. Drain the beans, place them in a crockery or glass bowl and let rest, covered with a wet kitchen towel or wet paper towels, until needed.

Meanwhile, squeeze the lemon halves into a large crockery or glass bowl of cold water, add a little salt, and soak the shrimp for half an hour.

To make the sauce, finely chop the garlic, marjoram, and parsley together on a cutting board. Heat the olive oil in a large skillet over medium heat; when the oil is warm, add the chopped mixture and the bay leaves and sauté for 1 minute. Season with salt and pepper. Drain the shrimp, pat them dry with paper towels, and thread them onto the skewers.

To cook the shrimp, lightly flour the skewered shrimp and add them to the skillet. Season with salt and pepper and lightly sauté on both sides until cooked, about 2 minutes per side.

Arrange the radicchio as a bed on a serving platter. Transfer the skewers of shrimp to another platter and immediately add the reserved beans to the skillet along with the wine, and let reduce for 2 minutes over high heat.

Place the beans and all the sauce over the radicchio and place the shrimp on top of the beans. Serve with sprigs of fresh marjoram and bay leaves.

GRANSEOLA ALLA TRIESTINA
Crabmeat Trieste Style

Makes 4 main-course or 8 antipasto servings

The large red crabs of the Adriatic have given rise to many special dishes, especially in Veneto and the coastal part of the region of Friuli called Venezia-Giulia. The crabmeat here is simply sautéed with garlic, parsley, and white wine in a most classical treatment of seafood. Venezia-Giulia really has a separate history from mountainous Friuli. Trieste first was ruled by Venice, but when it was annexed by the Austrian Empire, it became a major port until the First World War brought it back to Italy. Its culture is a fascinating mixture of Central European and Mediterranean. Trieste was Austria's only great port and was for a while the second most important port of Europe, just after London. It has its own distinct and important culinary culture, very Italian but different from that of Venice.

2 medium-size cloves garlic, peeled

10 large sprigs fresh Italian parsley, leaves only

½ cup extra virgin olive oil

½ cup very fine unseasoned bread crumbs, preferably homemade, lightly toasted

½ cup dry white wine

Salt and freshly ground black pepper

1 pound lump crabmeat, picked over for cartilage and shells

Finely chop the garlic and parsley together on a cutting board. Heat the olive oil over medium heat in a medium-size heavy casserole or saucepan. When the oil is warm, add the garlic mixture and sauté for 2 minutes, then add the bread crumbs, mix very well with a wooden spoon, and cook, stirring, until the crumbs turn golden, about 2 minutes more. Add the wine and let it reduce for 5 minutes. Taste for salt and add abundant black pepper. Add the crabmeat, mixing very well but gently to amalgamate the sauce with the crabmeat, and let cook for 2 minutes to heat through. Transfer to a serving dish and serve immediately.

VARIATIONS: Omit the bread crumbs and wine.

Don't chop the parsley with the garlic. Place the crabmeat in a serving dish, pour the sautéed garlic-and-crumbs mixture over it, then sprinkle on the uncooked coarsely chopped parsley.

TIELLA DI RISO E VONGOLE
Rice and Clams Cooked in a Clay Pot
Makes 6 to 8 servings

Tiella is the name of the terra-cotta pot used for making this wonderful *amonimous* ("of the same name") layered dish of clams, rice, onions, potatoes, and tomatoes. Clams in Italy are very small; the normal *vongole veraci* are usually smaller than Manila clams, and the treasured *arselle,* common in Tuscany, are even smaller. Littleneck and cherrystone clams are gigantic by comparison, but can be used if Manila or other small types are not available.

Tomatoes, potatoes, and onions are combined in many dishes of diverse Mediterranean cuisines, but this one is really special—so special that the people of Puglia have a pot reserved just for making it. Cherry tomatoes are not used very much in most of Italy, though they are featured in a number of dishes from Puglia. They are almost never used in salads.

1 pound clams (Manila or other very small clams)

½ cup extra virgin olive oil

10 sprigs fresh Italian parsley, leaves only, finely chopped

3 large cloves garlic, peeled and finely chopped

Salt and freshly ground black pepper

1 cup dry white wine

FOR THE LAYERING:

12 ounces raw short-grain rice (1½ heaping dry cups), preferably Italian Arborio

15 sprigs fresh Italian parsley, leaves only, finely chopped

2 large cloves garlic, peeled and finely chopped

½ tablespoon extra virgin olive oil

1 pound red onions, cleaned and very thinly sliced

1 pound all-purpose potatoes, peeled and thinly sliced (about ¼ inch thick)

1 pound cherry tomatoes, cut in half

¼ cup freshly grated Pecorino Romano cheese

Salt and freshly ground black pepper

TO SERVE:

Sprigs fresh Italian parsley

Rinse the clams many times in cold running water. Heat ¼ cup of the olive oil in a medium-size skillet over medium heat; when the oil is warm, add the parsley and garlic mixed together and sauté for a few seconds. Add the clams, increase the heat to high, cover the skillet, and cook for 1 minute, shaking the skillet two or three times. Season with salt and pepper, add the wine, and let evaporate for less than 2 minutes. At this point the clams should be a little undercooked. Transfer the clams, without their juices (reserve these), to a crockery or glass bowl and cover to keep the clams from getting dry. Discard any clams that have not opened.

Preheat the oven to 375 degrees and rinse the rice under cold running water. Transfer the rice to a bowl, add the parsley and garlic, and mix very well.

Lightly oil the *tiella* clay pot or an ovenproof casserole. Use half of the onions to make a layer on the bottom, place half the potatoes over them, and then arrange half the tomatoes over that. Pour all the seasoned rice on top of the tomatoes and sprinkle the cheese over that. Make a layer on top of the cheese with the remaining tomatoes, then with the remaining potatoes, and finally with the remaining onions. Season with salt and pepper.

Mix the reserved clam juices with the remaining ¼ cup olive oil and add enough cold water to make enough liquid to reach half an inch above everything. Bake, covered, for 35 to 45 minutes without mixing or stirring. By that time all the ingredients should be almost cooked. Arrange the clams over the top, cover, and bake another 5 minutes.

Remove the *tiella* from the oven and let it rest for 5 minutes before serving. Serve with the parsley sprigs. This dish may be eaten at room temperature as well.

CALAMARI ALL'ARRABBIATA
Hot and Spicy Calamari

Makes 4 to 6 servings

Fried calamari in tomato sauce with hot red pepper is one of the most classic ways of preparing it. The dish is most characteristic of the Naples area, though it shares the combination of ingredients with Calabria as well. Italians coat calamari very lightly, often just throwing a little flour over it and shaking the colander to remove any excess, as is common in Tuscany. The next lightest coating, as in this recipe, is to dip it in egg after being lightly floured. If the oil is hot enough, the coating should seal instantly and not allow oil to enter, resulting in fried calamari that is crisp, very light, and not greasy. When frying is heavy and unhealthy, it is usually because the cook doesn't know how to fry properly.

In the mid-twentieth century, it became accepted wisdom that it was better to fry with seed vegetable oils than with olive oil, the latter being too heavy. A little olive oil was sometimes included just for flavor. But opinion seems to be changing now, and olive oil is coming back for frying, its supposed heaviness having been revealed as a bit of a myth.

1½ pounds small calamari, cleaned

1 lemon, cut in half

Coarse-grained salt

FOR THE TOMATO SAUCE:

2 pounds ripe tomatoes or canned tomatoes, preferably imported Italian

¼ cup extra virgin olive oil

4 large cloves garlic, peeled

1 large yellow onion, cleaned and thinly sliced

Salt and freshly ground black pepper

Hot red pepper flakes

TO COOK THE CALAMARI:

2 cups vegetable oil (½ sunflower oil and ½ corn oil)

1 cup extra virgin olive oil

3 extra-large eggs

Pinch of salt

About 1½ cups unbleached all-purpose flour

TO SERVE:

20 sprigs fresh Italian parsley, leaves only

3 large cloves garlic, peeled and chopped

Cut the stomach of the calamari into about 1-inch-thick rings. Squeeze the lemon halves into a bowl of cold water, add the salt and the calamari, and soak for half an hour.

Meanwhile, prepare the sauce. If fresh tomatoes are used, cut them into large pieces. Place the fresh or canned tomatoes, olive oil, and garlic in a medium-size nonreactive skillet set over medium heat. Cook, stirring with a wooden spoon every so often. Soak the onion slices in a bowl of cold water for 15 minutes, drain, and add to the tomato sauce. Season with salt and black and red pepper. Cook until onions are translucent and almost fully cooked, but not overcooked, adding a little lukewarm water if the sauce becomes too dry. The tomatoes should not be allowed to fall completely apart. Finely chop the parsley and garlic together on a cutting board.

When ready, drain the calamari rings, rinse them under cold running water, and pat them dry with paper towels. Heat the vegetable oil and olive oil together in a deep-fryer or large skillet over medium heat. Use a fork to very lightly beat the eggs together with the salt in a small bowl. When the oil is hot, about 400 degrees, put the calamari in a large colander, pour the flour over the calamari, and vigorously shake the colander to remove the excess flour. Dip each piece of fish in the beaten eggs, then add to the hot oil. Add enough calamari to have only one layer in the skillet. Cook until the rings are golden all over, 3 to 4 minutes for small calamari. Use a slotted spoon to transfer them to a platter lined with paper towels in order to remove excess oil. Repeat with the remainder.

Arrange the tomato sauce on a large platter, transfer the calamari onto it, then sprinkle with the parsley leaves and garlic and serve hot.

POULTRY

❖

POLLO ALLA CALABRESE
Baked Chicken Calabrian Style

Makes 6 servings

This very savory Calabrian chicken dish layers sliced potatoes, chicken pieces, and sliced tomatoes and covers them with a sauce of olive oil, oregano, and black and red pepper. Baked, covered, the three main ingredients emerge perfectly cooked and having absorbed each other's flavors. As most Calabrian dishes are, it is quite spicy. In some regions a whole fish is sometimes baked between the potato and tomato slices, though not always as highly spiced.

1 pound all-purpose potatoes (not new potatoes)

1 chicken (about 3 pounds), washed, patted dry with paper towels, and cut into 12 pieces

1½ pounds ripe tomatoes

¾ cup extra virgin olive oil

3 large cloves garlic, peeled and coarsely chopped

Large pinch of hot red pepper flakes

Large pinch of dried oregano

Salt and freshly ground black pepper

TO SERVE:

25 large sprigs fresh Italian parsley, leaves only, coarsely chopped

Peel the potatoes and cut them into slices less than ½ inch thick. Heavily oil a terra-cotta or glass baking dish and layer the potatoes in the bottom of it. Place the chicken pieces over the potatoes. Cut the tomatoes into slices the same thickness as the potatoes and arrange them over the chicken. Preheat the oven to 375 degrees.

In a small crockery or glass bowl, mix the olive oil, garlic, red pepper flakes, and oregano together, season with salt and pepper, and pour the mixture over the tomatoes in the baking dish. Bake, covered, for 50 minutes; by that time the chicken should be cooked and very juicy and the potatoes and tomatoes tender. Sometimes at this point in Calabria the potatoes and tomatoes are roughly mashed together with a fork. Serve directly from the baking dish, sprinkling the parsley over each serving.

POLLO E RISO ALLA CACCIATORA
Chicken and Rice Hunter Style

Makes 6 to 8 servings

Unlike the many types of *paella* in Spain, Italian dishes in which the rice is combined with the meat or fish as part of a single dish are very rare. Rice, like pasta, usually forms a dish in itself, with its own sauces and seasonings, whether as risotto or employing other methods of cooking. A very close pairing is the Milanese *ossobuco*, which is eaten together with *risotto alla Milanese*, often on the same plate, but which are prepared separately and simply eaten together. The most notable combination dish is the *tiella* from the Puglia region (page 210), in which the rice is cooked with the clams. Another is this dish, in which chicken is combined with rice.

In the many regional versions of chicken *alla cacciatora*, the fowl, cut up but on the bone, is prepared quickly, with ingredients that are readily available in that area, in a manner that is practical for people who are busy hunting.

1 large chicken (about 3½ pounds), washed
    and patted dry with paper towels
3 large cloves garlic, peeled
15 sprigs fresh Italian parsley, leaves only
4 ounces pancetta or prosciutto, in one
    piece
3 tablespoons extra virgin olive oil
1 tablespoon (½ ounce) sweet butter, cut
    into pats

Salt and freshly ground black pepper
Coarse-grained salt
¾ cup raw short-grain rice, preferably
    Italian Arborio
About 1½ cups completely defatted chicken
    broth, preferably homemade
¼ cup freshly grated Parmigiano cheese
Fresh Italian parsley and basil leaves

Cut the chicken into 8 pieces. Finely chop the garlic and parsley together on a cutting board. Coarsely grind the pancetta or prosciutto, using a meat grinder. Place a casserole (large enough to arrange the chicken in a single layer) with the olive oil over low heat; when the oil is warm, add the ground pancetta and sauté for 2 minutes. Then add the garlic mixture, stir, arrange the chicken pieces in the casserole in a single layer, and sauté for 2 minutes. Turn the chicken pieces, arrange the pats of butter all over them, and season with salt and pepper.

Meanwhile, place a medium-size saucepan of cold water over medium heat and when the water reaches a boil, add coarse salt to taste, then the rice. Stir and cook the rice for 15 minutes. As the rice cooks, continue browning the chicken on all sides. When the rice is ready, the chicken should be almost cooked.

Drain the rice, arrange it over the chicken, and pour in the broth. Let simmer until chicken and rice are perfectly cooked and all the broth is completely absorbed, about 5 minutes. Sprinkle the Parmigiano all over, mix very well, and transfer the contents of the casserole to a large warmed serving platter. Serve hot with the parsley and basil leaves sprinkled over.

POLLO ALLE CIPOLLE
Savory Chicken "Spezzatino"

Makes 4 to 6 servings

Chicken cut up on the bone is cooked with a great variety of sauces, and this important category is called *spezzatino*. This recipe combines many ingredients—onions, yellow and red peppers, bay leaves, hot red pepper and black peppercorns, and both red wine vinegar and white wine. The results are very savory, indeed, the flavors integrating into a wonderful unity.

FOR THE SAUCE:

1 very large or 2 medium-size red onions, cleaned

3 tablespoons extra virgin olive oil

3 bay leaves

Salt and freshly ground black pepper

Large pinch of hot red pepper flakes

¾ cup cold water

¾ cup dry white wine

¾ cup red wine vinegar; if very strong, use ½ cup

15 black peppercorns

1 large yellow bell pepper

1 large red bell pepper

FOR THE CHICKEN:

1 large chicken (about 3½ pounds), washed, patted dry with paper towels, and cut into 16 pieces

3 tablespoons extra virgin olive oil

Salt and freshly ground black pepper

TO SERVE:

Fresh Italian parsley leaves

Preheat the oven to 400 degrees.

Prepare the sauce. Thinly slice the onions and soak them in a bowl of cold water to remove the bitter taste. Heat the oil in a large skillet over medium heat; when the oil is warm, drain the onions and add them to the skillet along with the bay leaves. Sauté for 15 minutes until very light in color, stirring every so often with a wooden spoon. Season with salt, black pepper, and red pepper flakes. Add the water, wine, and vinegar and cook until reduced by half, about 20 minutes.

While the onions are reducing, remove all the fat from the chicken, pour the olive oil into a large baking dish, and arrange the chicken pieces over the oil. Sprinkle with salt and pepper and bake for 20 minutes.

As the chicken is baking, add the peppercorns to the sauce and mix very well. Cut the peppers into ¼-inch-thick rings, discarding the stems and seeds, and soak the rings in a bowl of cold water for 10 minutes.

Return to the chicken. Turn the pieces over, season with more salt and pepper, and bake for another 20 minutes. Meanwhile, the onions should have become quite soft and the liquid reduced by one third.

Drain the pepper rings, mix well with the onion mixture, cover and cook until the peppers are soft, about 15 minutes more, adding some lukewarm water as needed.

When the sauce is ready, the chicken should be cooked through and golden.

Remove the chicken from the oven, using a slotted spoon to transfer to a large serving platter. Discard the cooking juices, pour the onion sauce over the chicken, sprinkle the parsley leaves over the top, and serve hot.

TUSCANY

POLLO RIPIENO ALLA LUNIGIANA
Poached Boned Stuffed Chicken

Makes 6 to 8 servings

This ambitious preparation survives from the Renaissance boiled course served at important banquets, when the *serviti*, or courses, each consisted of about thirty dishes—hot and cold *antipasti*, the boiled course, the fried or roasted course, and sweets.

The chicken is boned but left whole, stuffed with spinach and/or chard, with ricotta used as the binder, and poached with aromatic vegetables. It is the clove and cinnamon that reveal the Renaissance origins of the dish. The green herb sauce is one of many *salse verdi* that were developed in that period, some of which, like Tuscan *salsa verde* and Ligurian pesto, are still very much in use. Its unusual ingredient is ground carrot.

The whole stuffed chicken, with its green sauce and the sweet and hot *mostarda* with preserved whole fruits, should make an impressive presentation for a formal dinner.

This dish survives in the Lunigiana area of Tuscany.

1 chicken (about 3½ pounds) with the neck and feet left on if possible

FOR THE STUFFING:

2 pounds fresh spinach (see Note), large stems removed

2 pounds fresh Swiss chard (see Note), large stems removed

Coarse-grained salt

½ pound ricotta, very well drained

4 ounces Parmigiano cheese, freshly grated

4 ounces Pecorino Romano cheese, freshly grated

Freshly ground black pepper

Freshly grated nutmeg

4 extra-large eggs

FOR THE POACHING BROTH:

15 cups cold water

All the bones from the boned chicken and its neck and feet if available

1 carrot, scraped and cut into large pieces

1 large red onion, cleaned and quartered

2 stalks celery, cut into large pieces

2 cloves garlic, peeled

5 sprigs fresh Italian parsley

Coarse-grained salt

1 clove

Pinch of ground cinnamon

TO WRAP THE CHICKEN:

¼ pound sliced prosciutto

FOR THE *SALSA VERDE* (GREEN SAUCE):

15 sprigs fresh Italian parsley, leaves only

5 medium-size fresh basil leaves

1 small clove garlic, peeled

2 medium-size carrots, scraped

3 tablespoons capers in wine vinegar, drained

Salt and freshly ground black pepper

¾ cup extra virgin olive oil

1 tablespoon fresh lemon juice

TO SERVE:

Mostarda di cremona (sold in bottles at gourmet shops)

Detach the neck and feet from the chicken and set them aside. Bone the chicken from inside the cavity, without cutting the skin. To do this, first cut the two tendons at the end of each of the two legs. Free the bone on the inside by hand (there is nothing to cut here) and push out a little bit. Free each thigh bone by cutting the tendon between the leg and thigh. Push the thigh bone from one end and pull from the other. Starting from the cavity end, with a knife, little by little scrape the meat without breaking it off the inside of the central carcass. Remove the large central bone in one piece. Cut off the two outer sections of each wing. Remove the bone and the inner section in the same way you did the legs. Tuck the legs and wings inside.

Prepare the stuffing. Soak the spinach and Swiss chard in a large bowl of cold water for half an hour. Bring a large pot of cold water to a boil and add salt to taste. Drain and rinse the greens and add them to the pot to boil for 5 minutes; they should be very soft. (Boiled in a large amount of salted water, they will keep their green color very well.) Drain, cool under cold running water, and lightly squeeze them to remove excess water. Finely chop the greens on a cutting board, then transfer to a crockery or glass bowl. Add the ricotta, Parmigiano, and Pecorino and mix very well. Season with salt, pepper, and nutmeg and add the eggs. Mix very well, using a wooden spoon. Let the stuffing rest, covered, in the refrigerator until needed.

As you assemble the stuffing, prepare the poaching broth. Bring the water to a simmer in a large casserole over medium heat. Add all the bones from the chicken and its neck and feet if available and the carrot, onion, celery, garlic, and parsley. Simmer for 25 minutes, then season with salt. Simmer another 15 minutes. Remove from the heat and let the broth rest in its pot until lukewarm, about half an hour.

Stuff the chicken. With a trussing needle, sew up all the cavities but one. Use a spoon or a pastry bag to fill the chicken completely with the prepared stuffing. Do not overstuff it, or the skin will break while poaching. Sew up the last opening. Wrap the chicken with the prosciutto slices, then wrap it in cheesecloth, and tie it like a salami (see page 5). Place the chicken in the poaching broth, add the clove and cinnamon, set the casserole over medium heat, and simmer until tender and cooked through, about 45 minutes. Let the chicken rest in the broth for 15 minutes, then transfer it to a flat serving platter and place a weight of about 6 pounds on it. Let rest for 1 hour, then refrigerate, the weight still on it, overnight.

Prepare the *salsa verde*. Place the parsley, basil, garlic, carrots, and capers in a blender or food processor and process almost to a paste. Transfer to a small crockery or glass bowl, season with salt and pepper, pour in the olive oil and lemon juice, and mix very well. Refrigerate, covered, until needed.

The next day, unwrap the chicken, discard the prosciutto slices, and cut it into slices less than ½ inch thick. The chicken may also be sliced and served lukewarm after resting only 15 minutes, but the slicing will be more difficult and so the slices should be thicker. Serve the chicken slices with some of the *salsa verde* and *mostarda di Cremona* (fruit mustard from Cremona).

NOTE: Instead of using equal amounts of spinach and Swiss chard, you can use 4 pounds of either spinach or Swiss chard.

POLPETTONE VESTITO
Wrapped Chicken Loaf
Makes 8 servings

This is a galantine in which the forcemeat is wrapped only in the skin of the chicken rather than in the chicken opened down the back, boned, and stuffed. This type of galantine is eaten warm, unlike the usual type, which is served cold. However, it has a succulent sauce made from porcini mushrooms, some of which is mixed with the stuffing of ground veal and chicken breast, while the rest is served as a dressing for the slices of the *polpettone*.

There is an excellent alternate sauce, made with green peppercorns, which are peppercorns that have not yet dried. They therefore must be preserved in brine and have quite a different flavor from the dried black peppercorns. The fresh green ones are always used whole or smashed and cannot be ground like black peppercorns.

The slices of *polpettone* may be "remade" as delicious cutlets by dipping them in egg and frying them. Eaten hot, they become a completely new dish.

FOR THE MUSHROOM SAUCE:

2 ounces dried porcini mushrooms

3 cups lukewarm water

1 large clove garlic, peeled

10 sprigs fresh Italian parsley, leaves only

¼ cup extra virgin olive oil

Salt and freshly ground black pepper

1 tablespoon fresh thyme leaves or large pinch of dried thyme

½ cup dry red wine

3 tablespoons tomato paste, preferably imported Italian

1½ cups completely defatted chicken or meat broth, preferably homemade

FOR THE CHICKEN LOAF:

1 chicken (about 3½ pounds), washed and patted dry with paper towels

¼ pound sliced prosciutto

1 pound ground veal or additional ground chicken breast

1 cup heavy cream

Salt and freshly ground black pepper

TO BAKE THE CHICKEN:

1 teaspoon extra virgin olive oil

TO SERVE:

Sprigs fresh thyme

continued

Soak the mushrooms in the lukewarm water for half an hour. Meanwhile, finely chop the garlic and parsley together on a cutting board. Remove the mushrooms from the water and clean them, removing all the sand attached to the stems, then coarsely chop them. Clean the soaking water by passing it several times through a double thickness of paper towels or a coffee filter. The water should be absolutely clear with no sand at all.

Place a medium-size nonreactive saucepan with the olive oil over low heat; when the oil is lukewarm, add the chopped garlic mixture and sauté for 5 minutes. Add the mushrooms and sauté for another 5 minutes. Season with salt and pepper and add the thyme. Pour in the wine and let it evaporate for 5 minutes. Start pouring in the mushroom water ½ cup at a time. Dissolve the tomato paste in the broth and when all the water from the mushrooms has been used up, start adding the broth ½ cup at a time. When the broth has been added, the sauce should have a smooth but not very thick consistency. Remove from the heat and measure out a scant ½ cup of the solids of the sauce.

Bone the chicken. Cut through the two tendons at the end of the two legs. Cut the skin of the chicken lengthwise down the back and, using a paring knife, carefully remove the entire skin in one piece. It is this skin, and the breast meat, that you want for the dish, so save the rest of the chicken for another use.

Spread the skin out on a board with the inside facing up. Cover the skin completely with a layer of all the prosciutto slices. Remove the skinned breast from the chicken and coarsely grind it in a meat grinder into a crockery or glass bowl. Add the ground veal or chicken breast, then the heavy cream along with the ½ cup of the mushroom sauce. Season with salt and pepper. Mix the ingredients together very well with a wooden spoon. Transfer the stuffing onto one end of the prepared chicken skin and roll it up like a salami (see page 5). Oil the shiny side of a large sheet of aluminum foil and place the wrapped meat loaf on the prepared foil. Wrap it completely like a package and refrigerate it for half an hour (in this way you prevent the cream from leaking).

Preheat the oven to 375 degrees. Bake the loaf in a baking dish for 1 hour, turning the package once. Remove from the oven and let rest, wrapped, for half an hour.

Reheat the sauce, skimming off the extra oil from the top, then unwrap the meat and cut it into eight slices. For each serving, place one slice of the loaf on one side of the plate and spoon the sauce onto the other side, then serve with a sprig of fresh thyme over the meat.

VARIATION: You can prepare the *polpettone* without adding the mushroom sauce to the stuffing, or you may add ½ cup of the alternative sauce that follows.

SALSA AL PEPE VERDE

Green Peppercorn Sauce

Makes 8 servings

3 tablespoons green peppercorns preserved in brine, drained and rinsed

¼ cup extra virgin olive oil

Salt and freshly ground black pepper

1 medium-size clove garlic, peeled and finely chopped

2 tablespoons (1 ounce) sweet butter, at room temperature

1 flat tablespoon unbleached all-purpose flour

1 scant cup lukewarm completely defatted chicken or meat broth, preferably homemade

1 tablespoon fresh lemon juice

1 tablespoon red wine vinegar

Finely chop the peppercorns on a cutting board and transfer to a small crockery or glass bowl. Add the olive oil and season with salt and pepper. Mix well with a wooden spoon and let stand until needed.

Place the chopped garlic in another small crockery or glass bowl. Add the butter and flour and combine with a fork until a thick paste is formed. Then add the broth, lemon juice, and vinegar and mix again with a wooden spoon, adding a pinch of salt and pepper.

Place the chopped peppercorn mixture in a small heavy saucepan and set it over low heat. Sauté gently for 2 or 3 minutes, stirring occasionally with a wooden spoon. Then add the garlic mixture and combine very well to be sure no lumps remain. Simmer for about 10 minutes. By that time a smooth sauce should have formed. Serve hot with the *polpettone*.

COTOLETTE DI POLPETTONE VESTITO
Chicken Loaf Cutlets

Makes 8 servings

1 *Polpettone Vestito* (page 219), baked and left
  to rest in the refrigerator overnight

2 extra-large eggs

Pinch of salt

1 cup vegetable oil (½ sunflower oil and
  ½ corn oil)

1 cup very fine unseasoned bread crumbs,
  preferably homemade, lightly toasted

TO SERVE:

Enough arugula leaves to make a bed on a
  serving platter

Fine salt

1 lemon, cut into wedges

Cut the cold *polpettone* into six slices. Using a fork, lightly beat the eggs with the salt in a small bowl.

Heat the vegetable oil in a large heavy skillet over medium heat. When the oil is hot, about 375 degrees, dip the *cotolette* into the eggs, then coat them evenly with the bread crumbs. Fry them until lightly golden on both sides. Transfer to a serving platter lined with paper towels to absorb excess oil. When all the *cotolette* are fried, transfer them to the platter containing the arugula. Sprinkle some fine salt over them and serve hot with the lemon wedges.

❖

ANITRA RIPIENA DI FARRO

Duck Stuffed with Farro

Makes 6 servings

The duck, with the bones left in, is stuffed with the wonderful soft wheatberries called *farro* in Italian, spelt in English. These are first boiled, then seasoned with ground prosciutto, garlic, rosemary, and olive oil and placed in the cavity. The duck is then sewn up and browned by sautéing, then baked for almost two hours. No fat should be removed while baking. The duck emerges very crisp, with all the fat rendered and the bird itself greaseless.

The duck is carved in a most interesting way. It is cut through—meat, bones, and stuffing—and served as rings, with the boiled and sautéed carrots on the side.

1 duck (about 5 pounds), Long Island type

FOR THE STUFFING:

4 ounces (¾ cup) raw farro (page 19)

Coarse-grained salt

3 ounces prosciutto or pancetta, in one
    piece

3 tablespoons rosemary leaves, fresh or
    preserved in salt (page 2)

3 large cloves garlic, peeled

Salt and freshly ground black pepper

2 tablespoons extra virgin olive oil

FOR COOKING:

¼ cup extra virgin olive oil

Salt and freshly ground black pepper

TO ACCOMPANY THE DUCK:

2 pounds carrots, tops removed

Coarse-grained salt

2 tablespoons extra virgin olive oil

Salt and freshly ground black pepper

2 tablespoons very fine unseasoned bread
    crumbs (optional), preferably
    homemade, lightly toasted

Wash the duck very well, pulling off any fat inside the cavity. Pat dry with paper towels and set aside.

Prepare the stuffing. Soak the farro in a bowl of cold water for 45 minutes. Then bring a large saucepan of cold water to a boil, add coarse salt to taste, drain the farro, and add it to the boiling water. Reduce the heat to medium and simmer for 45 minutes. Drain the farro and place it in a small crockery or glass bowl to cool completely, covered with a dampened kitchen towel or paper towel, about half an hour. Finely process the prosciutto or pancetta, rosemary, and garlic together. Put the ground mixture in a medium-size crockery or glass bowl, season with salt and pepper, and add the olive oil. Stir very well, then add the cooled farro and mix again.

continued

Transfer the stuffing to the cavity of the duck, stuffing it loosely, and sew up the cavity, using a normal-size needle, *not* a trussing needle, and plain white thread for normal sewing. Then, tie the duck with string so that the wings and legs are pulled tightly against the body.

To cook the duck, heat the olive oil in a large casserole over medium heat. When the oil is warm, put in the duck, season with salt and pepper, and sauté until lightly golden all over. Preheat the oven to 450 degrees. Transfer the duck to a roasting pan, breast side up, and bake for 1 hour and 45 minutes, turning the duck over two or three times. Do not remove any fat while baking.

Meanwhile, boil the carrots with their skins on in coarse-salted water to cover until tender, then, when cool enough to handle, remove the skins and cut them into large pieces. Transfer the cooked duck to a cutting board, remove the string, and, using poultry shears, detach the legs and wings. Then use the shears to cut the duck into 2-inch-thick disks, cutting across through meat, bones, and stuffing, producing attractive self-contained portions that have dark meat, breast, and stuffing.

To finish the carrots, heat the olive oil and 2 tablespoons of the duck juices over medium heat in a large saucepan. Add the carrots and lightly sauté until heated through. Season with salt and pepper and, if you choose, sprinkle the bread crumbs over them. Serve the duck with some of the carrots on one side.

FARAONA ALLA CRETA ALLA FRIULANA
Guinea Hen Baked in Cabbage Leaves

Makes 4 servings

Guinea fowl is much used in Italy as an alternative to chicken. It is not, strictly speaking, a game bird. The name comes from the word for pharaoh, as it was reputed to be the great favorite of the ancient Egyptian rulers. *Creta* refers to a kind of clay that contains nothing toxic and may be used to wrap food for baking in a brick oven. With such a wrapping, the bird loses none of its juices. While it comes from the Siena area in Tuscany, which has the most celebrated clay for terra-cotta and many dishes made in this manner, here we have a version from Friuli, in which the guinea hen is first wrapped in cabbage and then covered. Since it is not easy to obtain completely nontoxic clay that is safe for food in the United States, this adaptation uses a crust that becomes very hard and is not to be eaten, but that seals in the juices in the same manner as the *creta*.

1 guinea hen, washed and patted dry with
    paper towels
2 cups dry white wine
4 teaspoons grappa or brandy
4 ounces prosciutto, in one piece
1 head Savoy cabbage (about 3 pounds)
Coarse-grained salt
¼ cup extra virgin olive oil
6 bay leaves
6 medium-size cloves garlic, peeled
Salt and freshly ground black pepper
Large pinch of freshly ground caraway seeds
    (see Note)

2 sweet Italian sausages without fennel
    seeds, or 6 ounces ground pork
    seasoned with salt and freshly ground
    black pepper

FOR THE CRUST:
4 cups unbleached all-purpose flour
1½ cups fine salt

TO SERVE:
¼ cup peeled and freshly grated horseradish
¼ cup white wine vinegar or fresh lemon
    juice
Fresh Italian parsley leaves

Cut the guinea hen into four pieces. In a crockery or glass bowl, marinate the hen in the wine for 2 hours in a cool place or in the bottom part of your refrigerator. Drain the hen and discard the wine. Place the hen pieces on a serving platter and pour 1 teaspoon of the grappa or brandy over each piece. Let rest until needed.

continued

Coarsely grind the prosciutto, then clean the cabbage, detaching all the leaves and discarding the very tough ones. Bring a large pot of cold water to a boil, add coarse salt to taste, and blanch the leaves four or five at a time in the boiling water for about 20 seconds. As the leaves are ready, transfer them to a bowl of cold water to cool, then onto paper towels or cotton kitchen towels dampened in cold water. Continue until all the leaves are on the towels.

Preheat the oven to 400 degrees. Place a large skillet with the olive oil over medium heat; when the oil is warm, add the ground prosciutto and cook for 2 minutes, stirring every so often with a wooden spoon. Put in the hen, bay leaves, and garlic cloves and cook until lightly golden on all sides. Season with salt and pepper and a pinch of ground caraway seeds. Transfer the hen with all the juices to a serving platter, discarding the bay leaves but keeping the garlic.

Spread two large sheets of parchment paper on a serving platter. Remove the tough middle vein from the blanched cabbage leaves and stack them. Arrange half of the leaves in a thick layer on the parchment. Place the hen pieces over the cabbage and pour on most of the juices. Remove the casings from the sausages and crumble the meat all over the hen. Use the other half of the cabbage leaves to make a layer over the hen. Wrap the parchment around the cabbage and hen, making a package.

Prepare the crust by arranging the flour in a mound on a work surface and making a well in the center of it. Place the salt and enough water in the well to form a very rough dough once you incorporate the flour into it. Knead for a few seconds, then use a rolling pin to roll it out into a ½-inch-thick layer. Wrap the package of cabbage and hen in the dough, being careful that there are no holes. Then transfer the wrapped package to a jelly-roll pan to bake for 1 hour. By that time the crust will have the consistency almost of a brick. Remove from the oven and let rest for 2 minutes. Then hit the crust with a hammer or something similar to open and remove it. Unwrap the parchment to reveal an incredibly succulent fowl that has kept all its juices and its flavor sealed within. Transfer the cabbage and hen to a serving platter. Serve the meat with some cabbage and juices and with the horseradish mixed with vinegar on one side and parsley leaves sprinkled on top.

NOTE: Caraway seeds are very hard and difficult to grind; they must be ground using a mortar and pestle, both made of marble. You'll find it impossible to grind less than 1 tablespoon of the seeds at a time. These seeds of what is called "mountain fennel" in Italian are typical of the cooking of mountainous areas such as Friuli.

POLENTA CON TOCCO DI FUNGHI ALLA GENOVESE
Polenta with Mushroom Meat Sauce

Makes 6 servings

Stone-ground cornmeal is cooked with pancetta, onion, and sage, then dressed with a uniquely Genoese meat sauce made from a solid piece of meat that is long-cooked with aromatic vegetables and herbs in red wine and broth and, most important, with dried porcini mushrooms. But the meat is not served in this dish, though it may be eaten at another meal. There are no pieces of meat in the sauce at all, just its essence. Typical of Genoese cooking is the use of the dried porcini mushrooms and their soaking water. The Genoese love to refer to their sauces as *con tocco di. . . ,* meaning "with a touch of . . . ," as in this case, "with a touch of mushrooms."

1 ounce dried porcini mushrooms

3 cups lukewarm water

1 pound boneless top sirloin, in one piece

2 tablespoons extra virgin olive oil

¼ cup (2 ounces) sweet butter

1 medium-size red onion, cleaned

1 medium-size carrot, scraped

15 sprigs fresh Italian parsley, leaves only

1 cup dry red wine

1 tablespoon unbleached all-purpose flour

1 pound drained canned tomatoes,
    preferably imported Italian

Completely defatted chicken or meat broth,
    preferably homemade, as needed

Salt and freshly ground black pepper

FOR THE POLENTA:

4 ounces pancetta, in one piece

2 fresh sage leaves

1 medium-size red onion, cleaned

¼ cup (2 ounces) sweet butter

1 tablespoon extra virgin olive oil

3 cups cold water or completely defatted
    chicken or meat broth, preferably
    homemade

1 cup coarse stone-ground yellow Italian
    cornmeal

Salt and freshly ground black pepper

TO SERVE:

Freshly grated Parmigiano cheese

Fresh Italian parsley leaves, coarsely chopped

continued

Soak the mushrooms in the lukewarm water for 30 minutes. Tie the meat like a salami (see page 5) if the butcher has not done so. Place a medium-size nonreactive casserole with the olive oil and butter over medium heat; when the butter is melted, add the meat and lightly brown all over. Finely chop the onion, carrot, and parsley together on a cutting board and add them to the casserole. Add the wine to the casserole and let evaporate for 10 minutes, turning the meat over two or three times. When ready, sprinkle the flour over the sautéed vegetables and mix very well. Cut the canned tomatoes in half without removing the seeds and add them to the casserole. Meanwhile, clean the mushrooms very well, removing all the sand attached to the stems, and strain the soaking water by passing it several times through paper towels or a coffee filter. Add the mushrooms, whole or coarsely chopped, to the casserole and enough broth to cover the meat completely, and season with salt and pepper. If you wish, you can also add some of the mushroom soaking water. Cover the casserole and simmer for 2 hours.

Start preparing the polenta when the sauce still has an hour to cook so they may be ready at the same time. Finely grind or chop the pancetta and sage leaves together and finely chop the onion. Place the butter and olive oil in a medium-size stockpot over medium heat; when the butter is melted, add the pancetta mixture and onion and sauté for 3 or 4 minutes. Add the water or broth and simmer for 15 minutes. Dissolve the cornmeal in the cold water and add it to the stockpot. Mix very well with a wooden spoon and keep stirring until the polenta reaches a boil, then reduce the heat to a simmer. Since this type of polenta is not very thick, you can stir only occasionally to be sure it does not stick to the bottom of the pot. The cooking time is 45 minutes from the time you add the cornmeal. The finished polenta should be a very uniform paste. Season with salt and pepper.

When the sauce is ready, remove the meat (use it for a different preparation) and pass the sauce through a food mill fitted with the disk with the smallest holes into a another, clean saucepan to reduce over medium heat to a rather thick sauce. When the polenta is ready, taste for salt and pepper and immediately ladle the polenta into individual serving bowls and pour some of the sauce over it. Top with the Parmigiano and parsley.

BEEF AND VEAL

❖

GOLAS ALLA FRIULANA
Goulash Friuli Style

Makes 6 servings

Friuli was ruled by the Hapsburg family, rulers of Austria as kings, emperors of Austria-Hungary, and even Holy Roman emperors, from the fourteenth century until 1918. So we should not be surprised that it shares certain traditions with Hungary. The Tocai wine, aside from the name, however, is not one of them. Hungarian Tokay is made from a different grape, and the Italian version of the name has existed since the early Middle Ages.

But undoubtedly *golas* and goulash are cousins. Paprika was developed by the Hungarians from a pepper brought back from the Americas and went into *golas* along with onions, tomatoes (also a new American addition), garlic, and the authentic potato (another New World import) accompaniment. But *golas* is not simply a copy of goulash, and it should be enjoyed for its own sake. To compare and contrast it to goulash, as described by the great expert on Hungarian food George Lang, it has wine and a little flour, both inauthentic to the true Hungarian version, butter and olive oil rather than the Hungarian lard, no green peppers, and a host of more familiar Italian ingredients such as several fresh herbs rather than the required caraway seeds, aromatic vegetables along with the onions, plus a different cut of beef, the shank, very typical of Friuli itself, which also specializes in whole veal shank and in pork shank.

Enjoy your *golas*!

2 pounds boneless beef shanks

3 medium-size red onions, cleaned

1 large stalk celery

1 medium-size clove garlic, peeled

1 large carrot, scraped

1½ teaspoons rosemary leaves, fresh or
    preserved in salt (page 2)

½ cup extra virgin olive oil

2 tablespoons (1 ounce) sweet butter

1 teaspoon fresh marjoram leaves or pinch
    of dried marjoram

3 cloves

1 bay leaf

5 cups cold water

1½ teaspoons hot paprika

1 tablespoon sweet paprika

1 tablespoon unbleached all-purpose flour

2 tablespoons tomato paste, preferably
    imported Italian

1 cup dry red wine

Salt

1½ pounds boiling potatoes (don't use new
    potatoes)

Coarse-grained salt

Cut the beef into 2-inch cubes. Finely chop the onions, celery, garlic, carrot, and rosemary together on a cutting board. Place a large heavy nonreactive casserole, preferably made of enamel, over medium heat with the olive oil and butter; when the butter is melted, add the onion mixture along with the marjoram, cloves, and bay leaf. Sauté until the onions are translucent, continuously stirring with a wooden spoon.

Meanwhile, bring the cold water to a boil in a small saucepan, then add both paprikas. Mix well with a wooden spoon, then remove the pan from the heat. When the vegetables are sautéed, add the meat cubes to the casserole and sprinkle the flour over them. Mix until the flour is well incorporated, then sauté for another 5 minutes. Add the tomato paste along with the wine and let the wine evaporate for 5 minutes. Then add the hot paprika water and simmer, uncovered, for 1 hour. Taste for salt, then let cook another 45 minutes.

Meanwhile, bring a large pot of cold water to a boil. Peel the potatoes and cut them into 2-inch cubes. When the water reaches a boil, add coarse salt to taste and then the potatoes and cook for 5 minutes. Drain the potatoes and add them to the casserole containing the meat. Mix well but gently, cover, and cook 10 minutes more. At that point the meat should be tender and a thick sauce formed. Discard the bay leaf, transfer the contents of the casserole to a large serving dish, and serve.

BRASATO AL BAROLO
Rump Roast Cooked in Barolo Wine
Makes 10 to 12 servings

The *brasato*, which roughly means "braised," is of the category of *stracotto* roasts, which exist in variant versions in most regions that produce full-bodied red wines. It involves a cut of meat, in this case rump of beef, which must be cooked for a very long time in a great deal of wine. The wine must be a "big" red, very full-bodied and capable of long aging. Barolo is one of the greatest of big Italian reds and, aside from the pleasure of drinking it, it is perfect for cooking a *stracotto*. It is not surprising that there are many variants of this recipe.

Perhaps the most celebrated Barolo is the one made on the estates of the Marchese Barolo, from which the wine got its name. Made from the Nebbiolo grape, it is one of the aristocrats of Italian wines.

Because the meat of a *stracotto* is usually quite dry, it is best to lard it and, in this recipe, even to coat it with butter during cooking.

2 ounces pancetta, in one piece, cut into thin strips

One 4-pound rump roast

10 sprigs fresh Italian parsley, leaves only

5 sage leaves, fresh or preserved in salt (page 2)

1 tablespoon rosemary leaves, fresh or preserved in salt (page 2)

2 medium-size cloves garlic, peeled

3 tablespoons (1½ ounces) sweet butter, at room temperature

Salt and freshly ground black pepper

Freshly grated nutmeg

½ cup unbleached all-purpose flour

FOR THE SAUCE:

1 large red onion, cleaned

2 medium-size carrots, scraped

1 stalk celery

4 bay leaves

¼ cup (2 ounces) sweet butter, at room temperature

2 tablespoons extra virgin olive oil

2 tablespoons unbleached all-purpose flour

1 cup dry red wine, preferably Barolo

1 bottle Barolo

Salt and freshly ground black pepper

continued

Insert the pancetta strips, one at a time, onto the larding needle, then thread the needle through the meat, leaving behind the pancetta. Finely chop the parsley, sage, rosemary, and garlic together on a cutting board, transfer the mixture to a small bowl, add the butter, season with salt, pepper, and nutmeg, and mix together very well. Refrigerate for half an hour. Coat the meat with the seasoned butter paste, then lightly flour it with the ½ cup flour.

Coarsely chop the onion, carrots, celery, and bay leaves together on a cutting board. Place a large casserole with the butter and olive oil over medium heat; when the butter is melted, add the meat and gently sauté until lightly golden all over. Transfer the meat to a serving platter and add the chopped vegetables to the casserole. Sauté for 3 or 4 minutes, then sprinkle the 2 tablespoons flour over them, mix again, add the cup of red wine, and cook, stirring, for 5 minutes. Return the meat to the casserole, then pour in the bottle of Barolo, cover, and let simmer covered for 2 to 2½ hours. By that time the meat should be extremely soft and very juicy.

Remove the meat to a platter and cover to keep it warm and juicy. Pass the sauce through a food mill fitted with the disk with the smallest holes into a second casserole over medium heat. Taste for salt and pepper and let the sauce reduce for about 5 minutes. Place the meat back in to reheat it completely. When ready, cut the *brasato* into rather thick slices, about 1 inch thick, and serve with its very rich sauce.

LAZIO

CODA ALLA VACCINARA
Oxtail Roman Style

Makes 4 servings

The two common Roman signature main dishes, those that shout "Roman cooking," are *abbacchio*, lamb roasted with garlic and with or without anchovies, and this oxtail cooked in a rich sauce. It is on most Roman menus and is difficult to find anywhere else in Italy.

Rome shares most of its main dishes with other parts of Italy, as historically its more refined cooking centered in the establishments of the cardinals, princes of the Church, who brought their own chefs and the dishes of their own provinces, or even their own countries. Therefore Rome is one of the few Italian cities in which you can find nonlocal food in Florentine and other Tuscan restaurants, as well as Bolognese, Abruzzese, and Sicilian restaurants and those of other regions.

This oxtail preparation started as a working-class dish and then was adopted by the rest of the native Romans, a distinct minority of the population of the great city.

2 pounds oxtail pieces

Coarse-grained salt

FOR THE SAUCE:

1 medium-size red onion, cleaned

1 medium-size carrot, scraped

15 sprigs fresh Italian parsley, leaves only

1 large clove garlic, peeled

3 large stalks celery

4 ounces pancetta, in one piece

¼ cup extra virgin olive oil

Salt and freshly ground black pepper

1 cup dry white wine

1½ pounds white stalks celery, cut into
1½-inch pieces

¼ cup tomato paste, preferably imported
Italian

3 cups lukewarm completely defatted
chicken or meat broth, preferably
homemade

TO SERVE:

Fresh Italian parsley leaves

Lightly toasted country-style bread slices

If the butcher has not done so, cut the oxtail into pieces at the joints and remove all the extra fat.

Bring a medium-size pot of cold water to a boil, and add coarse salt to taste, then the oxtail pieces. When the water returns to a boil, use a skimmer to transfer the oxtail to a serving platter. Discard the boiling water.

Finely chop or cut into very small pieces the onion, carrot, parsley, garlic, celery, and pancetta together on a cutting board. Put the onion mixture and olive oil in a medium-size casserole set over medium heat. Once the oil is hot, sauté, stirring with a wooden spoon, until lightly golden, then add the oxtail, season with salt and pepper, and brown the meat for 5 minutes, stirring. Add ½ cup of the wine, let it evaporate for 2 minutes, then mix very well and add the remaining ½ cup wine and cook another 2 minutes. Place the white celery in a bowl of cold water until needed.

Add the tomato paste to the casserole along with the broth. Cover and simmer, turning the meat three or four times, until very soft, 1½ to 2 hours. The meat should be very tender when fully cooked. When the meat is almost cooked and you feel it will be ready in about 20 minutes, drain the celery and add it to the casserole. Simmer the celery together with the meat until both are ready. (Most of the time it is easier to parboil the celery in some salted water, drain it, and add it to the sauce once it has reduced.) Transfer the meat and celery to a serving platter, cover to keep warm, and reduce the sauce by almost half over medium heat. Skim the extra fat from the sauce. Serve the meat and celery together with the sauce poured over them and the parsley sprinkled over, with the toasted bread on the side.

OSSOBUCO ALLA MONTANARA
Ossobuco Mountain Style

Makes 6 servings

The veal shank, sliced into *ossobuchi*, is popular in all regions of Italy and prepared in a great variety of ways. In this Emilia-Romagna mountain version, the emphasis is on the vegetable sauce and the accompanying carrots, using olive oil and none of the butter and cream of the Emilia plains. The browned meat is covered with the Marsala-flavored sautéed vegetables and the broth and is then baked to a succulent softness. It is served with a touch of the lemon, garlic, and parsley *gremolada*.

The food of this mountainous part of Emilia should be better known, as it is the healthiest of the region.

FOR THE SAUCE:

1 large red onion, cleaned

3 large cloves garlic, peeled

3 stalks celery

15 sprigs fresh Italian parsley, leaves only

1 teaspoon fresh marjoram or thyme leaves
    or ½ teaspoon dried

10 large fresh basil leaves

1 small carrot, scraped

½ cup extra virgin olive oil

Salt and freshly ground black pepper

¾ cup dry Marsala

1 cup completely defatted chicken broth,
    preferably homemade

FOR THE *OSSOBUCHI*:

6 large veal *ossobuchi,* about 1¾ inches thick

½ cup extra virgin olive oil

About 1 cup unbleached all-purpose flour

Salt and freshly ground black pepper

2 to 3 cups completely defatted chicken
    broth, preferably homemade

FOR SERVING:

Coarse-grained salt

2 pounds carrots

FOR THE *GREMOLADA*:

20 sprigs fresh Italian parsley, leaves only

1 very small clove garlic, peeled

Grated rind of 1 lemon (page 4)

3 tablespoons extra virgin olive oil

Salt and freshly ground black pepper

To make the sauce, coarsely chop the onion, garlic, celery, parsley, marjoram or thyme, basil, and carrot together on a cutting board. Place a medium-size skillet with the olive oil over medium heat;

when the oil is warm, add the onion mixture and sauté until the onion is translucent, mixing every so often with a wooden spoon to a rather thick consistency. Season with salt and pepper, then pour in the Marsala and let it evaporate for about 15 minutes. Add the broth and cook another 20 minutes.

Meanwhile, tie each *ossobuco* like a salami, using kitchen string (see page 5). Heat the olive oil in a large ovenproof casserole over medium heat. When the oil is warm, flour the cut sides of the meat, tap off any excess, then brown the shanks for 3 to 4 minutes on each side. Season with salt and pepper. Preheat the oven to 375 degrees.

When ready, transfer the contents of the skillet to the casserole containing the *ossobuchi*, arranging the sautéed vegetables on top of the meat. Pour in enough broth to completely cover the meat and bake, covered, until the meat is very soft and almost detached from the bones, about 50 minutes or more.

Meanwhile, bring a medium-size stockpot of cold water to a boil over medium heat. Add coarse salt to taste, then the carrots, and boil until tender, but still with a bite, about 20 minutes. Remove their skins under cold running water, cut the carrots into 1-inch-thick rounds, and let rest until needed.

When the *ossobuchi* are ready, tender and still very juicy, transfer them to a large serving dish and cover with a sheet of aluminum foil to keep the meat warm. Pass the contents of the casserole through a food mill fitted with the disk with the smallest holes into a clean casserole. Set this casserole over medium heat and cook until the sauce becomes quite thick, tasting for salt and pepper.

Meanwhile, prepare the *gremolada*. Finely chop the parsley and garlic together on a cutting board, place in a small crockery or glass bowl, add the grated lemon rind and olive oil, and season with salt and pepper. Mix very well. When the sauce is ready, put the meat back in the casserole and reheat for a few minutes, then add the carrots and cook for a few minutes more. Each serving will consist of an *ossobuco* with the string removed and some of the carrots, with sauce on both and, finally, some *gremolada* over the meat.

❖

STINCO DI VITELLA AGLI ODORI
Veal Shank in Vegetable Sauce
Makes 4 to 8 servings

The whole shank section of veal, beef, or pork is the basis of a number of characteristic main dishes from Friuli. In most of Italy, the shank of veal is usually cut into the very popular *ossobuchi*, but the Friulani like to cook the shank whole. It must be cooked for quite a long time and is made with a variety of flavorings and sauces. This light vegetable sauce, made from pureed aromatic vegetables and porcini mushrooms with two favorite herbs, results in a flavorful and colorful dish, which is impressive to serve and delicious to eat.

1 or 2 veal shanks, each about 2 pounds
    with the bone

FOR THE SAUCE (SEE NOTE):
1½ ounces dried porcini mushrooms
3 cups lukewarm water
3 stalks celery
3 large carrots, scraped
3 large cloves garlic, peeled
15 sprigs fresh Italian parsley, leaves only

6 large fresh basil leaves
¼ cup extra virgin olive oil
½ cup unbleached all-purpose flour
Salt and freshly ground black pepper
1 cup dry white wine
1 cup vegetable or completely defatted
    chicken broth, preferably homemade

Tie the veal shank or shanks like a salami (see page 5) if the butcher has not done so. Soak the porcini mushrooms in the lukewarm water for half an hour. Coarsely chop the celery, carrots, garlic, parsley, and basil together on a cutting board. Preheat the oven to 400 degrees, then place a heavy casserole with the olive oil over medium heat; when the oil is warm, lightly flour the shank or shanks and place in the casserole. Sauté until golden on all sides, then season with salt and pepper. Pour in the wine and let evaporate for 5 minutes.

Clean the mushrooms, removing the sand attached to the stems, and remove the sand from the soaking water by passing it several times through paper towels or a coffee filter. Add the chopped vegetables and herbs and the soaked porcini to the casserole, lightly seasoning them with salt and pepper, then pour the broth into the casserole along with 1 cup of the mushroom water and bake, covered, for 1 hour. Turn the meat over, stir the vegetables, and bake, still covered, for another 45 minutes. By that time the meat should be cooked and very soft. Remove the casserole from the oven, place the shank or shanks on a serving dish, and cover with a sheet of aluminum foil to keep the meat warm.

Pass all the cooked vegetables with their juices through a food mill fitted with the disk with the smallest holes directly back into the casserole. Taste for salt and pepper. Place the shank or shanks back in the casserole and spoon the sauce over the meat. Cover the casserole and bake for another 15 minutes. Remove from the oven and transfer the meat to a cutting board. Remove the bone or bones and cut the meat into slices about ½ inch thick. Serve the meat with some of the sauce on the side.

NOTE: The amount of sauce produced by the quantities above will suffice for either one or two shanks; it is not necessary to make additional sauce for the second shank.

The meat may be served with cannellini (white kidney) or borlotti (Roman) beans on the same plate. The beans should be boiled and then stewed in half of the meat sauce, whether the sauce is prepared with one or two shanks. The sauce (without the beans) may also be used for tossing with cooked dried pasta. This is one of the very few cases when pasta is eaten with the same sauce as the main course at the same dinner. The pasta will be served as a first course and the meat as the second.

TUSCANY

BRACIOLE RIFATTE ALLA FIORENTINA
Twice-Cooked Veal Cutlets

Makes 6 servings

Florentine cooking has a repertory of dishes made from leftovers. The people of that gastronomic center hate to eat food that is simply reheated, so they think of imaginative ways to transform what is left into a genuinely new dish. The name of the dish most often includes the word *rifatto,* or "remade." One very popular traditional cookbook from the Tuscan capital consists of nothing but several hundred recipes for "remaking" leftover meat, vegetables, pastas, etc.

These *braciole,* meaning thin slices of meat, are most often remade from veal scaloppine, but turkey cutlets have become popular in the style of scaloppine and so are also remade in the same way. In this recipe, I am assuming that you do not have the leftover scaloppine and so will make the dish from "scratch." If you do have the leftovers, of course you may start later in the recipe.

continued

6 veal or turkey cutlets (about 1½ pounds),
    lightly pounded
3 extra-large eggs
Pinch of salt

FOR THE SAUCE:
1½ pounds very ripe fresh tomatoes or
    drained canned tomatoes, preferably
    imported Italian
3 large cloves garlic, peeled
15 sprigs fresh Italian parsley, leaves only
10 fresh basil leaves
½ cup extra virgin olive oil
Salt and freshly ground black pepper

Pinch of hot red pepper flakes
1 large sprig fresh rosemary
6 large sage leaves, fresh or preserved in salt
    (page 2)

TO COOK THE CUTLETS:
About 1½ cups extra virgin olive oil
About 1 cup very fine unseasoned bread
    crumbs, preferably homemade, lightly
    toasted

TO SERVE:
Fresh basil leaves
Fresh Italian parsley leaves

Trim the cutlets very well of fat and skin and make several slits around the edges so the meat does not curl up when you fry it. Lightly beat the eggs together in a crockery or glass bowl with the salt. Add the cutlets and marinate them in the egg mixture, refrigerated, for at least 1 hour before cooking them. Soaking the meat in beaten eggs tenderizes the meat, but this is applied only when meat is to be fried. Otherwise, the egg taste is unwelcome.

Prepare the sauce. If using fresh tomatoes, cut them into pieces. Whether using fresh or canned tomatoes, pass them through a food mill fitted with the disk with the smallest holes into a crockery or glass bowl. Finely chop the garlic, parsley, and basil together on a cutting board. Place a large nonreactive skillet with the olive oil over low heat. When the oil is warm, add the garlic mixture and sauté for 2 minutes; the garlic still should be very light in color.

Add the tomatoes to the skillet and simmer for 20 minutes, stirring every so often with a wooden spoon. Season with salt, black pepper, and hot red pepper.

As you prepare the sauce, fry the cutlets. Heat the olive oil over medium heat in a large, heavy deep skillet. Place the bread crumbs on a plate or a sheet of aluminum foil. One by one, remove the cutlets from the egg marinade, letting the excess drip off, and bread them on both sides. When the oil reaches about 375 degrees, add the cutlets to the hot oil (you may have to do this in two batches) and fry them until lightly golden on both sides. Transfer the cutlets to a platter lined with paper towels to absorb any excess fat.

The cutlets may be prepared up to a day in advance and kept in the refrigerator until the last moment. When they are cooled and the tomato sauce reduced, arrange the cutlets over the sauce in one layer. Add the rosemary and sage leaves and simmer, covered, for 10 minutes, turning the meat over twice. Transfer the cutlets and sauce to a serving dish, sprinkle with the basil and parsley leaves, and serve hot. Boiled potatoes, cut into cubes, may be served on the same plate.

FEGATO ALLA VENEZIANA
Calf's Liver Venetian Style
Makes 4 servings

The first step in preparing this signature Venetian dish is to painstakingly make the "sofrito," in this case the sautéed onions, over the lowest of flames for a long time, carefully watched. Of the several types of famous Venetian onions, the white ones are used and any substitution should be with other white onions. The calf's liver should be sliced very thin, placed on top of the onions, and cooked very quickly over a high flame, leaving the inside still pink. The lemon juice is added just before mixing the liver and onions together.

Liver and onions are always served with grilled polenta instead of bread. In Venice polenta usually fulfills the function that bread does in most other parts of Italy.

1 pound white onions, cleaned	Juice of 1 medium-size lemon
2 tablespoons extra virgin olive oil	10 sprigs fresh Italian parsley, leaves only,
6 tablespoons (3 ounces) sweet butter	coarsely chopped
Salt and freshly ground black pepper	Polenta, as prepared in the first paragraph
1 pound calf's liver, cut into very thin slices	of Polenta con Mascarpone e Tartufi
(about ⅛ inch thick)	(page 252; optional), cooled and sliced

Slice the onions very thin and soak them in a bowl of cold water for half an hour. Place a medium-size skillet with the olive oil and butter over medium heat; when the butter is melted, drain the onions, pat dry, add them to the skillet, and sauté for 2 minutes. Cover the skillet, reduce to quite a low heat, and cook until the onions are completely cooked and still very juicy, 20 to 50 minutes. Season with salt and pepper.

Increase the heat to high, place the liver slices over the onions, sauté for a maximum of 1 minute on each side (the liver should still be pink inside), add the lemon juice, and mix the liver and onions together. Taste for salt and pepper, sprinkle the parsley over, mix again, and serve immediately accompanied by the polenta, if desired.

LAMB

❖

What Italians call lamb is what we would call baby lamb, and indeed it is usual for them to eat it only in the spring, which is the natural time of year in which it is found so young. The slightly older "lamb" is called *pecora*, that is, "sheep," and has its own repertory of dishes. And finally there are still recipes for the old mutton, requiring a longer cooking time and treated in an entirely different way. The distinction among these three is still very strong in Italy, and all three are used.

The two lamb dishes that follow form an excellent contrast between the more Northern cooking of Emilia-Romagna and the more Southern approach of Abruzzi, although both regions have distinctive *cucina*, not applicable to generic North and South. They both have names that suggest a very savory dish, but the strong flavor in Emilia-Romagna comes from the wine vinegar, whereas that of the Abruzzi comes from the hot red pepper that is almost omnipresent in that cooking. Emilia typically uses butter, but in this case it is mixed with olive oil, whereas Abruzzi uses purely olive oil. And both versions are most often served with polenta, the Abruzzi polenta being looser than that of Emilia.

AGNELLO ALLA DIAVOLA
Lamb in Peppery Wine Sauce

Makes 6 to 8 servings

6 pounds baby lamb or spring lamb, with
    bone, cut into 3-inch pieces

4 large cloves garlic, peeled

4 heaping tablespoons rosemary leaves,
    fresh or preserved in salt (page 2)

½ teaspoon hot red pepper flakes

4 medium-size carrots, scraped

½ cup extra virgin olive oil

Salt and freshly ground black pepper

1½ cups dry white wine

About 2 cups completely defatted chicken
    broth, plus some extra if using fresh
    peas, preferably homemade

20 ounces shelled fresh peas or two
    10-ounce packages frozen tiny
    tender peas

TO SERVE:

Sprigs fresh Italian parsley

Remove and discard the excess fat from the lamb. Finely chop the garlic, rosemary, hot pepper flakes, and carrots together on a cutting board or in a blender or food processor. Place a large skillet with the olive oil over low heat; when the oil is warm, add the carrot mixture and sauté for 2 minutes. Arrange the lamb pieces over the vegetables, increase the heat to medium, and cook for 5 minutes on each side. You'll probably have to do this in batches.

By that time the meat should be golden all over. Return all the meat to the skillet. Season with salt and pepper. Add the wine and let it evaporate over high heat for 3 or 4 minutes, then reduce the heat to medium and start to add the broth, ½ cup at a time. Cover the skillet and do not add any more broth until what you've added is completely absorbed by the meat. The full cooking time should be about 55 minutes from when the first ½ cup of the broth was added, or longer if the meat is not yet soft. Turn the meat over every time broth is added. Taste for salt and pepper, mix very well, and transfer the meat, completely cooked, to a serving platter. Cover the platter with a sheet of aluminum foil to keep it warm. Skim the fat off the top of the sauce in the skillet.

Add the peas to the juices in the skillet. If fresh peas are used, you will need to add some broth to cook them, but the meat juices are enough liquid to cook the frozen peas. For frozen peas the cooking time will be about 10 minutes, for fresh peas a bit more, depending on their size. Return the lamb to the skillet with the peas, mix very well, then transfer everything to a large serving platter. Each serving will consist of one or two pieces of lamb mixed with some of the peas and a sprig of fresh parsley on top.

The lamb may be served with a quite loose polenta (see page 242), prepared with coarse cornmeal and broth, the polenta placed on the bottom of each plate, with the lamb, peas, and sauce over it.

AGNELLO ALL'ARRABBIATA CON POLENTA
Lamb in Savory Sauce

Makes 6 servings

3 pounds boneless lamb shoulder

¼ cup (2 ounces) sweet butter

1 tablespoon extra virgin olive oil

Salt and freshly ground black pepper

1 cup dry white wine

½ cup red wine vinegar

About 1 cup completely defatted
   chicken or meat broth, preferably
   homemade, if necessary

FOR THE POLENTA:

2 tablespoons (1 ounce) sweet butter

1 tablespoon extra virgin olive oil

1 large clove garlic, peeled

1 tablespoon rosemary leaves, fresh or
   preserved in salt (page 2)

Salt and freshly ground black pepper

8 cups cold completely defatted chicken or
   meat broth, preferably homemade

6 ounces (scant 1¼ cups) coarse stone-
   ground yellow cornmeal, preferably
   imported Italian

FOR THE *GREMOLADA*:

2 tablespoons rosemary leaves, fresh or
   preserved in salt (page 2)

4 medium-size cloves garlic, peeled

2 whole anchovies preserved in salt
   (see Note on page 10) or 4 anchovy
   fillets packed in oil, drained

½ cup completely defatted chicken or meat
   broth, preferably homemade, if necessary

Salt and freshly ground black pepper

TO SERVE:

2 bell peppers preserved in wine vinegar
   (available in gourmet stores), cut into
   very thin strips

Fresh Italian parsley leaves

Remove all the fat from the lamb and cut it into 2-inch cubes. Place a medium-size casserole with the butter and olive oil over medium heat; when the butter is melted, add the lamb and sauté for 5 minutes, turning the meat several times. Season with salt and pepper. Add the wine and let evaporate for 15 minutes. Add the vinegar, cover the casserole, and simmer for another 20 minutes, stirring every so often with a wooden spoon. By that time the lamb should be cooked and very soft; otherwise, add some of the broth and cook longer—the final cooking time will depend on the age of the animal.

    As you cook the meat, start the polenta. Place a medium-size stockpot with the butter and olive oil over low heat. Finely chop the garlic and rosemary together on a cutting board. When the butter is melted, add the garlic mixture and sauté for 1 minute. Season with salt and pepper, add the cold broth, and bring to a boil. When the broth reaches a boil, start adding the cornmeal, a little at a time, in a thin stream, constantly mixing with a wooden spoon. When all the cornmeal is added, since this polenta is quite thin, stir for 1 minute, then let simmer for 45 minutes, stirring every so often. The lamb and polenta should be ready at the same time. When the meat is soft, transfer it to a serving dish using a slotted spoon and cover the dish to keep it warm.

Meanwhile, make the *gremolada*. Finely chop the rosemary, garlic, and anchovies together on a cutting board. Add this mixture to the casserole, along with the broth. Bring to a simmer and let simmer until the sauce is quite reduced, about 5 minutes. Taste for salt and pepper. Ladle some of the polenta onto individual plates, then some of the meat over the polenta, and finally pour some sauce on top. Sprinkle the pepper strips and parsley leaves over the top and serve.

VARIATION: This dish may also be prepared with chicken or rabbit cut into medium-size pieces.

PORK AND RABBIT

❖

SALSICCE CON CAVOLFIORE E PATATE
Sausages Baked with Cauliflower and Potatoes

Makes 6 to 8 servings

Broccolo means a hard flower. In Southern Italy, and even in Rome, the broccoli family includes many local variants as well as several types of what we call cauliflower. These vegetables are often prepared as a substantial separate course, highly flavored with meat, aromatic vegetables, and herbs. It is not surprising that the sausages used are the spicy ones containing hot red pepper. Fennel seeds are used in much of the sausage from the South, but far from all. This dish calls for sausage made without fennel seeds. Oregano is found all over Italy but is used much more in Southern Italy, and is available as the more delicate, less pungent fresh herb rather than dried.

1 large cauliflower (about 2½ pounds)

Coarse-grained salt

2 pounds boiling potatoes (don't use new potatoes)

6 hot Italian sausages without fennel seeds

½ cup extra virgin olive oil

Salt and freshly ground black pepper

2 large pinches of dried Italian oregano

15 sprigs fresh Italian parsley, leaves only, coarsely chopped

Soak the cauliflower in a bowl of cold water for half an hour. Bring a large pot of cold water to a boil over medium heat. Drain the cauliflower and clean it, discarding the green leaves and detaching all the florets. When the water reaches a boil, add coarse salt to taste, then the florets, and cook for 1 minute. Drain the cauliflower, cool under cold running water, and let rest, covered with a wet kitchen towel, until needed.

Peel the potatoes and cut them into slices less than ½ inch thick. Place them in a bowl of cold water until needed. Remove the casings from the sausages and cut them into 1-inch pieces.

Preheat the oven to 400 degrees. Drain the potatoes and put them in a large bowl with the sausage pieces. Pour the olive oil over them, season with salt, pepper, and oregano, mix very well, and transfer to a 13½ × 8¾-inch glass baking dish. Cover the dish with a sheet of aluminum foil and bake until the potatoes are soft, about 30 minutes. Mix very well and arrange the cauliflower on top. Bake, covered, for another 15 minutes. Serve hot, with a little chopped parsley.

CINGHIALE O CAPRETTO AL SALMI

Marinated Boar, Kid, or Beef Cooked with Aromatic Herbs

Makes 6 servings

Boar and kid, like most game meats, must be marinated for many hours in order to soften them for cooking. The same procedure should be used for the less tender cuts of beef if used in this recipe.

Sage and rosemary are used with the hearty red wine for the marinade, and the wine is saved to be used in the cooking. Ground mustard (common in medieval and Renaissance Italy but used now only in a few areas, such as Friuli in the extreme North) as well as the combination of butter and olive oil are then incorporated into the reduced sauce. Notable is the addition of refined grappa, which is one of the prides of mountainous Friuli.

The game (or beef) is often served in the manner of Veneto and Friuli, together with loose polenta (page 242).

2 pounds boneless boar or kid (goat) meat,
    any cut, or 4 pounds with bones,
    or 2 pounds boneless beef chuck

4 large sage leaves, fresh or preserved in salt
    (page 2)

1 tablespoon rosemary leaves, fresh or
    preserved in salt (page 2)

1 medium-size red onion, cleaned and
    quartered

2 medium-size carrots, scraped and cut into
    pieces

2 stalks celery, cut into pieces

2 large cloves garlic, peeled

5 cups dry red wine

TO COOK THE MEAT:

4 ounces pancetta or prosciutto, in one
    piece

½ cup (4 ounces) sweet butter

1 tablespoon extra virgin olive oil

2 tablespoons capers in wine vinegar,
    drained

Salt and freshly ground black pepper

1 teaspoon dry mustard dissolved in
    1 tablespoon cold water

¼ cup grappa or unflavored vodka

continued

Cut the meat, with or without bones, into 2-inch pieces and place them in a medium-size crockery or glass bowl. In another bowl mix together the sage, rosemary, onion, carrots, celery, and garlic, then arrange this mixture over the meat, pour the wine over, and refrigerate, covered with plastic wrap, for at least 8 hours or overnight.

Cut the pancetta or prosciutto into small pieces. Place a medium-size casserole with the butter and olive oil over medium heat.

Meanwhile, drain the meat and vegetables, saving the wine. Separate the meat from the vegetables and put it on a plate. When the butter in the casserole is melted, add the vegetables and pancetta along with the capers and sauté for 15 minutes, stirring every so often with a wooden spoon. Add the meat and sauté on all sides for 10 minutes. Start adding the marinating wine 1 cup at a time. Each cup should be reduced before adding the next one, and the entire cooking period is about 1 hour. Season with salt and pepper. By the time the wine is all used, the meat should be cooked and tender. Transfer it to a bowl, cover, and let stand until the sauce is finished.

Pass the remaining contents of the casserole through a food mill fitted with the disk with the smallest holes into a bowl. Return the sauce to the casserole and reduce over medium heat for 15 minutes, adding the dissolved mustard powder. Mix very well. Place the meat back in the casserole, add the grappa or vodka, and let cook for a final 10 minutes. Serve hot with or without polenta.

CONIGLIO CON LA PEPERONATA
Rabbit and Peppers Piedmont Style
Makes 4 to 6 servings

Rabbit has a low-fat white meat that is often compared to chicken, but some think it even better. It is widely eaten in Italy, originally because it was so much more plentiful than chicken, and hence much more affordable. In recent decades, however, it has come up in the world and is now more expensive than chicken and no longer considered a poor man's meat. Some countries have a prejudice against eating it, for a variety of reasons, and lack of familiarity compounds the problem. But once tried, few can deny how delicious it can be. Though technically not a game animal, it is best to begin by soaking it for a short time with some vinegar, to remove a slight gaminess.

Rabbit should not be confused with the true game animal, hare, which has dark meat and its own repertory of succulent dishes.

1 rabbit (about 2 pounds), cut into 8 pieces

2 tablespoons red wine vinegar

TO COOK THE RABBIT:

2 ounces pancetta or prosciutto, in one piece

1 heaping tablespoon rosemary leaves, fresh
  or preserved in salt (page 2)

¼ cup (2 ounces) sweet butter

1 tablespoon extra virgin olive oil

2 large bay leaves

Salt and freshly ground black pepper

1 cup completely defatted chicken broth,
  preferably homemade

TO COOK THE PEPPERS:

¼ cup (2 ounces) sweet butter

1 tablespoon extra virgin olive oil

3 whole anchovies preserved in salt
  (see Note on page 10) or 6 anchovy
  fillets packed in oil, drained

3 red or yellow bell peppers, seeded and
  cut into strips less than ½ inch wide

½ cup cold water

2 large cloves garlic, peeled and finely
  chopped

10 sprigs fresh Italian parsley, leaves only

¼ cup red wine vinegar

Salt and freshly ground black pepper

TO SERVE:

Fresh Italian parsley leaves

continued

Place the rabbit in a bowl of cold water with the vinegar and soak for half an hour. Cut the pancetta or prosciutto into very small pieces and finely chop the rosemary, then combine them or, even better, coarsely grind the pancetta and rosemary together.

Place a casserole with the butter and olive oil over medium heat; when the oil is warm, add the pancetta mixture and the bay leaves and sauté for 2 minutes. Meanwhile, quickly drain the rabbit pieces, pat them dry with paper towels, and add them to the casserole. Let them sauté until very lightly golden all over. Season with salt and pepper. Add the broth a small quantity at a time, turning the rabbit over several times, and cook until almost soft, about 25 minutes for a 2-pound rabbit.

As the rabbit cooks, prepare the peppers. Warm the butter with the olive oil in a large saucepan over low heat, then add the anchovies and mash them with a fork. Be sure the heat remains constantly low, so the anchovies do not crumble and become very fishy. Add the peppers and sauté for 5 minutes. Raise the heat, add the cold water, and cook the peppers for another 5 minutes; at that point the peppers should be half-cooked. Add the garlic, parsley, and vinegar and let the vinegar evaporate for 5 minutes. Taste for salt and pepper. Transfer the contents of the saucepan to the casserole containing the not yet completely cooked rabbit and mix well. Cook until the rabbit is soft. Transfer the meat to a bowl, leaving the peppers behind, and reduce the juices until the sauce is as thick as you like. Discard the bay leaves. Pass the contents of the casserole through a food mill fitted with the disk with smallest holes into a bowl, then return the sauce to the casserole and taste for salt and pepper. Mix very well and just reheat the sauce and rabbit. Serve with the parsley leaves sprinkled over each portion.

CONIGLIO ALLA GENOVESE
Rabbit with Rosemary Genoese Style

Makes 4 servings

Even in the days when rabbit was an inexpensive meat, there were very refined dishes based on it, usually involving boning the rabbit while leaving it whole and stuffing it, as with the cheese stuffing in this recipe or with the famous artichoke stuffing in a Tuscan version flavored with tarragon, called *dragoncello* in that region. The stuffed rabbit may be sliced through, showing the layers of meat and stuffing, in a very fine presentation, with sauce and olives.

In this Genoese version, a Ligurian fresh cheese is classically used in the stuffing, but it is very local and nowadays difficult to obtain even in its own area. The cheese is flavored with rosemary rather than the Tuscan tarragon, and it can be reasonably approximated in texture by the ricotta and grated Parmigiano suggested below.

1 rabbit (about 3 pounds)

3 tablespoons red wine vinegar

1 tablespoon rosemary leaves, fresh or preserved in salt (page 2)

2 medium-size cloves garlic, peeled

4 ounces very soft cheese, or 2 ounces very well-drained ricotta combined with 2 ounces Parmigiano cheese, freshly grated

Salt and freshly ground black pepper

About ¼ cup unbleached all-purpose flour

TO COOK THE RABBIT:

1 tablespoon (½ ounce) sweet butter

¼ cup extra virgin olive oil

1 stalk celery

1 medium-size carrot, scraped

1 very small red onion, cleaned

½ cup dry white wine

1 cup completely defatted chicken or meat broth, preferably homemade

Salt and freshly ground black pepper

1 pound very ripe tomatoes or drained canned tomatoes, preferably imported Italian

1 cup cold water

TO SERVE:

About 20 large black Greek olives

Salt and freshly ground black pepper

20 sprigs fresh Italian parsley, leaves only, coarsely chopped

continued

Wash the rabbit very well under cold running water, then soak it for half an hour in a bowl of cold water with the vinegar with just enough liquid to completely cover the rabbit. Remove the rabbit from the acidulated water and pat it dry with paper towels. Cut off the rabbit where the loin starts. Save the top part for later use and bone the lower part, being careful not to make holes.

Butterfly the boned rabbit by slicing through the thicker part of the loin, without detaching these slices, but rather opening them out in order to even out the thickness of the meat. Using a meat pounder, flatten it between two sheets of waxed paper moistened with cold water. Check to be sure there are no holes in the rabbit before preparing the stuffing.

Finely chop the rosemary and garlic together on a cutting board. Transfer the chopped ingredients to a small bowl, add the cheese, and season with salt and pepper. Mix very well. Spread this mixture over the rabbit, then roll it up from the long side and tie it like a salami (see page 5). Lightly flour it.

Place the butter and olive oil in a nonreactive medium-size casserole set over medium heat; when the butter has melted, put in the rolled-up rabbit and sauté for 5 minutes on all sides.

Meanwhile, coarsely chop the celery, carrot, and onion together on a cutting board.

Pour the wine into the casserole and let it evaporate for 2 minutes. Add the chopped ingredients to the casserole, ¼ cup of the broth, salt and pepper to taste, and the tomatoes, if fresh, cut into large pieces. Cover and cook for 30 minutes or longer, depending on the tenderness of the rabbit, adding more broth if needed. When ready, transfer the stuffed rabbit to a serving dish, cover, and let rest until needed.

Place the unboned part of the rabbit in the casserole. Add the cold water to the casserole. Cook until the vegetables are very soft, about 25 minutes. Discard the unboned part of the rabbit. Pass the contents of the casserole through a food mill fitted with the disk with medium-sized holes into a clean casserole. Reduce the sauce over medium heat until it is quite thick.

When ready, untie the meat and slice it like a salami. Add the olives to the sauce, season with salt and pepper, and mix well. Each serving will consist of stuffed rabbit slices, some of the sauce with olives on one side, and the parsley sprinkled over the meat.

The entire dish may be prepared a day in advance, reheating the sauce at the last moment. The meat may be reheated before slicing or sliced at room temperature and served with the warm sauce.

POLENTA

❖

Polenta, usually made with stone-ground cornmeal, is most often served as a main course. It is enriched with flavorful additions such as meat sauce, sometimes accompanied by game birds or pieces of meat or truffles with mascarpone and a rich mushroom meat sauce (page 227). Buckwheat polenta, called *taragna*, is still found in a few regions, usually together with a pork stew, but grains like millet and barley have been replaced by cornmeal, which is now the dominant grain for polenta. In the Veneto, polenta is allowed to cool and is sliced as an accompaniment to some other main dishes (see *Fegato alla Veneziana*, page 239, and *Cinghiale o Capretto al Salmi*, page 245). This sliced polenta may be toasted and used as the receptacle for *crostini* appetizers in place of bread. See also page 242 for *Agnello all' Arrabbiata con polenta,* served with a looser polenta.

POLENTA CON MASCARPONE E TARTUFI
Polenta with Mascarpone and Truffles

Makes 8 servings

This is a rich and wonderful dish, as unmindful of the expense of the white truffles as only a dish from Piedmont, where they are most plentiful, can be. The rich mascarpone, native to nearby Lombardy, enriches the polenta and carries it far from its rustic origins into an elegance that is appropriately crowned with the rare truffles.

3 quarts completely defatted chicken broth, preferably homemade

Coarse-grained salt

1 pound fine stone-ground Italian yellow cornmeal

Salt and freshly ground black pepper

2 tablespoons (1 ounce) sweet butter

16 heaping tablespoons mascarpone

Slivers of shaved fresh white truffle (optional), available at specialty food stores

Heat the broth in a large pot over medium heat; when the broth comes to a boil, add coarse salt to taste. Start to pour in the cornmeal in a very slow stream, stirring continuously with a flat wooden spoon. Be sure to pour the cornmeal slowly and to keep stirring, or the polenta will become very lumpy very easily. Stir slowly, without stopping, for 45 to 50 minutes from the moment the last of the cornmeal was added to the pot. Season with salt and pepper. If some lumps form, push them against the sides of the pot to crush them with the spoon.

Use the butter to lightly butter eight dinner plates. Put 1 heaping tablespoon of mascarpone in the center of each plate. Put the plates in the refrigerator until needed.

When the polenta is cooked, taste for salt and pepper, add the remaining mascarpone, mix well, then remove the pot from the heat. Immediately ladle some of the polenta over the cheese on the prepared plates. The polenta should cover the cheese completely. Serve as is or with the truffle shaved over.

DESSERTS

In Italy desserts are not a normal course in the everyday meal. Rather, they are associated with celebrations and holidays, and there are many that were traditionally made only once a year, for a holiday or saint's day. And often these sweets and pastries are to be eaten as a snack, not at the end of a meal. The normal finale to the Italian meal is fresh fruit or, very occasionally, cheese. Most of these desserts have a story behind them and a long history as well. A good many belong to a particular city or region and were originally made only there.

We should not be surprised that with the increase of travel in the twentieth century, desserts that were particularly loved spread beyond their homes and were made throughout Italy. And some are now made all through the year, not just to celebrate their own day. So what has been lost is a part of their story, their specific meaning. But what we've gained is the possibility of eating them anywhere, at any time, as much as we like.

It is now generally known and taken for granted by "those in the know" that many of the classic pastries of highly refined cuisines originated in Italy and were taken to France, Austria, and other countries from there.

ZABAIONE IN TAZZA ALLA PADOVANA
Zabaione with Cinnamon Butter Padova Style

Makes 6 servings

The liquid of zabaione varies according to the locality and may range from many kinds of dessert wines, such as Marsala, to a variety of red wines. This old zabaione from Padova, near Venice, combines the eggs with white wine. A simple white wine is used here because the area produces no reds and no dessert wines.

The unusual flavoring for this zabaione and what makes it instantly recognizable and widely copied is the cinnamon, so easily obtainable in earlier times because nearby Venice was the major spice importer from exotic places.

FOR THE ZABAIONE:

6 extra-large egg yolks

¾ cup granulated sugar

¼ cup (2 ounces) sweet butter, at room temperature

¼ teaspoon ground cinnamon

1 cup dry white wine

FOR THE WHIPPED CREAM:

1 cup heavy cream

3 tablespoons granulated sugar

2 teaspoons confectioners' sugar

Bring some water to a boil in the bottom of a double boiler. Put the egg yolks in a crockery or glass bowl and add the granulated sugar, butter, and cinnamon. Stir with a wooden spoon, always in the same direction, until the sugar and butter are completely incorporated and the mixture turns a light yellow. Add the wine and mix together. Transfer the mixture to the top part of the double boiler. When the water in the bottom part is boiling, insert the top. Stir constantly with a wooden spoon, always in the same direction. Just before it boils, the zabaione should be thick enough to coat the wooden spoon. Absolutely do not allow it to boil. Remove the top of the double boiler from the heat and stir for 2 or 3 minutes longer. Transfer the zabaione to six individual dessert glasses.

Using a wire whisk and a chilled metal bowl, whip the cream with the granulated and confectioners' sugars until stiff peaks form. Using a pastry bag with a scalloped point, place a *ciuffo* (wisp) of the cream on top of the still lukewarm zabaione and serve immediately. Mixed berries, very cold, may be served with the zabaione, topped with the whipped cream.

ZABAIONE D'ARANCIO
Orange Zabaione
Makes 8 servings

Zabaione often is used as a filling for many different tarts or cakes. A favorite dessert is zabaione combined with whipped cream, as in this recipe. It is sometimes given the fuller name *crema zabaione*. Zabaione-flavored gelato is also a great favorite.

When served as a separate dessert, zabaione is generally eaten cold; one of the few exceptions is *Zabaione in Tazza alla Padovana* (page 254). Hot zabaione is considered a "tonic" for the weak or aged in Italy, more a medicine than a dessert. Grating the orange rind, we get the full-flavored taste of the orange rind without the bitter aftertaste of the white part beneath the rind.

5 extra-large egg yolks

5 heaping tablespoons granulated sugar

½ cup orange juice, preferably fresh

1 tablespoon dark or light rum

Grated rind of 1 large orange with
    thick skin (page 4)

TO FINISH THE ZABAIONE:

1½ cups heavy cream

2 tablespoons granulated sugar

1 tablespoon confectioners' sugar

TO SERVE:

1½ pints fresh berries for sprinkling

Bring some water to a boil in the bottom of a double boiler or in a medium-size stockpot. Put the egg yolks in a crockery or glass bowl, add the sugar, and stir with a wooden spoon, always in the same direction, until the sugar is completely incorporated and the egg yolks turn a lighter color. Then slowly pour in the orange juice, mixing steadily. When all the juice is incorporated, add the rum and grated orange rind. Transfer the contents of the bowl to the top part of the double boiler or to a copper bowl set over the pot of boiling water. The water should not touch the bottom of the insert or the copper bowl. Stir continuously with a wooden spoon, always in the same direction. Just before it boils, the zabaione should be thick enough to coat the spoon—that is the moment it is ready. Absolutely do not allow it to boil. Immediately remove the insert from the boiling water and stir for a few seconds more. Transfer the zabaione to a crockery or glass bowl to cool for about half an hour, then cover with plastic wrap, making some holes in the plastic, and refrigerate for at least 1 hour before finishing it. Zabaione may be left in the refrigerator overnight before mixing it with the whipped cream.

Chill a metal bowl and wire whisk, or improvise a "cold" double boiler by placing the metal bowl over a bowl full of ice. Whip the cream together with the granulated and confectioners' sugars until quite firm peaks form. Add the cooled zabaione and, with the whisk, incorporate it into the whipped cream. You may serve immediately or hold for several hours in the refrigerator. Serve sprinkled with the berries.

SARDINIA

TORTA AL LATTE
Lemon Custard Mold

Makes 6 to 8 servings

This custard mold from Sardinia is flavored with grated lemon peel and coffee powder, which is then strained off. An unusual touch is the egg whites beaten stiff, then folded into the custard before baking. The medieval recipe for *Torta di Latte* was an early version of quiche, and was savory. Whether this near namesake has any connection with that older dish is worth pondering.

6 extra-large eggs	1 tablespoon finely ground espresso
2 extra-large eggs, separated	powder, preferably imported Italian
½ cup plus 10 tablespoons granulated sugar	2½ cups whole milk
1 tablespoon confectioners' sugar	1 cup heavy cream
Grated rind of 1 lemon with thick skin	2 tablespoons cold water
(page 4)	

Place the whole eggs and egg yolks, ½ cup of the granulated sugar, and the confectioners' sugar in a large crockery or glass bowl and mix very well, in a rotary motion, until the sugar is completely dissolved and the mixture turns a lighter color. Add the lemon rind and stir very well.

Wet the inside of a medium-size casserole with cold water (this will keep the milk from sticking to it). Place the espresso powder, milk, and cream in a medium-size crockery or glass bowl and mix very well. Transfer the mixture to the casserole and set over medium heat. Simmer for about 15 minutes, stirring every so often with a wooden spoon, then strain the mixture through paper towels, a coffee filter, or a very fine-mesh strainer to remove all the espresso granules. Let this mixture rest until lukewarm. You will need to have 2 cups of liquid.

Meanwhile, prepare the caramel by placing the remaining 10 tablespoons granulated sugar and cold water in a 9 × 5 × 2¾-inch metal loaf pan and set over low heat. Dissolve the sugar and keep the pan over the heat, shaking it several times until a very light-colored caramel forms. Carefully coat the loaf pan with it by turning the pan on its different sides until each side and the bottom are coated. Let the pan cool completely.

Preheat the oven to 375 degrees and prepare a water bath (*bagno Maria*) by placing paper towels or a kitchen towel in a large baking dish.

Add the cooled strained milk to the egg mixture and stir well. Use a wire whisk and a copper bowl to beat the egg whites until soft peaks form. Fold the whites into the egg mixture with a rubber spatula, then transfer to the prepared pan. Place the pan in the baking dish and add enough lukewarm water to reach almost to the level of the egg mixture in the loaf pan. Bake for about 1 hour. If the top of the custard is becoming too dark or very crusty after 15 minutes, cover with a sheet of aluminum foil. Remove from the oven (the custard should be resistant to the touch), place the pan on a wire rack, and let cool for 10 minutes before unmolding onto a serving dish, leaving the mold on the *torta* until cool, about 30 minutes. Remove the mold and serve the *torta* by slicing it into squares. This *torta* may be prepared a day in advance and eaten at room temperature.

LOMBARDY

CREMA CALDA AL CAFFÈ
Coffee Custard with Hazelnut Sauce

Makes 8 to 10 servings

Hazelnuts complete the triumvirate (almonds, walnuts, hazelnuts) of nuts that are favored in Italian *cucina*. (*Pignoli* are in a category of their own, being usually used whole.) Hazelnut is a favorite flavor in sweets, including gelato, and combined with chocolate makes up the traditional flavor called *gianduia*. These nuts as well as walnuts combine beautifully with coffee (and with chocolate), so this coffee-flavored custard pairs classically with its hazelnut sauce.

6 teaspoons finely ground espresso powder, preferably imported Italian

1 cup boiling water

3 cups heavy cream

12 extra-large egg yolks

1 cup granulated sugar

2 extra-large eggs

1 tablespoon (½ ounce) sweet butter

FOR THE SAUCE:

3 ounces hazelnuts, blanched for 1 minute and lightly toasted in a 350-degree oven

3 extra-large egg yolks

¼ cup granulated sugar

2 cups heavy cream

1 cup lukewarm milk

1 tablespoon brandy (optional)

continued

Place the espresso powder in a coffee filter and pour through the boiling water. In a medium-size heavy saucepan, bring 2 cups of the cream to a boil over medium heat, reduce the heat to medium-low, and let simmer for a minute, then add the prepared coffee. Stir very well, remove the pan from the heat, cover, and let rest for half an hour.

Meanwhile, place the egg yolks in a large crockery or glass bowl, add the sugar, and stir with a wooden spoon until the sugar is completely incorporated and the yolks turn a lighter color. Pass the coffee-flavored cream through a second coffee filter, add it to the egg yolk mixture, and stir very well with a wooden spoon. Add the 2 whole eggs and the remaining cup of cream. Mix well and let rest for a few minutes.

Meanwhile, heavily butter a glass loaf pan and cool it in the freezer for a few minutes. Preheat the oven to 375 degrees. To prepare a water bath (*bagno Maria*) for the loaf pan, place a cotton kitchen towel or several layers of paper towels in the bottom of a large crockery or glass baking dish and add enough lukewarm water to reach the level of the custard. Remove the loaf pan from the freezer, stir the egg mixture very well, and pour it into the pan. Place the loaf pan in the baking dish and bake for 2 hours.

Meanwhile, prepare the sauce. Husk, then very finely grind the hazelnuts. Place the egg yolks in a crockery or glass bowl, add the sugar, and use a wooden spoon to mix until the egg yolks turn a lighter color. Add the hazelnuts, then the heavy cream and mix very well. Then pour in the lukewarm milk gradually, constantly stirring with a wooden spoon. Cook the sauce in a double boiler, still stirring with the wooden spoon, and when the sauce coats the spoon, transfer it to a crockery or glass bowl. Absolutely do not allow it to boil. Add the brandy, if used, at this point. Let cool for a few moments, then pour the sauce into an empty wine bottle. Cork the bottle and refrigerate until needed. The sauce should be cold when used. When custard is baked and still warm, unmold it onto a serving platter and cut it into slices. Cold sauce should be placed on the side of each serving.

BONET AL CAFFÈ
Piedmont Chocolate-Coffee Dessert

Makes 8 to 10 servings

A custard mold, this is unusually flavored with vanilla bean, rum, cocoa, coffee, and ground bitter almond amaretti cookies. Though of Piedmontese origin, it is famous all over Italy and a classic dessert. The ingredients blend exceptionally well into a single integrated flavor.

3½ cups whole milk

One 2-inch piece vanilla bean

7 extra-large eggs

1 cup granulated sugar

½ cup light rum

¼ cup unsweetened cocoa powder

½ cup finely ground espresso powder,
    preferably imported Italian

4 ounces amaretti (bitter almond cookies),
    preferably imported Italian, finely
    ground

TO SERVE:

A few drops of rum to pour over

Wet the bottom part of a medium-size casserole with cold water, then add the milk; this keeps the milk from sticking to the pan. Set the pan over medium heat with the vanilla bean and let simmer for 15 minutes. Strain the milk through a cheesecloth or paper towels into a crockery or glass bowl to remove the skin formed on the top. Let the milk cool completely, for about half an hour. Meanwhile, place the eggs in a large crockery or glass bowl, add the sugar, and mix very well, using a wooden spoon, until the eggs turn a lighter color. Add the rum and again mix very well. Take 1 cup of the cooled milk and dissolve the cocoa in it, then add it to the bowl with the other ingredients.

Preheat the oven to 375 degrees.

Add the espresso powder, the ground amaretti, then the remaining milk and stir very well to be sure the ingredients are well amalgamated. Lightly butter a nonstick 9 × 5 × 2¾-inch loaf pan. Prepare a water bath (*bagno Maria*) by placing a cotton kitchen towel or some paper towels in a baking dish. Pour the contents of the bowl into the loaf pan, cover it with foil, and place the pan in the prepared baking dish. Pour lukewarm water into the dish to at least three-quarters of the height of the custard. Bake for 1 hour and 20 minutes. Remove from the oven, transfer the loaf pan to a rack, and let cool for half an hour before refrigerating it for at least 1 hour. Remove from the refrigerator, unmold onto a serving dish, and serve with a few drops of rum poured over.

CREMA FRITTA ALLA VENEZIANA
Fried Pastry Cream Venetian Style

Makes 8 to 10 servings

Crema Fritta is one of the most famous Venetian desserts. Though its present name means literally "fried cream," in the old days the custard cream was not fried; it was poured in a thin layer onto a dinner plate and allowed to cool, then sprinkled with sugar. Nowadays the cooled cream is cut into a variety of shapes—though round disks seem to be prohibited—dipped in egg whites, breaded, and fried.

Try it, for it is an extraordinarily good dessert.

5 extra-large egg yolks

6 tablespoons granulated sugar

4 ounces unbleached all-purpose flour

Grated rind of 1 large lemon with thick skin
    (page 4)

Pinch of salt

4 cups whole milk

TO FRY:

5 extra-large egg whites

About 1½ cups very fine unseasoned bread
    crumbs, preferably homemade, lightly
    toasted

2 cups vegetable oil (½ corn oil and
    ½ sunflower oil)

2 tablespoons (1 ounce) sweet butter

TO SERVE:

Confectioners' sugar

Strips of zests of 1 lemon and 1 orange with
    thick skins (page 4)

Mix the egg yolks with the granulated sugar in a crockery or glass bowl until light-colored, then add the flour and mix completely. Mix in the grated lemon rind and salt. Pour in the milk little by little, mixing constantly with a wooden spoon. When all the milk is used up, transfer the mixture to a medium-size casserole. Place the casserole over low heat and keep mixing until it starts to simmer. Continue to mix until the cream is rather thick and has the consistency of paste. Pour the cream into a well-buttered 13½ × 8¾-inch crockery or glass baking dish. Let rest for half an hour, then refrigerate, covered with plastic wrap, overnight.

    When ready, cut the custard into diamonds, squares, rectangles, or almond shapes, but not into disks. Lightly beat the egg whites with a fork and place the bread crumbs on a plate. Heat the vegetable oil with the butter in a large deep-sided heavy skillet. When the butter is melted and the oil is about 375 degrees, dip each cut piece of cream in the egg whites, then coat evenly with bread crumbs. Place several in the skillet at a time and fry the custard cream until golden all over. Transfer to a dish lined with paper towels to remove excess oil. When all the pieces are cooked, transfer to a serving platter, sift the confectioners' sugar over them all around, and serve with the lemon and orange zests.

BUDINI DI ARANCE CANDITE
Candied Orange Rind Budini

Makes 6 servings

These small soufflé-like molds are of candied orange rind soaked in rum with ground walnuts, sugar, cookie crumbs, and egg whites beaten stiff. *Budini* are cooked in a water bath (*bagno Maria*) and, when served, a cream with caramelized sugar is poured over each.

2 ounces candied orange rind, cut into tiny
    pieces

¼ cup light rum

2 ounces shelled walnuts

⅓ cup plus 3 tablespoons granulated sugar

1 ounce tea biscuits or champagne puffs

¼ cup (2 ounces) sweet butter, at room
    temperature

3 extra-large eggs, separated

Grated rind of 1 orange with thick skin
    (page 4)

TO BAKE THE *BUDINI*:

¼ cup granulated sugar

FOR THE PASTRY CREAM:

3 extra-large egg yolks

6 tablespoons granulated sugar

1 cup lukewarm milk

½ cup cold heavy cream

TO SERVE:

6 teaspoons rum (optional)

In a small crockery or glass bowl, soak the candied orange rind in the rum for half an hour.

Meanwhile, in a food processor or blender, finely grind the walnuts, 2 tablespoons of the sugar, and the biscuits together. Transfer the mixture to a bowl and set aside. Place ⅓ cup of the sugar and the butter in a large crockery or glass bowl and use a wooden spoon to mix very well until the sugar is completely incorporated and the color is much lighter. Add the walnut mixture a little at a time, constantly stirring with a wooden spoon. Then add the egg yolks one at a time and mix well after each addition. Add the grated orange rind. Drain the candied orange rind, discarding the rum, and add it to the mixture.

Preheat the oven to 375 degrees and place paper towels or a cotton kitchen towel in the bottom of a large crockery or glass baking dish. Heavily butter six glass custard cups and coat them with the sugar. Use a copper bowl and a wire whisk to beat the egg whites until stiff peaks form, adding the remaining tablespoon sugar. Gently fold the whites into the batter. Distribute this equally among the custard cups. Place the cups in the baking dish. Add lukewarm water to the dish to make a water bath (*bagno Maria*) equal to the level of the batter in the molds. Place the dish in the oven. Bake until the batter has risen to the top of the cups and the tops are golden, about 45 minutes. If you serve the *budini* straight from the oven, they will unmold very easily. But if you plan to unmold them even 10 minutes after cooked, they will be quite difficult to unmold. In that case, either don't coat the cups with sugar, to make unmolding easier, or unmold immediately and serve later.

When the *budini* are almost ready, prepare the pastry cream. Mix the egg yolks and 3 tablespoons of the sugar together in a medium-size bowl until well combined. Add the milk and heavy cream and mix well. Transfer the mixture to the top part of a double boiler. Bring some water to boil in the bottom of the double boiler and insert the top part. Stir constantly with a wooden spoon, always in the same direction, until the mixture is thick enough to coat the spoon. Absolutely do not allow it to boil.

Melt the remaining 3 tablespoons of sugar over medium heat in a small saucepan to a light golden syrup. Add it to the pastry cream in the double boiler and stir to combine.

Serve the *budini* with some of the warm cream on one side. A teaspoon of rum may be poured on top of each *budino*.

TIMBALLI DI RICOTTA
Little Ricotta Budini

Makes 8 servings

In Italy this *budino* is made with sheep's milk ricotta, but it also works very well with cow's milk. The ricotta in Italy is very dry, so the ricotta used here must be drained very well before using. These *timballi* are really small soufflés, but Italians prefer them to be unmolded, so they do fall a little. They may also be eaten at room temperature, in which case they become the lightest of cheesecakes.

12 ounces whole-milk ricotta, drained

1½ ounces candied orange rind, cut into
very small pieces

1½ tablespoons dark or light rum

½ cup plus ¼ cup superfine sugar

4 extra-large eggs, separated

Pinch of salt

1 tablespoon potato starch (*not* potato flour;
see Note on page 284)

Grated rind of 1 small lemon with thick
skin (page 4)

Pinch of ground cinnamon

Granulated sugar as needed

TO SERVE:

About 2 tablespoons confectioners' sugar

Strips of zest of 1 medium-size orange with
thick skin (page 4)

Be sure the ricotta is very well drained and smooth. Soak the candied orange rind in the rum for 1 hour. Preheat the oven to 375 degrees and line the bottom of a large baking pan with paper towels or a cotton kitchen towel, to be used later as a water bath (*bagno Maria*).

Add the ½ cup sugar to the ricotta in a large bowl and mix very well. Add the egg yolks one at a time and mix as each is added. Then add the salt, potato starch, grated lemon rind, and cinnamon. Let rest, covered with plastic wrap, in the refrigerator, for at least 1 hour before using.

Butter eight custard cups or ramekins and coat them with granulated sugar. When ready, drain the candied orange rind and add it to the ricotta, discarding the unabsorbed rum. Beat the egg whites with the remaining ¼ cup sugar in a large copper bowl with a wire whisk until soft peaks form. Gently fold the whites into the ricotta mixture, then ladle into the prepared cups. The cups should be no more than two-thirds full. Place the cups in the baking pan and pour in enough lukewarm water to almost reach the level of the ricotta filling. Bake until the tops of the *timballi* are golden and very puffy, about 25 minutes.

Remove the cups from the water bath, run a paring knife all around the molds to be sure nothing is attached to the sides, then unmold onto individual dessert plates with the golden side on top. Using a very fine sieve, sprinkle the confectioners' sugar over, then a few orange zest strips. Serve hot.

VARIATIONS

- Use candied citron instead of orange rind.
- Use grated orange rind instead of lemon rind.
- Sprinkle unsweetened cocoa powder over the tops instead of confectioners' sugar.
- Do not unmold the *timballi*.

SEMIFREDDO DI ALBICOCCHE
Apricot Semifreddo

Makes 8 to 10 servings

Meringues have been popular in Italy since very early times and were first documented in a Florentine cookbook of the 1300s. Egg yolks were used for many purposes at that time, not only in emulsions with oil by chefs, but also by fresco painters who belonged to the same guild as the chefs. The egg whites were given to the cooks to be used for the many "white" category dishes, including frittate with the whites alone, which were common then.

Generally meringues are baked and used in a variety of desserts. Since the *semifreddo* is a frozen cream, the meringue must remain uncooked. However, when mixed with the very hot syrup, it reaches a temperature that makes it safe to eat; it may then be allowed to cool and to freeze.

2 ounces dried apricots

½ cup brandy

FOR THE CUSTARD CREAM:

7 extra-large egg yolks

¼ cup granulated sugar (for imported apricots such as Turkish; if using California apricots, at least double the amount of sugar)

1 tablespoon confectioners' sugar

1 cup dry white wine

1 teaspoon pure lemon extract or 1 drop imported Italian lemon extract

FOR THE SYRUP:

½ cup cold water

½ cup granulated sugar

2 or 3 drops fresh lemon juice, to your taste

TO FINISH THE MERINGUE:

4 extra-large egg whites

1 tablespoon granulated sugar

FOR THE WHIPPED CREAM:

2 cups heavy cream

1 tablespoon granulated sugar

1 tablespoon confectioners' sugar

Coarsely chop the apricots on a cutting board, then soak them in the brandy in a small crockery or glass bowl for 1 hour.

When ready, mix the egg yolks with the granulated and confectioners' sugars in a crockery or glass bowl using a wooden spoon; when the mixture turns a lighter color, add the wine and lemon extract and mix very well. Drain the apricots, discarding all the brandy but 1 tablespoon, then add them to the egg mixture and mix again.

Bring some water to a boil in the bottom of a double boiler. Transfer the mixture to the top part of the double boiler. When the water in the bottom part is boiling, insert the top. Stir constantly with a wooden spoon, always in the same direction, until the mixture is thick enough to coat the spoon. Absolutely do not allow it to boil. Transfer the prepared custard to a crockery or glass bowl and let rest until completely cold, about 1 hour.

Meanwhile, prepare the Italian meringue, starting with the syrup. Place the water, granulated sugar, and lemon juice in a heavy medium-size nonreactive saucepan over medium heat. Simmer until a thin syrup forms (soft ball stage), brushing the entire inside of the pan with cold water to prevent the sugar from crystallizing. Meanwhile, beat the egg whites with the granulated sugar in a copper bowl with a wire whisk until stiff peaks form. When the syrup is ready, remove from the heat, let cool for 2 minutes, then pour in a thin stream into the beaten egg whites, continuously beating the whites with the whisk until all the syrup is evenly incorporated. Immediately whip the heavy cream with the granulated and confectioners' sugars in a chilled metal bowl until soft peaks form.

When ready, assemble the *semifreddo*. Add the cooled custard cream to the whipped cream and whisk very well, then fold in the Italian meringue, using a rubber spatula so that a lot of air will also be incorporated. Transfer the *semifreddo* to a large serving bowl or individual cups and place in the freezer for at least 2 hours before serving.

Semifreddo may be kept in the freezer for up to two weeks.

TORTA PAESANA DELLA BRIANZA
Peasant Torte from Brianza

Makes one 10-inch torte; 10 to 12 servings

Cakes made from leftover bread form a very old tradition. We must remember that bread, because it required very finely ground wheat, was labor intensive and therefore a food of the rich from Roman times through the Middle Ages. Because of this, bread was not wasted. Many dishes were developed to use leftover, no-longer-fresh bread. Once these dishes became traditional they held a place in the cuisine long after bread became inexpensive and incorrectly became associated with the working classes and farmers.

An irony of this "peasant" dessert is that, being from Lombardy, the "simple" bread base is elaborated into quite a rich dish, incorporating butter, cream, and amaretti. But it has remained popular quite simply because it is delicious and well loved.

4 to 4½ cups whole milk, depending on the dryness of the bread

¼ cup heavy cream

8 ounces 3-day-old whole-wheat bread, cut into pieces

3 ounces tea biscuits or champagne puffs

3 ounces amaretti (bitter almond cookies), preferably imported Italian

¼ cup (2 ounces) plus 2 tablespoons (1 ounce) sweet butter, at room temperature

¾ cup granulated sugar

2 tablespoons confectioners' sugar

1 teaspoon pure vanilla extract or 1 drop imported Italian vanilla extract

3 extra-large eggs

Grated rind of ½ orange with thick skin (page 4)

2 ounces semisweet chocolate, grated

4 ounces raisins

1 cup lukewarm water

FOR THE WHIPPED CREAM:

1½ cups heavy cream

2 tablespoons granulated sugar

1 tablespoon confectioners' sugar

TO SERVE:

2 tablespoons granulated sugar

Place the milk and cream in a large crockery or glass bowl, then add the bread, biscuits, and amaretti. Soak for 2 hours, mixing every so often.

Place the ¼ cup butter, the granulated sugar, and confectioners' sugar in a blender or food processor and blend well. Add the vanilla, eggs, orange rind, and chocolate and blend again. Add the bread and cookies with the soaking milk to the blender or food processor and process until smooth. Remove the batter to a crockery or glass bowl and mix very well with a rubber spatula.

Preheat the oven to 375 degrees. Soak the raisins in the lukewarm water for 15 minutes. With the remaining 2 tablespoons butter, butter and lightly flour a 10-inch round double cake pan (one with 3-inch-high sides) and line the bottom with a piece of parchment paper. Drain the raisins and add them to the cake batter. Mix very well, then pour the batter into the prepared pan. Bake for 1 hour and 45 minutes. The *torta* is done when it is golden, resistant to the touch, and detached from the sides. Remove from the oven and let the *torta* rest for at least half an hour before unmolding it onto a large round serving platter.

Whip the cream in a chilled metal bowl together with the granulated and confectioners' sugars until stiff peaks form. Arrange the cream all over the *torta*, sprinkle with the granulated sugar, and serve. If the cake is cold, you can place the whipped cream over the *torta* as much as an hour before serving, but wait to sprinkle the sugar over until the very last moment.

DOLCE AL CAFFÈ
Coffee Liqueur Cake

Makes one 10-inch cake; 8 servings

This flourless cake is based on ground walnuts and flavored with cocoa as well as coffee. The coffee liqueur-flavored pastry cream forms the filling between the two layers of cake, while the chocolate glazing fulfills the promise of the cocoa. It is best to prepare the entire cake a day in advance of serving. This very rich cake is the kind of dessert typically associated with Emilia-Romagna.

½ cup strong brewed coffee, preferably
    Italian espresso

¼ cup unsweetened cocoa powder

4 extra-large eggs, separated

7 tablespoons granulated sugar

1 ounce blanched almonds

7 ounces shelled walnuts

FOR THE COFFEE PASTRY CREAM:

4 extra-large egg yolks

¼ cup granulated sugar

1 tablespoon confectioners' sugar

2 tablespoons (1 ounce) sweet butter

¼ cup coffee liqueur

¾ cup dry white wine

1 tablespoon potato starch (*not* potato flour; see Note on page 284)

FOR THE *GLASSA* (GLAZE):

4 ounces semisweet chocolate

1 tablespoon granulated sugar

1 tablespoon water

3 tablespoons (1½ ounces) sweet butter

In a small saucepan heat the coffee over medium heat until lukewarm. Place the cocoa powder in a medium-size bowl, then pour in the coffee, stir very well with a wooden spoon until the cocoa is completely dissolved, and let rest until cold, about half an hour. Place the egg yolks in a crockery or glass bowl, add ¼ cup of the granulated sugar, and stir very well with a wooden spoon until the sugar is completely absorbed and the egg yolks turn a lighter color. Add the cooled coffee-cocoa mixture, stir very well, then transfer the contents of the bowl to a larger bowl and let stand until needed. Using a food processor or blender, finely grind together the almonds, walnuts, and the remaining 3 tablespoons granulated sugar and add to the egg mixture.

    Preheat the oven to 375 degrees. Lightly butter and flour the bottom and sides of a 10-inch round double cake pan (one with 3-inch-high sides) and fit a disk of parchment paper over the bottom of the pan. Using a copper bowl and wire whisk, beat the egg whites until stiff peaks form. Gently fold them into the egg mixture in a rotating motion, using a rubber spatula. Pour this batter into the prepared pan and bake for about 45 minutes. Unmold onto a wire rack lined with parchment paper, remove the baked-on parchment, and let rest for half an hour.

Meanwhile, prepare the coffee pastry cream. Mix the egg yolks, sugars, and butter together well in a medium-size bowl. Add the liqueur and wine and mix well again, then stir in the potato starch. Transfer the mixture to the top part of a double boiler. Bring some water to a boil in the bottom part of the double boiler and insert the top part. Stir constantly with a wooden spoon, always in the same direction, until the mixture is thick enough to coat the spoon. Absolutely do not allow it to boil. Transfer to a crockery or glass bowl and let rest until needed.

Prepare the glaze. Coarsely chop the chocolate and place a medium-size pot with cold water over medium heat. When the water reaches a boil, remove the pot from the burner, place the chopped chocolate, sugar, and the tablespoon of water in a metal bowl and insert it on top of the pot. Be sure the bottom part of the bowl is not touched by the very hot water. Let rest for 10 minutes, then gently mix; the chocolate will be completely melted and very smooth. Remove the bowl from over the hot water and, constantly stirring with a wooden spoon, add the butter, incorporating it into the chocolate. Let the glaze rest for 15 minutes before using it.

Cut the cake in half horizontally, pour the pastry cream over the bottom part and spread it evenly around. Be sure the pastry cream does not drip around the cake. Place the top of the cake over the pastry cream. Use a narrow metal spatula to glaze the cake all over. Transfer the cake to a serving platter and let it rest for half an hour before serving.

❖

DOLCE AGLI AMARETTI

Bitter Almond Cake

Makes one 10-inch cake; 8 to 10 servings

The most common way to obtain the bitter almond taste that is so popular in Italian cakes is to use ground commercial amaretti cookies. There are several high-quality brands imported from Italy. The cookies are very hard, and a box lasts almost indefinitely. Very small quantities of the cookie yield a strong bitter almond flavor. It is very easy to grind these superfine with a food processor or blender.

Though the bitter almond flavor blends very well with chocolate, it is important not to allow the chocolate to overwhelm or cover it. The cakes of Emilia are most often very rich, with butter-and-cream or chocolate stuffings, sauces, and even glazes.

FOR THE CAKE:

4 ounces amaretti (bitter almond cookies),
      preferably imported Italian
½ cup (4 ounces) sweet butter
6 tablespoons granulated sugar
6 extra-large eggs, separated
3 ounces unbleached all-purpose flour
1 tablespoon baking powder
1½ ounces bittersweet chocolate, in one
      piece
1 tablespoon confectioners' sugar

FOR THE CHOCOLATE SAUCE:

8 ounces bittersweet chocolate, cut into
      small pieces
½ cup whole milk
¼ cup heavy cream

TO SERVE:

Confectioners' sugar

Finely grind the amaretti in a food processor or a blender. Melt the butter in a metal bowl over boiling water and let it rest for 10 minutes before using it.

Place the butter in a crockery or glass bowl or in the bowl of a stand mixer fitted with the paddle attachment. Add the granulated sugar and mix very well. When the sugar is completely incorporated, add the egg yolks one at a time, and mix until the yolks turn a lighter color. Combine the flour, ground amaretti, and baking powder together and add this mixture to the eggs ¼ cup at a time. Meanwhile, melt the chocolate in a metal bowl over hot water. When all the flour has been added, pour the melted chocolate into the bowl and mix for 30 seconds to be sure all the ingredients are well amalgamated. Preheat the oven to 350 degrees, heavily butter a 10-inch round double cake pan (one with 3-inch-high sides) and line the bottom of it with a piece of parchment paper.

Use a copper bowl and wire whisk to beat the egg whites with the confectioners' sugar to soft peaks. Gently fold the whites into the thick batter, using a rubber spatula. Transfer everything to the prepared pan and bake until the cake pulls away from the sides of the pan, about 45 minutes. Remove from the oven and let the cake rest on a wire rack at least 15 minutes before unmolding it. Remove the parchment paper and reverse the cake.

Prepare the chocolate sauce by placing the chocolate, milk, and cream in a small saucepan over low heat, mixing every so often with a wooden spoon. When the chocolate is completely melted and the sauce very smooth, it is ready to be served.

Serve the cake by slicing it like a pie. Sprinkle some confectioners' sugar over each serving and pour some of the chocolate sauce on one side.

PAZIENTINA PADOVANA
Almond Sponge Cake from Padua
Makes one 10-inch cake; 12 servings

The use of egg whites beaten stiff to help baked desserts rise is documented in Italian cookbooks of the 1300s; one even finds recipes for baked meringues. Sponge cakes are an Italian invention; indeed, in France they are known as *bisquit Italien*. The *pazientina* is a three-layer cake with an almond base and two layers of sponge cake. Syrup is poured over each layer and zabaione is the filling between the layers. Finally the assembled cake is covered with a chocolate glaze.

The sponge-cake part of this dessert is made with the lighter potato starch instead of flour and is flavored with grated orange peel. Ground almonds, once the sole ingredient of the base, are supplemented by flour. The egg whites are lightly mixed with the other ingredients but not beaten stiff. It is the baking powder that helps the cake rise a little and makes it lighter.

continued

5 very crisp ladyfingers (Savoiardi), preferably imported Italian

About 3 tablespoons (1½ ounces) sweet butter

FOR THE ALMOND BASE:

10 tablespoons granulated sugar

6 tablespoons (3 ounces) sweet butter

3 ounces almonds, all but 4 of them blanched

3 ounces unbleached all-purpose flour

1½ teaspoons baking powder

½ cup whole milk

4 extra-large egg whites

FOR THE SPONGE CAKE:

8 extra-large eggs, separated

Generous ½ cup granulated sugar

8 ounces potato starch (*not* potato flour; see Note on page 284)

Pinch of salt

1 tablespoon baking powder

Grated rind of 1 large orange with thick skin (page 4)

¼ cup whole milk

FOR THE ZABAIONE:

6 extra-large egg yolks

½ cup granulated sugar

1 tablespoon potato starch (*not* potato flour; see Note on page 284)

1 cup dry Marsala

FOR THE SYRUP:

3 cups cold water

1½ cups granulated sugar

2 drops fresh lemon juice

¾ cup dry Marsala

FOR THE *GLASSA* (GLAZE):

10 ounces semisweet chocolate, in one piece

2 tablespoons (1 ounce) sweet butter

¼ cup cold water

TO SERVE:

2 tablespoons crystallized sugar

Preheat the oven to 375 degrees. Finely grind the ladyfingers and heavily butter two 10-inch round double cake pans (ones with 3-inch-high sides), then line the bottoms with parchment paper and coat the sides evenly with the ladyfingers crumbs, discarding any left over.

Prepare the almond base. Place the granulated sugar and butter in a stand mixer fitted with the paddle attachment and beat until the sugar is completely amalgamated with the butter and the butter is almost whipped.

Place the blanched and unblanched almonds and flour in a blender or food processor and finely grind together. Combine the baking powder with the flour mixture and start adding this mixture to the almost whipped butter a little at a time, alternating with a little milk. Finally add the egg whites and keep mixing for 30 seconds after the last ingredient has been added. Transfer the batter to one of the prepared cake pans and bake for 10 minutes, then reduce the oven temperature to 350 degrees for 15 minutes, and finally reduce it to 325 degrees and bake for another 30 minutes. You can prepare this "base" of the cake a few hours before serving.

Prepare the sponge cake. Preheat the oven to 350 degrees. Place the egg yolks and granulated sugar in a crockery or glass bowl or in the bowl of a stand mixer fitted with the paddle attachment and mix until the egg yolks turn a lighter color and are almost whipped. Combine the potato starch, salt, and baking powder and sift them together. Start adding this mixture, along with the grated orange rind and milk, to the egg yolk mixture. Stir very well for 30 seconds. Beat the egg whites in a copper bowl with a wire whisk until soft peaks form, then fold them into the batter. Transfer this batter to the second prepared pan and bake until the top of the cake is golden and very puffy, about 35 minutes. The top of the cake should be golden and very puffy.

Prepare the zabaione with the ingredients and quantities listed above according to the directions on page 254, cook it in a double boiler, then cool it, covered, in a crockery or glass bowl.

Prepare a syrup with the cold water, granulated sugar, and lemon juice in a small saucepan over medium heat. When it becomes rather thick, after about 20 minutes, remove from the heat and let rest until lukewarm, about 15 minutes, then add the Marsala.

Place the almond base on a round serving platter lined with parchment paper cut in half. Drizzle some of the syrup all over. Use half of the cooled zabaione to make a layer over the almond base.

Slice the sponge cake in half horizontally and fit the bottom part over the layer of zabaione. Pour more syrup over the sponge cake, then the other half of the zabaione. Top it with the other half of the sponge cake and drizzle more syrup over.

Put the chocolate, cut into pieces, the butter, and water in the top part of a double boiler or in a metal bowl. Bring a medium-size pot of cold water to a boil over medium heat; when the water reaches a boil, remove the pot from the heat and immediately insert the top of the double boiler or the bowl containing the chocolate. Be sure the bottom part of the insert is not touched by the hot water. Let rest until the chocolate is completely melted and very smooth. Stir with a spoon to amalgamate all the ingredients, then, with a metal spatula, glaze the entire cake, sides and top, reheating the chocolate if it hardens too much. Sprinkle the top of the cake with the crystallized sugar. Let the cake rest until the glaze hardens a bit. Cut it into wedges and serve.

DOLCE DI RISO CON ALBICOCCHE
Apricot Rice Cake

Makes one 10-inch cake; 8 to 10 servings

It is commonly said in Italy that rice desserts and cakes are more often found in the areas that do not grow rice, such as Tuscany and Veneto, though the latter is close to Lombardy and Piedmont, important rice-growing centers. This cake, made with dried apricots soaked in rum, with eggs and cream as binders, is one of the delicious Venetian rice desserts.

6 ounces dried apricots

½ cup light rum

1 quart whole milk

Grated rinds of 2 large oranges with thick
    skins (page 4)

One 1-inch piece vanilla bean

8 ounces (1 heaping cup) raw short-grain
    rice, preferably Italian Arborio

6 cups cold water

Pinch of salt

¼ cup (2 ounces) sweet butter, cut into pats

¾ cup granulated sugar

4 extra-large eggs

1 cup heavy cream

TO SERVE:

Strips of zest of 1 lemon with thick skin
    (page 4)

Cut the apricots into very small pieces and place them in a small bowl. Pour in the rum and mix very well. Dampen the bottom of a medium-size casserole with a few drops of cold water (so the milk does not stick), then pour the milk into it. Add half the grated orange rind to the apricots and the remaining half to the milk. Add the piece of vanilla bean to the milk and set the casserole over medium heat. When the milk reaches a boil, remove it from the heat, cover, and let rest until luke-warm.

Meanwhile, place the rice in a bowl of cold water and let soak for 10 minutes. Bring the 6 cups cold water to a boil in a medium-size saucepan, add the salt, then drain the rice and add it to the pan. Cook the rice for 10 minutes. Drain the rice and let it rest in a colander until the milk is ready.

Strain the milk through a very fine-mesh strainer, discarding the orange zest and vanilla bean, then return it to the casserole over medium heat; when it again reaches a boil, add the rice, stir very well, and cook for 5 minutes. Remove the casserole from the heat and let rest, covered, for half an hour. Preheat the oven to 375 degrees and lightly butter and flour the bottom and sides of a 10-inch springform pan.

Drain the rice and transfer it to a large crockery or glass bowl. Add the butter pats, the sugar, reserving 2 tablespoons of it, the eggs, heavy cream, and apricot mixture with its rum and mix very well, using a fork to avoid breaking the rice grains. Pour the mixture into the prepared pan, sprinkle with the remaining 2 tablespoons sugar, and bake until the cake detaches from the side of the pan, about 1 hour. Remove from the oven and let the cake rest for 10 minutes before releasing the sides of the pan.

Arrange the lemon zests over the top of the cake, cut it into wedges, and serve.

SICILY

DOLCE DI ARANCI
Flat Orange Cake

Makes one 10-inch cake; 8 servings

This is one of Italy's numerous flourless cakes, undoubtedly a survival from the Renaissance, when ground nuts, here Sicily's almonds, were used instead of flour. A modern addition is the ground ladyfingers and potato starch, added to the ground nuts. The orange flavor is provided by the juice and the grated orange rind, augmented by a bit of lemon rind. The baking powder helps the cake rise and makes it lighter than it probably was in earlier times.

8 ounces unblanched almonds

8 ounces confectioners' sugar

Grated rind of 1 orange with thick skin
    (page 4)

Grated rind of ¼ lemon with thick skin
    (page 4)

3 crisp ladyfingers (Savoiardi), preferably
    imported Italian, finely ground

1 tablespoon (½ ounce) sweet butter

6 tablespoons (3 ounces) sweet butter,
    melted and cooled to room temperature

4 extra-large eggs, separated

½ cup fresh orange juice

3 ounces potato starch (*not* potato flour;
    see Note on page 284)

2 teaspoons baking powder

TO SERVE:

Grated rind of 1 orange with thick skin
    (page 4)

3 heaping tablespoons granulated sugar

continued

Blanch the almonds in boiling water for a few minutes, squeeze off their skins, then dry them in the oven preheated to 375 degrees for 10 minutes. Leave the oven on. Place the almonds, half of the sugar, and the orange and lemon rinds in a blender or food processor and process until the almonds are ground to a flour.

Butter a 10-inch round double cake pan (one with 3-inch-high sides), then line the sides of it with the ground ladyfingers. Place a piece of parchment paper on the bottom of the pan. Place the soft butter in a medium-size mixing bowl, add the egg yolks, and whisk very well with an electric mixer fitted with a whisk until the butter is almost whipped. Still with the whisk on, add the almond flour a little at a time, then the orange juice, the potato starch mixed with the baking powder, and finally the remaining sugar. Mix it all together until well integrated; be sure this thick batter is uniform.

Use a copper bowl and wire whisk to beat the egg whites to soft peaks, then fold the whites into the batter, using a rubber spatula. Pour the batter into the prepared pan and lightly smooth the top. Bake until the sides of the cake pull away from the pan, about 45 minutes. Remove from the oven, let the cake cool on a rack for 10 minutes, then unmold it onto a round serving platter. Remove the parchment paper from the top of the cake. Mix the grated orange rind very well into the granulated sugar and sift it over the cake. Serve lukewarm or after a few hours at room temperature.

FRIULI

GUBANA
Classic Friuli Fruit-Nut Cake
Makes 10 to 12 servings

Gubana is from the town of Cividale, founded by Julius Caesar, and the pastry is one of the oldest documented in Europe. It is probably the granddaddy of all "coffee-cake"/Viennese/Danish pastries. The line of passage is most likely first through the Hapsburgs, who ruled Cividale as the then capital of Friuli beginning in the Middle Ages, the pastry then passing through to the rest of Central, Eastern, and Northern Europe during the later Middle Ages and the Renaissance.

Using a buttery yeast dough, it combines aspects of both puff pastry (as we know, a Florentine invention) and brioche pastry. *Gubana* reveals its medieval origins in the abundant dried and candied fruits and nuts that form the basis of most desserts of that time, such as the famous Sienese *panforte*.

The wine in which the raisins are soaked was probably originally a sweet white wine such as Malvasia (Malmsey), since dry white wines had not yet been extensively developed. Marsala, though it did not exist before the early nineteenth century, is most often used now.

FOR THE SPONGE:

½ cup unbleached all-purpose flour

Pinch of salt

1 ounce compressed fresh yeast or
    2 packages active dry yeast

6 tablespoons lukewarm or hot milk,
    depending on the yeast used

FOR THE FILLING:

3 ounces unblanched almonds

3 ounces shelled walnuts

3 ounces raisins

½ cup Marsala, not very dry, or white wine

3 ounces dried figs

3 ounces candied orange rind

2 ounces pine nuts (*pignoli*)

6 tablespoons granulated sugar

Pinch of ground cinnamon

6 tablespoons (3 ounces) sweet butter

2 ounces very fine unseasoned bread
    crumbs, preferably homemade, lightly
    toasted

3 extra-large eggs, separated

2 ounces bittersweet chocolate, grated

FOR THE DOUGH:

14 ounces unbleached all-purpose flour plus
    2 ounces for kneading

¼ cup lukewarm milk

¼ cup granulated sugar

Grated rind of ½ orange with thick skin
    (page 4)

Grated rind of ½ lemon with thick skin
    (page 4)

¼ cup (2 ounces) sweet butter

TO BAKE:

1 tablespoon (½ ounce) sweet butter

Enough unbleached all-purpose flour to
    dust the mold

1 extra-large egg

1 tablespoon cold water

2 tablespoons granulated sugar

TO SERVE:

Grappa (optional)

Confectioners' sugar

Prepare the sponge. Place the flour, seasoned with the salt, in a medium-size bowl and make a well in the flour. Dissolve the yeast in the lukewarm or hot milk and pour it into the well. With a wooden spoon, mix all the ingredients together into a thick batter. Let the sponge rest, covered, in a warm place away from drafts until doubled in size, about 1 hour.

    Preheat the oven to 375 degrees. Prepare the filling. Blanch the almonds and walnuts in boiling water for 1 minute, then drain and remove their skins. Place the nuts on a cookie sheet to let them dry in the oven for 5 or 6 minutes. Keep the oven on. The nuts should be very dry but not toasted. Let the nuts cool. Once the almonds and walnuts are dry and cool, coarsely grind them in a blender or food processor. Soak the raisins in the Marsala or white wine for half an hour. Coarsely grind the figs and candied orange rind together in a blender or food processor. Combine the nut and fig mixtures in a crockery or glass bowl, add the pine nuts, sugar, and cinnamon and stir. Place the butter in a saucepan over low heat; when it is almost melted, add the bread crumbs and lightly sauté until lightly golden, about 2 minutes. Let cool for a few minutes, then add them to the bowl containing the other ingredients.

Drain the raisins, discarding the soaking wine, and add them to the bowl of ingredients along with the egg yolks. Mix very well. Add the chocolate and mix again. When the sponge is ready, start mixing the soft butter with the yolks in a crockery bowl or in a stand mixer fitted with a paddle, until the egg yolks turn a lighter color. Add the 14 ounces of flour, a little at a time, and the milk along with the sugar and the orange and lemon rinds. Keep stirring until the dough is rather thick but smooth and shiny. Let the dough rest, covered, until doubled in size, about 1 hour. Spread out the remaining 2 ounces of flour on a pastry board. Transfer the dough onto the board and knead, incorporating one-quarter of the flour. Stretch the dough into a long rectangle about 6 × 20 inches. Cut the butter into pats and distribute them over the dough. Fold the dough into thirds, then, starting from one open side, with a rolling pin stretch the folded dough to the size of about 6 × 20 inches. Repeat this folding and stretching two more times, without resting between these "turns."

Finally stretch the dough into an even longer rectangle, about 6 × 30 inches, being careful not to make any holes. Use a copper bowl and wire whisk to beat the egg whites until soft peaks form and gently fold them into the prepared filling. Arrange the filling in the middle of this long rope of dough, then fold one side over to meet the other end for the entire length of the rope. Seal the two ends together. Heavily butter and lightly flour a 10-inch round double cake pan (one with 3-inch-high sides).

Turn the stuffed rope into a spiral, trying to keep the inside starting point a little higher than the outside. Carefully transfer to the cake pan. Let rest, covered, for half an hour. By that time the dough will rise so that it becomes about one-third higher. Mix the egg with the water and brush the top of the dough, then sprinkle the sugar over the top. Bake until the cake pulls away from the side of the pan and a toothpick inserted in the center of the cake comes out clean, about 50 minutes. Remove from the oven and let the *gubana* rest on a rack for at least 20 minutes before unmolding it onto a second rack. Turn the cake again and let it cool for 20 minutes more before serving.

Gubana is just as good at room temperature and may last for several days. You may eat it sliced, as it is, or moistened with a few drops of grappa and the confectioners' sugar.

DOLCE ALLE PESCHE
Peach Cake with Almonds

Makes one 10-inch cake; 6 to 8 servings

This peach "upside-down cake" from Piedmont is made with a single crust based on almonds and the bitter almond flavor of ground amaretti. The eggs are incorporated whole, and baking powder is used to help the cake rise and to lighten it.

FOR THE CAKE PAN:

¼ cup (2 ounces) sweet butter, at room temperature

3 tablespoons granulated sugar

3 ounces amaretti (bitter almond cookies), preferably imported Italian

2 ounces blanched almonds

FOR THE CAKE:

4 large peaches, blanched for 1 minute, peeled, pitted, and cut into eighths

½ cup granulated sugar

¼ cup (2 ounces) sweet butter, at room temperature

2 extra-large eggs

5 ounces unbleached all-purpose flour

4½ teaspoons baking powder

Large pinch of ground cinnamon

2 tablespoons superfine sugar

½ cup milk

1 tablespoon potato starch (*not* potato flour; see Note on page 284)

Grated rind of 1 medium-size orange with thick skin (page 4)

1 teaspoon pure orange extract or 2 drops of imported Italian orange extract, mixed together with 1 tablespoon milk

TO BAKE:

2 tablespoons (1 ounce) sweet butter, cut into pats

Heavily butter a 10-inch round double cake pan (one with 3-inch-high sides).

Put the ¼ cup butter and the sugar, amaretti, and almonds in a food processor and process until the cookies and nuts are finely ground. Arrange the mixture evenly over the bottom of the cake pan. Refrigerate until needed.

If the peaches are not very ripe and sweet, sprinkle 2 extra tablespoons of granulated sugar over them and let rest until needed.

Place the ½ cup sugar and the butter in a medium-size bowl and blend very well. Add the eggs, then the flour sifted together with the baking powder and cinnamon, then the remaining cake ingredients one at a time, continuously blending, and continue to mix for 1 more minute after the last ingredient, the orange extract, is added.

Preheat the oven to 375 degrees. Arrange the peaches over the almond mixture on the bottom of the cake pan, leaving a little space between the fruit and the sides of the pan. Then pour the batter over the peaches. Distribute the pats of butter over the surface and bake for 50 minutes. At that point, the pastry should have detached from the sides of the pan and the cake should be soft to the touch and golden. Remove from the oven, let rest for 20 seconds, then unmold it onto a round serving platter. The layer of golden amaretti/almond crumbles will be on top and the peaches just below. The cake is best when eaten lukewarm. Serve, slicing it like a pie.

ELBA

"CROSTATA" DI MELE ALLA CREMA
Italian Apple Cake with Cookie Crust

Makes one 10-inch cake; 6 to 8 servings

In a crust of cookie and amaretti crumbs, the apple filling is covered with custard cream and everything is baked together in a springform pan. Such a baked custard cream layer on top is not rare among Italian pastries.

Vin Santo wine is used to flavor the cooked apples. This Tuscan dessert wine is very special but may be hard to obtain, so sherry can be substituted.

2 pounds Golden or Red Delicious apples,
   cored, peeled, and cut into quarters

1 large lemon, cut in half

½ cup granulated sugar

¼ cup raisins

¼ cup Vin Santo wine or dry sherry

FOR THE CUSTARD CREAM:

5 extra-large egg yolks

6 tablespoons granulated sugar

1 tablespoon confectioners' sugar

3½ tablespoons potato starch (*not* potato
   flour; see Note on page 284)

2 cups lukewarm heavy cream

1 teaspoon pure lemon extract or 1 drop of
   imported Italian lemon extract

FOR THE COOKIE CRUST:

3 tablespoons (1½ ounces) sweet butter,
   very soft

3 ounces tea biscuits or champagne puffs,
   finely ground

3 ounces amaretti (bitter almond cookies),
   preferably imported Italian, finely
   ground

TO SERVE:

2 tablespoons granulated sugar

Grated rind of 1 large lemon with thick skin
   (page 4)

Place the quartered apples in a medium-size nonreactive casserole with enough cold water to cover them. Squeeze the lemon halves over the water, then add the granulated sugar and raisins. Set the casserole over medium heat and cook until the apples are soft but still retain their shape, about 30 minutes. Drain the apples and raisins, discarding the poaching water. Let the fruit rest until cold, about 1 hour.

Meanwhile, prepare the custard cream. Put the egg yolks in a crockery or glass bowl and add both sugars and the potato starch. Stir with a wooden spoon, always in the same direction, until the mixture is light yellow. Add the heavy cream and lemon extract and mix together. Transfer the mixture to the top part of a double boiler. Bring some water to a boil in the bottom part of the double boiler and insert the top part. Stir the mixture constantly with a wooden spoon, always in the same direction, until the mixture thickens enough to coat the spoon. Absolutely do not allow it to boil. Transfer the cooked custard to a crockery or glass bowl and let rest until cool, about 1 hour. Preheat the oven to 375 degrees.

Wth a fork, coarsely mash the cooled apples, being careful to leave the raisins whole. Add the Vin Santo and mix very well. Heavily butter a 10-inch springform pan and coat the bottom and sides with the mixed-together ground biscuits and cookies; keep applying the cookie crumbs until the sides and bottom are thickly lined. Arrange the apples in the bottom of the pan, then pour the cooled custard over them. Level it with a rubber spatula. Bake until the cake pulls away from the side of the pan, about 45 minutes. Remove from the oven and let rest for at least 15 minutes before releasing its sides. Transfer to a serving platter, then mix together the granulated sugar and grated lemon rind and sprinkle this mixture over the cake before serving.

DOLCE DI MELE ALLA ROMANA
Apple Cake Roma Style

Makes one 10-inch cake; 8 to 10 servings

Most regions have their own apple cakes, but this one from Rome is unique in that the apples, cut into small pieces, are ground into the batter itself, so that when the cake is baked it has tiny pieces of apple in it.

FOR THE APPLES:

2 Golden or Red Delicious apples

3 tablespoons granulated sugar

FOR THE BATTER:

¾ cup granulated sugar

¾ cup (6 ounces) sweet butter, at room
    temperature

3 extra-large eggs

Grated rind of 1 large orange with thick
    skin (page 4)

6 ounces unbleached all-purpose flour

1 tablespoon potato starch (*not* potato flour;
    see Note on page 284)

1 tablespoon baking powder

Pinch of salt

TO SERVE:

Sifted confectioners' sugar

Peel the apples, then quarter and core them. Finely slice each quarter and place it in a crockery or glass bowl. Sprinkle the 3 tablespoons of sugar over them. Heavily butter a 10-inch springform pan and line the bottom with a piece of parchment paper.

Preheat the oven to 375 degrees. Place the sugar and butter in a crockery or glass bowl and blend very well. Add the eggs one at a time and mix for 1 minute more. Mix in the grated orange rind. Combine the flour, potato starch, baking powder, and salt, and add one-quarter of this mixture at a time to the egg mixture, mixing for 1 minute after each addition. Add the apples with all their juices and mix again for 30 seconds. In this way a lot of the apples will break into tiny pieces. Transfer the batter to the prepared pan and bake until the cake is golden, very puffy, resistant to the touch, and detached from the sides of the pan, about 55 minutes. If during this time the top of the cake begins to turn too dark, place a sheet of aluminum foil over it. Remove from the oven and let the cake rest on a wire rack for at least 15 minutes before releasing the sides. Transfer the cake to a serving platter. Sprinkle the confectioners' sugar over the top and serve.

DOLCE DI CAROTE E NOCI
Carrot-Walnut Cake from Parma

Makes one 10-inch cake; 8 servings

Still another from the very large category of old flourless cakes is this traditional carrot cake, whose origins stretch back long before current health food fashions. Ground nuts, here walnuts and almonds, are, as usual, found in place of the flour. The cinnamon is likely an original ingredient, but post-Renaissance potato starch was undoubtedly added later to help bind the pastry. The glaze is a simple white one, the most common "icing" made with confectioners' sugar and water, here with a little lemon juice added.

6 ounces shelled walnuts

2 ounces blanched almonds

1 cup plus 5 tablespoons granulated sugar

Grated rind of 1 large lemon (see page 4)

5 extra-large eggs, separated

2 ounces potato starch (*not* potato flour; see Note on page 284)

8 ounces very thin carrots (12 ounces if carrots are large), scraped

Large pinch of ground cinnamon

FOR THE *GLASSA* (GLAZE):

8 ounces confectioners' sugar

2 tablespoons fresh lemon juice, strained very well

3 tablespoons cold water

TO SERVE:

Strips of zest of 1 lemon with thick skin (page 4)

Place the walnuts, almonds, 1 cup of the sugar, and the rind of the lemon, reserving the lemon, in a food processor or blender and finely grind together. Transfer the mixture to a large bowl. Next mix the egg yolks and ¼ cup of the sugar together very well to completely incorporate the sugar. Add the potato starch and mix again.

    Cut the carrots into small pieces. The carrots should be very thin so they are not woody in the center, otherwise you will have to cut out and discard the tough inner part. (If you must use larger carrots, begin with 12 ounces so the net yield will be 8 ounces.) Place the carrots in a food processor or blender with the egg mixture and process until a very smooth batter forms.

continued

Preheat the oven to 375 degrees. Line the bottom of a 10-inch round double cake pan (one with 3-inch-high sides) with parchment paper and butter and flour the sides. Combine the carrot mixture with the nut mixture and mix very well. Squeeze the reserved lemon, strain the juice, and add it to the bowl with the carrot-and-nut mixture along with the cinnamon. Mix again. In a copper bowl, add the remaining tablespoon sugar to the egg whites and use a wire whisk to beat them to form stiff peaks. Fold them gently into the thick batter using a rubber spatula. Be sure to incorporate a lot of air into the mixture. Transfer the batter to the prepared cake pan and bake for 35 minutes. Increase the oven temperature to 400 degrees and bake until the cake is puffy and pulls away from the side of the pan, about 25 minutes more. Remove from the oven and let the cake rest on a wire rack for 10 minutes. Then cover a cake stand with two half moons of parchment paper, overlapping the stand itself by several inches, and unmold the cake onto them. Peel off the baked-on parchment paper.

Prepare the lemon glaze. Sift the confectioners' sugar onto a board, then transfer it to a small nonreactive saucepan. Add the lemon juice and water. Mix very well with a wooden spoon. Set the saucepan over low heat and stir constantly with the spoon. The sugar will dissolve completely in a few minutes. With a metal spatula, spread the *glassa* all over the top and sides of the cake. Let the *glassa* dry completely. Reduce the temperature of the oven to 250 degrees. Pull away the parchment paper overlapping the cake stand and place the detachable top of the stand, with the cake on it, in the preheated oven for 2 minutes. The *glassa* will become very shiny and translucent. Remove from the oven, transfer to a serving platter, and decorate the top with the lemon zest.

NOTE: Potato starch is available in some gourmet shops and the kosher section of many supermarkets.

PANE DEL VESCOVO
The Bishop's Fruit-Nut Cake for Christmas

Makes one 12-inch cake; 6 to 8 servings

This Christmas cake from Friuli is a traditional chopped dried fruit/ground nut cake. It is an ancestor of the family of Christmas cakes now made with yeast dough found throughout Italy, the famous *panettoni* of Milan and the lesser known Tuscan *panettone*. The density of fruit and nuts recalls the very ancient *dolci* like *panforte* of Siena. The medieval cakes without yeast may have evolved into the lighter yeast-dough cakes, which retain just a reminiscence of the dried fruit. Nowadays, Pane Del Vescovo is lightened with a little baking soda.

5 tablespoons raisins	4 ounces shelled walnuts
1 cup lukewarm milk	8 extra-large eggs, separated
4 ounces dried figs, preferably moist Turkish ones, small stems removed	1 cup granulated sugar
	8 ounces plus ½ cup unbleached all-purpose flour
4 ounces dried apricots or peaches	
4 ounces blanched almonds	½ teaspoon baking soda

Soak the raisins in the lukewarm milk for half an hour.

Meanwhile, coarsely chop the figs and apricots or peaches together. In a food processor, finely grind the almonds and walnuts together. Set aside.

Place the egg yolks in a large crockery or glass bowl, add the sugar, and, using a wooden spoon, mix very well until the mixture turns a lighter color. Add the 8 ounces of flour and mix very well until smooth.

Drain the raisins and pat them dry with paper towels. Place the raisins, figs, and apricots or peaches in a colander. Lightly flour all the fruit by sprinkling the remaining ½ cup flour over them and shaking the colander very well to remove any excess flour.

Heavily butter and flour a 12-inch round double cake pan (one with 3-inch-high sides). Preheat the oven to 375 degrees.

Add the ground nuts to the egg yolk mixture and mix very well, then add the chopped fruit and mix again to incorporate fully. Use a large copper bowl and wire whisk to beat the egg whites until stiff peaks form. Add the baking soda to the fruit batter, then fold in the egg whites. Transfer the batter to the prepared pan and bake for 50 minutes. Remove from the oven and let the cake rest for half an hour before unmolding it. Then let it cool completely on a wire rack before slicing.

MIGLIACCIO DELLE VALLI DI ROMAGNA
Romagna Fruit Cake

Makes one 10-inch cake; 8 to 10 servings

Emilia and, to a lesser extent, Romagna are known for the richness of their food, using copious amounts of butter, cream, cheese, eggs, and pork. There are, however, areas in the mountains and valleys of both Emilia and Romagna that have extraordinary, lesser known food that is low fat and healthy, what Italians call *cucina povera,* that is, "poor" food, meant in a most complimentary way. The "riches" that are lacking are the fats. This flat cake doesn't contain much butter, has no cream, and utilizes dried fruit, nuts, and ricotta (in Italy made with little or no fat) to make a delicious and healthy dessert. This is just one of many low-fat dishes, including many vegetable recipes, that one can find in this great gastronomic region if one knows the region deeply.

2 cups cold water	6 ounces raisins
2 cups whole milk	1½ pounds ricotta, drained
4 ounces (heaping ½ cup) raw short-grain rice, preferably Italian Arborio	1 tablespoon unsweetened cocoa powder
Pinch of coarse-grained salt	Pinch of freshly grated nutmeg
2 ounces blanched almonds	2 tablespoons Vin Santo wine or dry sherry
2 ounces pine nuts (*pignoli*)	4 extra-large eggs
8 ounces dried figs, preferably moist Turkish ones, small stems removed	½ cup granulated sugar
	2 ounces confectioners' sugar
Grated rind of 1 large lemon with thick skin (page 4)	TO SERVE:
	Confectioners' sugar

Mix together the water and milk in a medium-size casserole and bring to a boil. Add the rice and salt and simmer for 15 minutes, stirring every so often with a wooden spoon. Drain the rice and let it cool for at least 15 minutes.

Place the almonds and pine nuts in a blender or food processor. Cut the figs into small pieces and add them to the nuts. Coarsely grind everything together, then transfer it to a large crockery or glass bowl. Add the lemon rind, raisins, ricotta, cocoa, and cooled rice and mix well with a wooden spoon. Season with the nutmeg. Add the wine and mix again.

Preheat the oven to 375 degrees. Lightly butter the bottom and sides of a 10-inch springform pan and dust it with flour. Place the eggs and granulated and confectioners' sugars in a medium-size crockery or glass bowl and mix with a wooden spoon until the sugar is incorporated and the mixture lightens in color. Combine the almost whipped eggs with the nut/fruit mixture and stir very well with a wooden spoon. Transfer the mixture to the buttered pan and bake until the cake pulls away from the side of the pan, about 1 hour. By that time a very thin crust will have formed on top of the cake but the inside should be still quite soft and moist.

Transfer the pan to a wire rack and let stand for at least 20 minutes before releasing the sides. Transfer to a serving platter and serve immediately warm, or later when it has cooled. While letting it cool, cover with a large metal bowl to keep it from drying out. Sprinkle the confectioners' sugar over the top right before serving (even when the cake is served warm).

PIEDMONT

SCHIACCIATA D'UVA
Schiacciata of Grapes Piedmont Style

Makes 6 to 8 servings

Piedmont and Tuscany are two of the main wine-producing regions of Italy, and each has its *schiacciata*, made with bread dough and the grapes of the harvest and wine-making season. There are similarities between the two but there are, as well, important differences.

Schiacciata is a very flat layer of bread dough. Most types are savory rather than sweet. The most famous one is topped with olive oil and rosemary and has been documented as early as the Etruscan tombs of Chiusi, many centuries earlier than the similar Neapolitan pizza. Both the Tuscan and Piedmontese versions of the grape *schiacciata* are made with olive oil. In Tuscany the olive trees are on the higher slopes of the vineyards themselves, though the oil harvest comes after that of the grapes, so the olive oil used is that of the previous season. Piedmont produces no olive oil, instead importing it from neighboring areas such as Liguria, so it is unexpected that such a signature local dish would utilize it.

The Tuscan version has two layers of dough and two of grapes, with grapes on top; that of Piedmont places all the grapes between the two dough layers. Also, the Piedmont version adds sugar to the dough making it more like a dessert, and it is flavored with anise seeds rather than the fennel seeds of the Tuscan version.

continued

2 pounds red wine grapes or seedless ruby
    red grapes
6 tablespoons granulated sugar
1 level tablespoon anise seeds

FOR THE SPONGE:

4 ounces plus 1 tablespoon unbleached
    all-purpose flour
1 ounce fresh compressed yeast or
    2 packages active dry yeast
¾ cup lukewarm or warm water, depending
    on the yeast

FOR THE DOUGH:

12 ounces unbleached all-purpose flour
2 tablespoons extra virgin olive oil
6 tablespoons granulated sugar
½ cup lukewarm water
Pinch of salt

TO BAKE:

2 tablespoons extra virgin olive oil

TO SERVE:

2 tablespoons granulated sugar

Remove the stems from the grapes and carefully wash them under cold running water, then pat dry with paper towels. Place them in a crockery or glass bowl. Let rest, covered, in the refrigerator until needed.

Meanwhile, prepare the sponge. Put the 4 ounces flour in a bowl and make a well in the center of it. Dissolve the yeast in the lukewarm or warm water and pour it into the well. Mix the dissolved yeast with a wooden spoon, incorporating the flour from the edges of the well. Sprinkle the remaining tablespoon flour over the sponge. Loosely cover the bowl with plastic wrap, then place a kitchen towel over it. Let it rest in a warm place, away from drafts, until the sponge has doubled in size, about 1 hour. The indications that the sponge has doubled are the disappearance of the tablespoon of flour or the formation of large cracks on top.

Prepare the dough. Arrange the flour in a mound on a large pastry board, then make a well in the center of it. Place the sponge in the well along with the olive oil, sugar, water, and salt. Use a wooden spoon to mix together the ingredients in the well. Then start mixing with your hands, incorporating the flour from the inside rim of the well little by little. Keep mixing until all but about 5 tablespoons of the flour is incorporated. Then knead the dough with the palms of your hands, incorporating the remaining flour in a folding motion, until the dough is smooth, about 2 minutes. Lightly oil a crockery or glass bowl and place the ball of dough in it. Cover with plastic wrap, then place a kitchen towel on top and let rest until doubled in size, about 1 hour.

Preheat the oven to 400 degrees. Use 1 tablespoon of the olive oil to oil a 12-inch pizza pan. When ready, divide the dough into two pieces of one-third and two-thirds. Use a rolling pin to stretch the larger piece into a disk about 16 inches in diameter. Transfer this disk to the prepared pan to cover completely the bottom and sides. Sprinkle 3 tablespoons of the sugar and ½ tablespoon of the anise seeds over the dough. Arrange all the grapes over this, then sprinkle the remaining 3 tablespoons sugar and ½ tablespoon anise seeds over them. Stretch the second piece of dough out to the size of the pan. Fit the disk of dough over the grapes and firmly seal together the edges of the two disks of dough with your fingers. With a fork, prick the top layer of dough in three or four places and brush it with the remaining tablespoon oil. Bake until the top crust is golden, about 35 minutes. Remove from the oven, sprinkle the sugar over, and let rest for 10 minutes before serving. Slice it like a pie. *Schiacciata* is very good at room temperature as well.

STRUDEL O STRUCCOLO DI MELE
Apple-Stuffed Pastry
Makes 8 to 10 servings

The regions of Trentino and Friuli border Austria and make a rolled pastry stuffed with apples that has much in common with the Austrian strudel. There are two types of strudel pastry. The first consists of many layers of paper-thin flaky pastry made with oil. It originated with the Byzantines and spread to the areas they ruled or that neighbored them and is still found in Turkey, the Middle East, and the Balkans, where it is sometimes called by the Greek name *phyllo*. This type of pastry is used in Hungarian strudel.

The second is a single thin, but not paper-thin, layer of pastry made with butter and eggs. The Austrians share this butter pastry for strudel with Northern Italy, but the Italians use far less butter in their version.

FOR THE PASTRY:

10 ounces unbleached all-purpose flour plus
    more for kneading

Pinch of salt

2 level tablespoons granulated sugar

About ½ cup lukewarm water

1 extra-large egg

3 tablespoons (1½ ounces) sweet butter, at
    room temperature

FOR THE FILLING:

2½ pounds Red or Golden Delicious apples

¼ cup granulated sugar, or more to your taste,
    depending on the ripeness of the apples

Grated rind of 1 large lemon with thick skin
    (page 4)

Ground cinnamon

¼ cup (2 ounces) sweet butter

¼ cup very fine unseasoned bread crumbs,
    preferably homemade, lightly toasted

4 ounces Muscat raisins or golden raisins

TO SERVE:

Sifted confectioners' sugar or ½ cup
    granulated sugar mixed with the grated
    rind of 1 large orange, with thick skin
    (page 4)

continued

Prepare the pastry. Sift the flour, salt, and sugar together into a large bowl. Make a well in the center of the flour and place the water, egg, and butter in it. Mix the ingredients in the well, then start incorporating the flour from the edges of the well. When a rather stiff dough forms, gather together all the pieces to make a ball. Knead the dough on a large pastry board for at least 5 minutes, then start "beating" the dough by throwing it against the pastry board until very elastic, about 2 minutes. Wrap the dough in a lightly dampened cotton kitchen towel and wrap the towel with plastic wrap. Refrigerate the dough for 1 hour.

When almost ready to stretch the dough, preheat the oven to 350 degrees and start the filling. Peel the apples, quarter, then core and coarsely grate them. Transfer the apples to a crockery or glass bowl and add the sugar, grated lemon rind, and cinnamon. Mix very well.

Place a small saucepan with the butter over low heat; when the butter is melted, add the bread crumbs and lightly sauté for a few seconds. Let the crumbs rest a few minutes before adding them to the apple mixture. Soak the raisins in lukewarm water to cover for 5 minutes.

Lightly butter a 15 × 10½-inch jelly-roll pan and unwrap the dough. Divide the dough into two pieces of two-thirds and one-third. Before stretching the dough, drain the raisins, add them to the filling, and mix well.

Knead the two pieces of dough for a few seconds with both the board and your hands very well floured. Use a rolling pin to stretch the two pieces of dough into two rectangles, one large enough to cover the pan and its sides and the second, smaller one just large enough to cover the top part of the pan. Gently line the pan with the larger sheet of pastry and gently arrange all the filling over it, then fit the second sheet of pastry on top. Seal the edges of the two sheets of pastry together, using your fingers. With a thin needle, prick the top layer all over. Bake for 40 minutes. Remove from the oven and let the *struccolo* rest for 10 minutes before cutting it into "pastries" about 3 inches square. Sift the confectioners' sugar over them, transfer to a serving platter, and serve.

SICILY

TORTA DI ARANCE
Orange Tart

Makes one 11-inch tart; 6 to 8 servings

This dessert from Sicily is undoubtedly more modern than *Dolce di Aranci* (page 275), in which the fruit plays a bigger role. Included are orange slices, the juice and the zest, intensified by lemon extract and zest. In addition to the flour, we have ground nuts—walnuts this time—and butter, not olive oil, as in the orange cake. In the earliest post-Roman Italian cookbooks, from about 1300, there is excitement about butter, so it might have been a recent discovery for them.

FOR THE CRUST:

7 ounces unbleached all-purpose flour

¼ cup shelled walnuts

Pinch of salt

1 tablespoon confectioners' sugar

½ cup (4 ounces) cold sweet butter, cut
    into pats

⅓ cup cold water

1 tablespoon vegetable oil

FOR THE FILLING:

5 large oranges with thick skins

1 cup granulated sugar

5 extra-large egg yolks

1 cup heavy cream

1 teaspoon pure lemon extract or 1 drop
    imported Italian lemon extract

TO SERVE:

Strips of zest of 1 large lemon with thick
    skin (page 4)

Place the flour and walnuts in a blender or food processor and blend very well. Add the salt, confectioners' sugar, and butter and pulse for 20 seconds. Pour in the cold water, pulse again for a few seconds, and finally add the vegetable oil and pulse again. Transfer the dough to a sheet of parchment paper, flatten it a bit, and refrigerate, completely wrapped in the parchment, for at least 1 hour.

Prepare the filling. Peel 2 of the oranges, being careful to remove the woody white pith, and cut each orange into 5 slices. Place a large nonreactive skillet with ½ cup of the granulated sugar over low heat, arrange the orange slices over the bottom of it in a single layer, and cook for about 10 minutes, shaking the skillet every so often. Meanwhile zest the skins of the 3 remaining oranges into thin strips and place them in a bowl of cold water. Squeeze the 3 oranges and strain the juices very well. If you do not have a full cup of orange juice, add enough cold water to make up the difference.

When the sugar in the skillet turns lightly golden, add the orange juice, carefully turn the orange slices over, and simmer for about 10 minutes more. By that time the juice should be almost evaporated. Remove the skillet from the heat and let rest until cool, about 1 hour.

Roll the dough between two sheets of parchment paper into a disk about 16 inches in diameter. Carefully transfer the dough to an 11-inch fluted tart pan with a removable bottom. Press the overhanging dough against the side of the pan and cut off and discard any extra. Lightly prick the pastry all over with a fork. Place a sheet of parchment paper over the pastry and put pastry weights or dried beans on it. Place the tart pan in the freezer for half an hour.

Preheat the oven to 375 degrees. When ready, put the tart pan in the oven for 25 minutes, then remove the weights and paper and bake for 5 minutes longer.

Meanwhile, mix the egg yolks and the remaining ½ cup granulated sugar together very well, add the cream and lemon extract, and mix again. Remove the tart pan from the oven, arrange the caramelized orange slices over the tart in a single layer, pour the egg mixture over, and bake until the crust is crisp, about 20 minutes. Remove from the oven and let the tart cool for at least 1 hour before transferring it to a round serving platter.

Drain the orange zests, combine them with the lemon zests, sprinkle them over the top of the tart, and serve. The tart may also be served at room temperature after a few hours.

TORTA DI FICHI
Fig Tart

Makes one 9½-inch tart; 6 to 8 servings

Fruit tarts are very popular in Central Italy, the fruit used varying according to the season. Uncooked fresh fruit is a very popular feature for these desserts, sometimes also called *crostate*, but if cooked, the approach is to bring out the flavor of the particular fruit at the moment of its fullness, and not to cover it with too elaborate a treatment.

FOR THE CRUST:

5 ounces plus 2 tablespoons unbleached
  all-purpose flour
¼ cup (2 ounces) very cold sweet butter,
  cut into pats
¼ cup Vin Santo wine or dry sherry
Pinch of salt

FOR THE FILLING:

18 fresh or dried Turkish figs, small stems
  removed
2 cups dry white wine
3 tablespoons granulated sugar
1 tablespoon confectioners' sugar

1 clove
1 large piece lemon rind (page 4)
2 cups cold water

FOR THE ZABAIONE:

5 extra-large egg yolks
5 tablespoons granulated sugar
¼ cup Vin Santo wine or dry sherry
½ cup syrup of the baked figs

TO SERVE:

1½ cups heavy cream
1 tablespoon granulated sugar
1 teaspoon confectioners' sugar

Prepare the crust. Sift the flour onto a large pastry board, then transfer to a blender or food processor. Add the butter, blend for a few seconds, then add the Vin Santo and salt and blend for a few seconds more. The dough will resemble *pastine* (very small soup pasta, like orzo). Gather all the pieces of dough together and return to the board. Wrap the dough in a dampened kitchen towel and refrigerate for 1 hour.

Meanwhile, cook the figs. Preheat the oven to 375 degrees. Wash the figs very well, pat dry with paper towels, and place in a baking dish. Add the wine, granulated and confectioners' sugars, clove, lemon rind, and water and bake for about 1 hour. By that time, the fruit should be soft but retain its shape. Transfer the figs to a serving dish and cover so they do not dry out. Transfer all the juices from the figs to a medium-size casserole and bring to a simmer over low heat. Reduce until a thin syrup forms, about 45 minutes. Let the syrup rest until cool, about 30 minutes.

Dust the pastry board with a little of the flour and lightly butter a 9½-inch tart pan with a removable bottom. Unwrap the dough and knead it for a few seconds. Then, using a rolling pin, roll out the dough into a round sheet about 16 inches in diameter. Roll up the sheet of dough onto the rolling pin, then unroll it over the buttered pan. Gently press the dough into the bottom of the pan. Cut off the overhanging pastry by rolling the pin over the pan. With a fork, make several punctures in the pastry to keep it from puffing up. Fit a sheet of aluminum foil loosely over the pastry and put weights or dried beans on the foil to keep the shell from rising while it bakes. Refrigerate the prepared pastry for 15 minutes.

Bake the crust for 30 minutes, remove it from the oven, remove the aluminum foil with the weights, and return the pastry to the oven for 15 minutes more. Remove from the oven, let cool, and remove the pastry from the pan to a serving platter

Prepare the zabaione with the egg yolks, sugar, Vin Santo, and cooled syrup according to the directions on page 254. Transfer the zabaione to a crockery or glass bowl and let stand until cool, then cover and refrigerate until needed.

Cut all the figs but 4 in half. Arrange the half figs inside the pastry shell all around the edges. Spoon the cooled zabaione in the center. Use a chilled metal bowl and wire whisk to whip the cream with the granulated and confectioners' sugars until stiff peaks form. Place the cream in a pastry bag with or without a tip and pipe over on top of the zabaione. Refrigerate for at least a half hour before serving. When ready to serve, place the remaining 4 whole figs on the platter next to the tart and lightly brush the cut-up figs with the remaining fig syrup. Serve it by slicing wedges every 2 half-figs.

❖

TORTA DI CILIEGE
Sour Cherry Torte

Makes one 10-inch tart; 6 to 8 servings

Friuli's numerous fruit tarts and cakes often feature plums and cherries instead of the apples and pears used all over Italy. The preference for these two fruits agrees with the Friuli liking of a little tartness together with the sweetness. Gnocchi stuffed with plums is Friuli's most famous dish utilizing that fruit.

This recipe is for one of several cherry tarts from the region. It is distinguished by the addition of walnuts to the fruit.

One 16-ounce can pitted tart cherries, drained

1 cup plus 2 tablespoons granulated sugar

3 ounces shelled walnuts

¾ cup (6 ounces) sweet butter, at room temperature

3 extra-large eggs

6 ounces unbleached all-purpose flour

1 tablespoon baking powder

Grated rind of 1 medium-size orange with thick skin (page 4)

Pinch of salt

TO SERVE:

Sifted confectioners' sugar

Be sure the cherries are drained very well, then finely grind 6 tablespoons of the granulated sugar and the walnuts together in a blender or food processor. Gently mix the cherries and ground walnut mixture together. Combine the butter and the remaining ¾ cup granulated sugar in a stand mixer fitted with the paddle attachment and mix for 2 minutes, then add the eggs, one at a time, mixing well after each addition. Combine the flour with the baking powder and add the flour mixture ¼ cup at a time, mixing well after each addition. Add the grated orange rind and salt and mix for another minute.

Butter a 10-inch springform pan and line the bottom with a piece of parchment paper. Preheat the oven to 350 degrees. With a rubber spatula, gently incorporate the cherry mixture into the thick batter. Transfer the batter to the pan, lightly level the top, and bake until the sides of the cake pull away from the pan, about 50 minutes. If the top is becoming too brown, place a sheet of aluminum foil over it. Remove from the oven and let rest for a few minutes before opening the pan and transferring the *torta* to a serving platter. Sift the confectioners' sugar over it. This cake may be served lukewarm or at room temperature after several hours.

TARALLI DOLCI MARCHIGIANI

Sweet Taralli

Makes 20 taralli

There are many different versions of *taralli,* varying with the region. *Taralli* may be savory, that is, seasoned with black pepper, hot red pepper, fennel seeds, or anise seeds, or sweet, glazed with confectioners' sugar, among other possibilities. They are most often associated with Puglia in the South, but this sweet version comes from Marche in Central Italy.

Both the ring shape and the unique method of cooking *taralli* (boiling them first, then baking them) finds parallels in the bagel, so popular now in the United States, probably brought there from Poland. Did these two pastries arise independently, or were *taralli* brought to Poland with the well-documented importation of Italian art, music, and cooking during the fourteenth century?

I make *taralli* by the simpler method; the more complicated method, which I have observed in Puglia, is to drop a small ball of dough in the boiling water and to use the handle of a wooden spoon to pinch it and, with a rotating motion, while the dough is still in the water, to give it the shape of a ring.

1 pound unbleached all-purpose flour	Pinch of salt
6 tablespoons granulated sugar	Coarse-grained salt, for boiling
½ cup dry white wine	TO FINISH:
¼ cup extra virgin olive oil	2 tablespoons granulated sugar

Place the flour on a large pastry board, form it into a mound, and make a well in the center of it. Place the sugar, wine, olive oil, and pinch of salt in the well and start mixing them together. Start incorporating the flour from the edges of the well a little at a time until a very soft dough forms. Wrap the dough in a dampened cotton kitchen towel and refrigerate for half an hour.

Bring a casserole with cold water to a boil over medium heat; add a little coarse salt. Unwrap the dough and add a little more flour if too sticky. Preheat the oven to 375 degrees. Form small rings of dough by rolling 2 heaping tablespoons into a rope and closing the edges. Or form the 2 heaping tablespoons into a ball and then with your finger make a hole in the center. Carefully place them in the boiling water and cook for less than 1 minute. Use a skimmer to transfer the parboiled *taralli* to a wet kitchen towel. When all the rings have been parboiled, very lightly oil cookie sheets and arrange the *taralli* on them. Bake for 15 minutes. Sprinkle the granulated sugar over the *taralli* and bake until lightly golden and rather dry, about another 20 minutes.

BISCOTTI ALL'ARANCIO
Orange Biscotti

Makes 28 biscotti

In Italy many crusts for timbales, tarts, or cookies are made using hard-boiled egg yolks rather than raw eggs in the dough.

The very popular bulls-eye or *occhio di bue* cookies may be made with this dough. These are cookie "sandwiches" for which half of the cookies have their centers removed with a 1½-inch-diameter cookie cutter. The solid cookies are spread with a layer of fruit preserves or jam of apricot, peach, raspberry, etc., which is then covered with the cookies having a hole in them. This allows a small circle of preserves to be seen, in the shape of a bulls-eye.

5 extra-large eggs

¾ cup (6 ounces) sweet butter, at room temperature

2 ounces confectioners' sugar, sifted

Grated rind of 1 medium-size orange with thick skin (page 4)

6 ounces unbleached all-purpose flour plus 2 to 4 tablespoons for kneading

3 ounces potato starch (*not* potato flour; see Note on page 284)

Pinch of fine salt

2 tablespoons granulated sugar

TO SERVE:

2 tablespoons confectioners' sugar

Hard boil the eggs and, while they are still very hot, shell them, discard the whites, and place the yolks in a large bowl or in the bowl of a stand mixer fitted with the paddle attachment along with the butter, confectioners' sugar, orange rind, 6 ounces of the flour, the potato starch, and salt. Mix very well for 1 minute, then transfer the dough to a large pastry board and knead it, using 2 tablespoons of the flour, for less than a minute. Refrigerate, wrapped in plastic wrap, for half an hour.

Butter and lightly flour a cookie sheet and preheat the oven to 375 degrees. Use a rolling pin to stretch the dough to a thickness of ½ inch. With a 2-inch cookie cutter, cut out 28 disks, place them on the prepared cookie sheet, and refrigerate for at least half an hour. You can combine the pieces of pastry left over in cutting out the disks and roll them out to cut more disks.

When ready, bake for 10 minutes, then sprinkle the granulated sugar over the cookies, reduce the oven temperature to 300 degrees, and bake for another 15 minutes. Remove the cookie sheet from the oven and let the biscotti cool completely before dusting them thoroughly with the confectioners' sugar. Transfer the biscotti to a serving platter and serve.

VARIATIONS

- Grated lemon rind may be used instead of orange rind.
- Omit the orange rind and use 1 teaspoon pure vanilla extract instead.
- The granulated sugar sprinkled over the biscotti during baking may be replaced by confectioners' sugar, but it should be sprinkled over the biscotti when they are half-baked.
- The biscotti may be dipped halfway in melted chocolate, then allowed to cool to harden.

VENETO

TORTIGLIONI
Venetian Jewish Cookies
Makes 12 cookies

One of many types of Italian Jewish cookies or cakes made with ground nuts rather than flour, *tortiglioni* get their name from their twisted shape. These pastries date back to the Middle Ages and Renaissance, when many Italian desserts were made without flour. The flourless cakes are still much prepared during Passover, when yeast doughs are ritually forbidden, but they are justly so popular that they are found throughout the year and long ago found their way outside the Jewish community.

Venice has the oldest ghetto in Europe, still in existence long after its questionable function was abolished by Napoleon because it is so colorful and architecturally beautiful. Since its area was restricted by law, many of its buildings are taller and have more stories than the city's other architecture.

4 ounces unblanched almonds

1 ounce pine nuts (*pignoli*)

½ cup plus 1 tablespoon granulated sugar

Large pinch of ground cinnamon

1 heaping teaspoon grated lemon rind
    (page 4)

Confectioners' wafer papers (found in
    German and Hungarian specialty stores)
    or parchment paper

2 extra-large egg whites

continued

Blanch the almonds in boiling water for 1 minute, remove the skins, and let them dry for 15 minutes in a preheated 375-degree oven. Leave the oven on.

Combine the almonds with the pine nuts, ½ cup of the granulated sugar, the cinnamon, and grated lemon rind in a blender or food processor and grind until all the ingredients become like a flour. Butter one or two cookie sheets, if using the confectioners' wafer papers, or, if using parchment paper, lightly butter the paper. With a copper bowl and wire whisk beat the egg whites with the remaining tablespoon sugar until stiff peaks form. Gently fold the whites into the almond flour using a rotating motion. Transfer this thick batter to a pastry bag with a very large 1" serrated tip. Shape the *tortiglioni* by pushing enough batter from the bag to make an "S" shape, 4 to 5 inches long.

Bake for about 20 minutes at 375 degrees, then lower the oven temperature to 325 degrees and bake for 10 minutes more. Remove from the oven and let the *tortiglioni* cool for about 15 minutes. Cut the confectioners' wafers around the edges of the cookies in order to separate them, leaving the piece of wafer attached to each cookie, or if they are on the buttered parchment, detach them with a knife from the paper. They are very crisp when they come out of the oven but soften after a short time into a slightly chewy texture. Serve lukewarm or at room temperature.

FRAGOLE IN CAMICIA
Batter-Fried Strawberries

Makes 8 servings

Batter-fried apples, pears, and other fruit are an especially popular dessert in Tuscany, but the favorite fried fruit of all is probably strawberry—the large juicy, red kind, with white in the center. My favorite batter for strawberries is one containing a little alcohol to provide crispness and egg whites beaten stiff for lightness. The result is an incredible crust covering a delectable fruit.

FOR THE BATTER:

7 ounces unbleached all-purpose flour,
    sifted

Pinch of salt

2 teaspoons extra virgin olive oil

1 extra-large egg

2 extra-large eggs, separated

1 cup cold water

1 tablespoon granulated sugar

3 tablespoons brandy

TO PREPARE THE STRAWBERRIES:

24 large ripe strawberries

¼ cup granulated sugar

A few drops of fresh lemon juice

2 tablespoons brandy

TO COOK:

2 cups vegetable oil (½ sunflower oil and
    ½ corn oil)

1 cup extra virgin olive oil

TO SERVE:

1 cup granulated sugar

Grated rind of 1 large lemon with thick
    skin (page 4)

Thin strips of zest of 2 oranges with thick
    skins (page 4)

Prepare the batter. Place the flour in a bowl, add the salt, and mix.

Make a well in the flour and put in the olive oil, whole egg, and egg yolks. Then start stirring, adding the cold water little by little and incorporating the flour. When all the water is added and the flour incorporated, add the sugar and brandy and stir well for 2 minutes more. Make sure there are no lumps. Let the batter rest, covered, for at least 2 hours in a cool place; do not refrigerate.

Meanwhile, prepare the fruit. Carefully wash the berries, pat them dry with paper towels, then carefully remove the stems. Mix the sugar with the lemon juice and brandy in a small bowl and soak the berries for 1 hour.

When the batter is ready, use a wire whisk and copper bowl to beat the egg whites until stiff peaks form. Gently fold the beaten egg whites into the batter. Heat the vegetable and olive oils in a large skillet. When the oil is hot, about 400 degrees, dip each strawberry into the batter, being sure that the fruit is completely coated. Fry until golden all over. Transfer the fruit to a serving platter lined with paper towels to absorb excess oil. Place the sugar mixed with the grated lemon rind in a small dish, coat the strawberries, and transfer them to a clean platter. Sprinkle the orange zests over and serve hot.

SORBETTO DI UVA

Grape Sherbet

Makes 10 to 12 servings

Sorbetto is made with crushed fruit and a sugar-and-water syrup. It does not contain the custard base found in many *gelati* and has no cream at all. Some fruit *gelati* are made in a manner similar to *sorbetti*, without custard, milk, or cream. This grape *sorbetto* has a little flavoring of alcohol and lemon juice.

The invention of the general category of "ice cream" is associated with the late-sixteenth-century Florentine artist and designer Buontalenti and spread to Sicily, France, and then all over. It became popular in a cream-based rather than a custard-based version, that is, without eggs, in the United States as "Philadelphia Vanilla Ice Cream" in the nineteenth century.

2 pounds seedless grapes (about 1¾ pounds fruit)

1 large lemon, cut in half

½ cup granulated sugar

¼ cup grappa or brandy

FOR THE SYRUP:

1½ cups cold water

1 cup granulated sugar

1 tablespoon fresh lemon juice

TO SERVE:

Fresh grapes

Honey

½ cup granulated sugar

Carefully wash the grapes, removing all the stems. Pass the grapes through a food mill fitted with the disk with the smallest holes into a crockery or glass bowl. Squeeze the lemon and add the juice to the grape juice along with the sugar and grappa or brandy. Mix very well with a wooden spoon to dissolve the sugar completely, then use a fine-mesh strainer or coffee filter to strain the grape mixture. Refrigerate for 1 hour, stirring every so often to be sure the sugar is completely dissolved. To make the syrup, place the cold water, sugar, and lemon juice in a small saucepan and set the pan over medium heat. Simmer until half reduced. Transfer to a crockery or glass bowl and let cool for 15 minutes, then refrigerate until cold.

Start the ice-cream maker. Pour the juice along with the syrup into the container and start churning. The *sorbetto* will thicken enough in about 20 minutes. Transfer to a container and put it in the freezer for at least 1 hour.

Meanwhile, carefully wash the grapes for serving and dry them with paper towels. Lightly brush them with very little honey, then roll them in the sugar. Transfer the grapes to a plate and refrigerate for at least 1 hour before using. Serve the *sorbetto* topped with 2 or 3 grapes.

LIQUORE AL CEDRO
Citron Liqueur
Makes about 6 cups

Citrons resemble very large lemons and have a very distinctive flavor. They are particularly cultivated in Sicily. Sliced very thin, fresh citrons, when sprinkled with sugar, make a delicious snack or dessert. Candied, they are used, along with candied orange rind, as an ingredient in pastries such as *panettone* and fruitcake. And their special perfume permeates one of the best of all citrus-flavored liqueurs.

Obtain a piece of the whole candied citron rather than the packaged diced product, and dice it yourself to guarantee full flavor and high quality when making pastries.

In order to make the liqueur Cedrata, you need a whole fresh citron. If you cannot obtain one, make the liqueur with a whole fresh lemon. When in Sicily or Italy you can purchase a bottle of the already prepared liqueur as an alternative if you wish to taste it.

1 large citron

1 sprig fresh lemon verbena

3 cups pure grain alcohol or unflavored
    vodka

3 cups cold water

2 cups granulated sugar

Carefully wash the citron and lemon verbena and dry with paper towels. Wrap the citron and lemon verbena in a large piece of cheesecloth and tie it up like a package, leaving about 10 inches of the string on and cutting off almost all the leftover cheesecloth. You must have a glass jar with the lid made of glass as well, large enough to hold the citron attached to the inside part of the lid by the cheesecloth without the citron touching the alcohol in the jar.

continued

Pour the grain alcohol or vodka into the jar, hang the citron over, close the jar, and seal between the lid and the lower part of the jar with Scotch tape all around. Be sure no pieces of string or cheesecloth hang out from the jar, or not only the perfume of the citron and lemon verbena will escape but even the color will drip out.

Let the jar rest in a cool, dark place, but not in the refrigerator, for 1 month. By that time the citron will dry and become very hard and the alcohol will become colored with a yellowish or green shade, depending on the color of the citron. Prepare a very thin syrup by bringing the cold water to a boil in a medium-size saucepan over medium heat and adding the sugar. Simmer for 15 minutes. Let the syrup cool completely, then add it to the alcohol in the jar. Mix very well and let rest for about half an hour. Strain the mixture through a fine-mesh strainer or coffee filter into an empty bottle. Cork the bottle and let rest for about 1 week before using it. Serve it very cold.

INDEX

bean(s) *(continued)*
in Venetian vinegar sauce, 187
see also specific beans
beef:
in bread crumb gnocchi,
131–132
in cut ziti baked in a beehive
of pasta, 90–92
in goulash Friuli style,
229–230
marinated, cooked with
aromatic herbs, 245–246
oxtail Roman style, 232–233
in polenta with mushroom
meat sauce, 227–228
rump roast cooked in Barolo
wine, 231–232
in trenette pasta with meat
sauce Ligurian style,
84–85
beet:
red, gnocchi, 125–126
salad Roman style, 138
bigoli, whole-wheat, with an
onion anchovy sauce, 87
bigoli scuri in salsa, 87
biscotti, orange, 296–297
biscotti all'arancio, 296–297
bishop's fruit-nut cake for
Christmas, 285
bitter almond cake, 270–271
boar, marinated, cooked with
aromatic herbs, 245–246
bonet al caffè, 259
borlotti beans, *see* Roman beans
braciole rifatte alla fiorentina,
237–238
brasato al Barolo, 231–232
bread crumb(s):
gnocchi, 131–132
pasta with rosemary and, 81
toasting of, 5
broth, gnocchi in, 110
bruschetta, 23–30
artichoke, 28
with cabbage, 27
with cannellini beans, 25
with Pecorino cheese and
pepper, 26

with sautéed tomato slices, 24
with tomato and capers, 29
with truffle, 26–27
bruschetta, 23–30
di carciofi, 28
al cavolo, 27
ai fagioli, 25
di Pecorino al pepe nero, 26
ai pomodori, 24
al pomodoro e capperi, 29
umbra, 26–27
bucatini con peperonata
all'arrabbiata, 74–75
budini:
candied orange rind, 261–262
little ricotta, 262–263
budini di arance candite, 261–262
butternut squash:
in gnocchi in broth, 110
in squash gnocchi, 129–130
button or pearl onions Roman
style, 151

cabbage:
bruschetta with, 27
leaves, guinea hen baked in,
225–226
minestrone, 103–104
salad, Italian, 139
Savoy, stewed, with bay
leaves, 171
in "sharpshooter's" salad,
140–141
cakes:
almond sponge, from Padua,
271–273
apple, Roman style, 282
apricot rice, 274–275
bishop's fruit-nut, for
Christmas, 285
bitter almond, 270–271
carrot-walnut, from Parma,
283–284
classic Friuli fruit–nut,
276–278
coffee liqueur, 268–269
flat orange, 275–276
Italian apple, with cookie
crust, 280–281

peach, with almonds,
279–280
Romagna fruit, 286–287
calamari, hot and spicy, 211–212
calamari all'arrabbiata, 211–212
calf's liver Venetian style, 239
canapés:
of mozzarella and prosciutto,
31
of polpettone, 30
candied orange rind budini,
261–262
cannellini beans:
in beans and farro Elba style,
97–98
in beans Treviso style, 189
in beans with bay leaves,
184–185
bruschetta with, 25
and Swiss chard casserole, 186
in tortelli stuffed with bean
puree, 59–60
cannellini e bietola, 186
caper(s):
bruschetta with tomato and,
29
in rice timbale stuffed with
sole, 200–201
sauce, potatoes in, 143–144
-walnut sauce, string beans
in, 182–183
carciofi:
in agro dolce, 162–163
in umido o stufati, 164
cardoons, Roman "egg drop" soup
with, 94–95
carote in insalata, 134
carrot(s):
in duck stuffed with farro,
223–224
gnocchi with Ligurian garlic
sauce, 127–129
in lamb in peppery wine
sauce, 241
in Milanese vegetable salad,
144–145
in ossobuco mountain style,
234–235
salad, 134